D0194558

The Winning Investment Habits

of Warren Buffett and George Soros

THE WINNING

INVESTMENT HABITS

of Warren Buffett and George Soros

MARK TIER

T·T

TRUMAN TALLEY BOOKS

ST. MARTIN'S GRIFFIN

NEW YORK

www.stmartins.com

Design by Maura Rosenthal

Grateful acknowledgment is made to the following for permission to print previously published material:

The Alchemy of Finance by George Soros. Copyright © 1987, 1994 by George Soros. Reprinted by permission of John Wiley & Sons, Inc.

Buffett: The Making of an American Capitalist by Roger Lowenstein. Copyright © 1995 by Roger Lowenstein. Reprinted by permission of Random House, Inc.

Common Stocks and Uncommon Profits by Philip A. Fisher. Copyright © 1996 by Philip A. Fisher. Reprinted by permission of John Wiley & Sons, Inc.

Market Wizards: Interviews with Top Traders by Jack D. Schwager. Copyright © 1989 by NYIF Corp. Reprinted by permission of Berkley Publishing Group, a division of Penguin Group (USA), Inc.

Soros on Soros by George Soros. Copyright © 1995 by George Soros. Reprinted by permission of John Wiley & Sons, Inc.

Soros: The Life and Times of a Messianic Billionaire by Michael T. Kaufman. Copyright © 2002 by Michael T. Kaufman. Used by permission of Alfred A. Knopf, a division of Random House, Inc.

WARREN E. BUFFETT: Excerpts from various *Letters to the Shareholders of Berkshire Hathaway, Inc., An Owner's Manual,* and various quotations of Warren Buffett, copyright © 1981, 1982, 1983, 1984, 1985, 1987, 1989, 1990, 1991, 1992, 1993, 1995, 1996, 2000, and 2001 by Warren E. Buffett. Reprinted by permission of Warren E. Buffett.

ISBN-13: 978-0-312-35878-5
ISBN-10: 0-312-35878-4

Originally published by St. Martin's Press as *Becoming Rich: The Wealth-Building Secrets of the World's Master Investors Buffett, Icahn, Soros*

10 9 8 7 6 5

For Tamsin, Natasha, Shaun, and Bun—
so you don't need to repeat my mistakes

Contents

PART TWO
Making the Habits Your Own 269

PART ONE

The Winning Investment Habits of Warren Buffett and George Soros

The Power of
Mental Habits

WARREN BUFFETT AND GEORGE SOROS are the world's most successful investors.

Buffett's trademark is buying great businesses for considerably less than what he thinks they're worth—and owning them "forever." Soros is famous for making huge, leveraged trades in the currency and futures markets.

No two investors could seem more different. Their investment methods are as opposite as night and day. On the rare occasions when they have bought the same investment, it was for very different reasons.

What could the world's two most successful investors possibly have in common?

On the face of it, not much. But I suspected that if there *is* anything Buffett and Soros *both* do, it could be crucially important . . . perhaps even the secret behind their success.

The more I looked, the more similarities I found. As I analyzed their thinking, how they come to their decisions, and even their beliefs, I found an amazing correspondence. For example:

The World's Richest Investors

Forbes 2004 Rank	Billionaire	$bn	Source of Wealth	Company/ Country
2	Warren E. Buffett	42.9	Self-made	Berkshire Hathaway, USA
4	Prince Alwaleed Bin Talal Alsaud	21.5	Inherited	Saudi Royal Family, Saudi Arabia
31	Abigail Johnson	9.8	Inherited	Fidelity Investments, USA
47	Carl Icahn	7.6	Self-made	Icahn & Co., USA
54	George Soros	7.0	Self-made	Quantum Fund, USA
57	August von Finck	6.8	Inherited	Inheritance, Switzerland

Warren Buffett, Carl Icahn, and George Soros all began with nothing. The other billionaire investors on this list all had a head start.

- Buffett and Soros share the same beliefs about the nature of the markets.
- When they invest they're not focused on the profits they expect to make. Indeed, they're *not* investing for the money.
- Both are far more focused on *not losing* money than on making it.
- They *never diversify:* they *always* buy as much of an investment as they can get their hands on.
- Their ability to make predictions about the market or the economy has *absolutely nothing* to do with their success.

As I analyzed their beliefs, behaviors, attitudes, and decision-making strategies, I found twenty-three mental habits and strategies they *both* practice religiously. And every one of them is something you can learn.

THE MASTER INVESTORS

Warren Buffett *"The Sage of Omaha"*	George Soros *"The Man Who Broke the Bank of England"*
Born 1930, Omaha, Nebraska	Born 1930, Budapest, Hungary
Started managing funds in 1956 with the formation of the Buffett Partnership (dissolved in 1969). Now chairman and major owner, Berkshire Hathaway, Inc.	Began Quantum Fund in 1969 (originally called the Double Eagle Fund). Fund became the Quantum Endowment Fund in 2000.
$1,000 invested with Buffett in 1956 would now be worth $29,490,500.*	$1,000 invested with Soros in 1969 would now be worth $5,913,560.*
Annual compound rate of return: 24.4%	Annual compound rate of return: 28.2%
$1,000 invested in the S&P index in 1956 would now be worth $73,860.*	$1,000 invested in the S&P index in 1969 would now be worth $34,314.*
Number of losing years: 1 (2001)—compared to 13 down years for the S&P 500 since 1956.	Number of losing years: 4 (1981, 1996, 2000, 2002) compared to 9 down years for the S&P 500 since 1969.
*To 31 December 2003	*To 31 December 2003.

My next step was to "test" these habits against the behavior of other successful investors and commodity traders. The match was perfect.

The feared company raider Carl Icahn—whose net worth leapt an amazing 52 percent in 2003 to rocket him past George Soros on the *Forbes* list of the world's richest people; Peter Lynch, who produced an annual return of 29 percent during the years he ran the Fidelity Magellan Fund; legendary investors such as Bernard Baruch, Sir John Templeton, and Philip Fisher; and every one of dozens of other highly successful investors (*and* commodity traders) I've studied and worked with, all practice exactly the same mental habits as Buffett and Soros, *without exception*.

Cultural background makes no difference. A personally dramatic moment came when I interviewed a Japanese investor living in Hong Kong who trades futures in Singapore, Tokyo, and Chicago using Japanese candlestick charts. As the conversation proceeded, I checked off one habit after another from my list until I had twenty-two ticks.

And then he asked whether I thought he was liable for any tax on his profits from trading. That completed the list. (Thanks to Hong Kong's liberal tax regime, it was easy for him to legally do what he wanted: trade tax-free.)

The final test was to discover whether these habits are "portable." Can they be taught? And if you learned them, would your investment results change for the better?

I started with myself. Since I used to be an investment advisor, and for many years published my own investment newsletter, *World Money Analyst,* it's embarrassing to admit that my own investment results had been dismal. So bad, in fact, that for many years I just let my money sit in the bank.

When I changed my own behavior by adopting these Winning Investment Habits, my investment results improved dramatically. Since 1998 my personal stock market investments have risen an average of 24.4% per year—compared to the S&P, which went up only 2.3% per year.* What's more, I haven't had a losing year, while the S&P was down three out of those six years. I made more money more easily than I ever thought possible. You can, too.

It makes no difference whether you look for stock market bargains like Warren Buffett, trade currency futures like George Soros, scour the markets for undervalued takeover targets like Carl Icahn, use technical analysis, follow candlestick charts, buy real estate, buy on dips or buy on breakouts, use a computerized trading system—or just want to salt money away safely for a rainy day. Adopt these habits and your investment returns will soar.

---

*1 January 1998 to 31 December 2003.

Applying the right mental habits can make the difference between success and failure in anything you do. But the mental strategies of Master Investors are fairly complex. So let's first look at a simpler example of mental habits.

Why Johnny Can't Spell

Some people are poor spellers. They exasperate their teachers because nothing the teacher does makes any difference to their ability to spell.

So teachers assume the students aren't too bright, even when they display better-than-average intelligence at other tasks—as many do.

The problem isn't a lack of intelligence: it's the *mental strategies* poor spellers use.

Good spellers call up the word they want to spell from memory and *visualize* it. They write the word down by "copying" it from memory. This happens so fast that good spellers are seldom aware of doing it. As with most people who are expert at something, they generally can't explain what they do that makes their success possible . . . even inevitable.

By contrast, poor spellers spell words by the way they *sound*. That strategy doesn't work very well in English.

The solution is to teach poor spellers to adopt the mental habits of good spellers. As soon as they learn to "look" for the word they want to spell instead of "hearing" it, their spelling problem disappears.

I was amazed the first time I showed a poor speller this strategy. The man, a brilliant writer, had gotten a string of B's in school all with the comment: "You'd have gotten an A if only you'd learn how to spell!"

In less than five minutes, he was spelling words like "antidisestablishmentarianism," "rhetoric" and "rhythm," which had confounded him all his life. He already knew what they looked like; he just didn't know that he had to look.*

Such is the power of mental habits.

The Structure of Mental Habits

A habit is a learned response that has become automatic through repetition. Once ingrained, the mental processes by which a habit operates are primarily *subconscious*.

This is clearly true of the good speller: he is completely unaware of *how* he spells a word correctly. He just "knows" that it's right.

But doesn't most of what the successful investor does take place at the conscious level? Aren't reading annual reports, analyzing balance sheets, even detecting patterns in charts of stock or commodity prices conscious activities?

To an extent, yes. But consciousness is only the tip of the mental iceberg. Behind every conscious thought, decision, or action is a complex array of subconscious mental processes—not to mention hidden beliefs and emotions that can sabotage even the most determined person.

For example, if someone has been told "You can't spell" over and over again, that belief can become part of his identity. He can understand the good speller's strategy and with an instructor's guidance can even replicate the good speller's results. But left to his own devices, he quickly reverts to his old mental pattern.

Only by changing the belief that "I am a poor speller" can he adopt the good speller's mental habits.

Another, though usually minor, stumbling block is the lack of an associated skill. A tiny percentage of people simply can't create

---

*The Spelling Strategy was developed by Robert Dilts, codeveloper of the branch of applied psychology known as Neuro-Linguistic Programming.

an internal mental image: they have to be taught how to visualize before they can become good spellers.

Four elements are needed to sustain a mental habit:

1. a belief that drives your behavior;
2. a mental strategy—a series of internal conscious and subconscious processes;
3. a sustaining emotion; and
4. associated skills.

Let's apply this structure to analyze another process, one that's simpler than the habits of highly successful investors but more complex than the spelling strategy.

"IceBreakers"

Imagine we're at a party and we see two men eyeing the same attractive woman. As we watch, we notice that the first man starts to walk toward her but then stops, turns, heads over to the bar, and spends the rest of the evening being an increasingly drunken wallflower. A few moments later, we see the second man walk over to the woman and begin talking with her.

A while later we become aware that the second man seems to be talking to just about everybody at the party. Eventually, he comes over to us and initiates a conversation. We conclude that he's a really nice guy, but when we think about it later we realize he didn't say very much at all: We did most of the talking.

We all know people like this, who can walk up to a total stranger and in a few minutes be chatting away like they're lifelong friends. I call them "IceBreakers," and behind their behavior is the mental habits they practice:

1. **Belief:** They believe that *everybody* is interesting.

2. **Mental Strategy:** They hear their own voice inside their head saying: "Isn't he/she an interesting person."

3. **Sustaining Emotion:** They feel curious, even excited, at the prospect of meeting somebody new. They feel good about themselves, and their attention is focused externally. (If they're preoccupied with some problem or feeling depressed about something—internally focused—they won't be "in the mood" for conversation.)

4. **Associated Skills:** They establish rapport by making eye contact and smiling with their eyes. When they have a sense of rapport, they initiate a conversation with some innocuous remark and maintain it by listening rather than talking, keeping eye contact and focusing their attention on the person (giving that person a sense of importance), and by wondering what's going on in this person's mind.

You can get a taste of how this works by trying it out for yourself. Just imagine (if you don't already believe it) that you consider *all* people are interesting and hear your own voice saying, "Isn't he/she an interesting person." Then look around, and if you're alone, imagine that you're in the middle of a crowd. You should be able to feel the difference (if only for a moment).

The Wallflower, who ended up at the bar, had a very different mental strategy. After an initial flash of interest, he "ran a movie" in his head of all the times he had been hurt in a relationship, felt lousy—and went to have a beer to drown his sorrows. His emotional reaction was the expression of a subconscious, self-limiting belief that "I'm not good enough," or "I always get hurt in relationships."

Another pattern when meeting someone new is to continually wonder: *"Is this person interesting (to me)?"* This self-centered approach reflects a belief that only *some* people are interesting. And it has very different behavioral consequences.

On the next page is a chart of these three different mental habits.

	IceBreaker	Wallflower*	Self-Centered
Belief	People are interesting.	I'm not good enough/I always get hurt.	Some people are interesting.
Mental Strategy	*Internal voice:* "Isn't he/she an interesting person."	Recalls previous relationships.	*Internal voice: "Is* this person interesting (to *me*)?"
Mental Focus	External	Internal	Primarily internal
Emotion	Curiosity, excitement	Hurt	Uncertainty
Skills	Rapport, good listener	N/A	Questioning

*Note: This is only one of many variants of what we might call Wallflower strategies.

The Wallflower or the Self-Centered person can easily learn all the IceBreaker's skills: how to establish rapport, how to "smile with your eyes," how to be a good listener, and so on. He can even create an internal voice saying, "Isn't he/she an interesting person."

But what happens when the Wallflower actually tries to initiate a conversation with a complete stranger? His self-limiting beliefs override his conscious attempt to do something different—and nothing happens.

In the same way, an investor who subconsciously believes that "I don't deserve to make money" or "I'm a loser" cannot succeed in the markets no matter how many skills he learns or how hard he tries.

There are similar kinds of beliefs that lie behind many investors' losses, beliefs that I call *The Seven Deadly Investment Sins.*

The Seven Deadly Investment Sins

MOST INVESTORS ARE HURT BY mistaken beliefs about how to achieve investment success. These are beliefs that Master Investors such as Warren Buffett, George Soros, and Carl Icahn don't share. The most widely held of these damaging falsehoods are what I call *The Seven Deadly Investment Sins*.

The first step in putting these mistaken notions behind you is to see what's wrong with them . . .

DEADLY INVESTMENT SIN NO. 1
Believing that you have to predict the market's next move to make big returns.

REALITY:
Highly successful investors are no better at predicting the market's next move than you or I.

Don't take my word for it.

One month before the October 1987 stock market crash, George Soros appeared on the cover of *Fortune* magazine. His message:

"That [American] stocks have moved up, up and away from the fundamental measures of value does not mean they must tumble. Just because the market is overvalued does not mean it is not sustainable. If you want to know how much more overvalued American stocks can become, just look at Japan."[1]

While he remained bullish on American stocks, he felt there was a crash coming . . . in Japan. He repeated that outlook in an article in the *Financial Times* of October 14, 1987.

One week later, Soros's Quantum Fund lost over $350 million as the US market, *not* the Japanese market, crashed. His entire profit for the year was wiped out in a few days.

As Soros admits: *"My financial success stands in stark contrast with my ability to forecast events."*[2]

And Buffett? He simply doesn't care about what the market might do next and has no interest in predictions of any kind. To him, "forecasts may tell you a great deal about the forecaster; they tell you nothing about the future."[3]

Successful investors don't rely on predicting the market's next move. Indeed, both Buffett and Soros would be the first to admit that if they relied on their market predictions, they'd go broke.

Prediction is the bread-and-butter of investment newsletter and mutual fund *marketing*—not of successful investing.

DEADLY INVESTMENT SIN NO. 2
The "Guru" belief: If I can't predict the market, there's someone somewhere who can*—and all I need to do is find him.*

REALITY:
If you could really predict the future, would you shout about it from the rooftops? Or would you keep your mouth shut, open a brokerage account, and make a pile of money?

Elaine Garzarelli was an obscure number cruncher when, on October 12, 1987, she predicted "an imminent collapse in the stock market." That was just one week before October's Black Monday.

Suddenly, she became a media celebrity. And within a few years, she had turned her celebrity status into a fortune.

By following her own advice?

No. She became one of the highest-paid "gurus" in America, with a salary estimated between $1.5 and $2.0 million a year.

And money poured into her newly created mutual fund, reaching $700 million in less than a year. With a management fee of 3 percent, that's 21 million smackeroos per year. Not bad—though the fee went to Shearson Lehman Brothers, her employer and the manager of the fund, rather than Garzarelli herself.

In 1996, she started an investment newsletter that quickly grew to 82,000 subscribers.

The business benefits of guru-status made plenty of money for Shearson and for Elaine Garzarelli—but what about her followers?

By 1994, the mutual fund's asset base was eroding as it continued to underperform the market. The fund's managers quietly folded it into another of their funds. Average return over the life of the fund: 4.7 percent per annum, vs. 5.8 percent for the S&P 500.

Garzarelli's first newsletter was closed down in 1997, the year after it was launched, in the midst of a well-publicized fallout with her publisher. The publisher claimed the newsletter had lost about 30,000 subscribers and worried about her long-term ability to attract and retain subscribers. Garzarelli said only 15,000 subscribers had been lost and put some of the blame for that on her publisher, which she also said hadn't marketed the newsletter properly.

Her subsequent forays into fund management proved no more successful than her first. For example, the Foward Fund group hired her to manage its U.S. Equity fund in 2000. In the expectation that her name would bring investers flooding in, it was reincarnated as the Forward Garzarelli U.S. Equity Fund.

When she took over its management, the fund had assets of $35 million. When it was recast as the Sierra Club Stock Fund three years later, sans Garzarelli, its asset base had declined to $20 million.

Garzarelli has even admitted "I've learned that market timing can ruin you," she says. "If you're holding too much cash when the market moves, you're behind the eightball."[4]

Nevertheless, eighteen years after she first rocketed to the investing public's attention, Elaine Garzarelli still maintains her guru/media celebrity status. She is just one of a long line of such celebrity gurus whose star no longer shines so brightly.

Remember Joe Granville? He was the darling of the media in the early 1980s—until, when the Dow was around 800 in 1982, he advised his followers to sell everything and short the market.

Well, 1982 was the year the great bull market of the 1980s began. Nevertheless, Granville continued to urge people to short the market . . . all the way up to 1200.

Granville was replaced by Robert Prechter, who—unlike Granville—had predicted a bull market in the 1980s. But after the crash of 1987 Prechter declared the bull market finished and predicted that the Dow would plunge to 400 in the early 1990s. That's like missing the side of a barn with a double-barreled shotgun.

The dot.com boom of the 1990s produced another set of media heroes, most of whom disappeared from view soon after the NASDAQ began tanking in March 2000.

If someone actually exists who can make accurate market predictions consistently, he or she has escaped the relentless hunt for such people by the world's media. The sage Anonymous was right on the money when he said: "Prediction is difficult, especially when it concerns the future."

Media gurus make their money from talking about investments, selling their advice, or charging fees to manage other people's money. But as John Train put it in *The Midas Touch*, "The man who discovers how to turn lead into gold isn't going to give you the secret for $100 a year."[5] Or give it to you for nothing on CNBC.

That's why Buffett, Soros, Icahn, and other Master Investors who make money from actually investing *rarely talk about what they're doing or how they are thinking about the market.* Quite often, they won't even tell their own investors what's happening to their money!

DEADLY INVESTMENT SIN NO. 3
Believing that "inside information" is the way to make really big money.

REALITY:

Warren Buffett is the world's richest investor. His favorite source of investment tips is usually free for the asking: company annual reports.

George Soros earned the title of "The Man Who Broke the Bank of England" when he took a massive $10 billion short position against the pound sterling in 1992.

He wasn't alone. The signs that sterling was on the brink of collapse were there for anyone who knew how to look. Hundreds, if not thousands, of other traders also cleaned up when the pound plummeted.

But only Soros jumped in with both feet and took home $2 billion in profits.

Now that they are famous, Buffett and Soros have ready access to highly placed people. But when they began investing, they were nobodies and could expect no special welcome. What's more, both Buffett's and Soros's investment returns were higher then, when they were unknown, than they are today. So if either now draws on insider information in any way, it clearly isn't doing him much good.

As Buffett says, "With enough inside information and a million dollars you can go broke in a year."[6]

DEADLY INVESTMENT SIN NO. 4.
Diversifying.

REALITY:
Warren Buffett's amazing track record comes from identifying a half dozen great companies—and then taking huge positions in only those companies.

According to George Soros, what's important is not whether you're right or wrong about the market. What's important is how much money you make when you're right about a trade and how much money you lose when you're wrong. The source of Soros's success is exactly the same as Buffett's: a handful of positions that produce huge profits that more than offset losses on other investments.

Diversification is the exact opposite: Having many small holdings assures that even a spectacular profit in one of them will make little difference to your total worth.

Highly successful investors will all tell you that diversification is for the birds.

But that's not a message you're likely to hear from your Wall Street advisor.

DEADLY INVESTMENT SIN NO. 5
Believing that you have to take big risks to make big profits.

REALITY:
Like entrepreneurs, successful investors are highly risk averse *and do everything they can to avoid risk and minimize loss.*

At a management conference a few years ago, one academic after another presented papers on "the entrepreneurial personality." The academics pretty much disagreed with each other except on one thing: Entrepreneurs have a high tolerance for risk and, indeed, most love taking risks.

At the end of the conference, an entrepreneur in the audience stood up and said that he was flabbergasted by what he had heard. As an entrepreneur, he did everything he could to avoid risk, he said. He also knew many other successful entrepreneurs and said it would be hard to find a bunch of people anywhere who were more risk averse.

Just as successful entrepreneurs are risk averse, so are successful investors. *Avoiding* risk is fundamental to accumulating wealth. Contrary to the academic myth, if you take big risks you're more likely to end up making big losses than banking giant profits.

Like entrepreneurs, successful investors know it's easier to lose money than it is to make it. That's why they pay more attention to avoiding losses than to chasing profits.

DEADLY INVESTMENT SIN NO. 6
The "System" belief: Somebody, somewhere has developed a system—some arcane refinement of technical analysis, fundamental analysis, computerized trading, Gann triangles, or even astrology—that will guarantee investment profits.

REALITY:

This is a corollary of the "Guru" belief—if an investor can just get his hands on a guru's system, he'll be able to make as much money as the guru says he does. The widespread susceptibility to this Deadly Investment Sin is why people selling commodity trading systems can make good money.

The root of the "Guru" and "System" beliefs is the same: the desire for a sure thing.

As Warren Buffett responded to a question about one of the books written about him in a scathing tone of voice: "People are looking for a formula."[7] They hope that by finding the right formula, all they'll have to do is plug it in to the computer and watch the money pour out.

DEADLY INVESTMENT SIN No. 7

Believing that you know what the future will bring—and being certain that the market must "inevitably" prove you right.

REALITY:

This belief is a regular feature of investment manias. Virtually everyone agreed with Irving Fisher when he proclaimed: "Stocks have reached a new, permanently high plateau"—just a few weeks before the stock market crash of 1929. When gold was soaring in the 1970s, it was easy to believe that hyperinflation was inevitable. With the prices of Yahoo, Amazon.com, eBay, and hundreds of "dot-bombs" rising almost every day, it was hard to argue with the Wall Street mantra of the 1990s that "Profits don't matter."

This is a more powerful variant of the first Deadly Investment Sin, that you have to be able to predict the future—but far more tragic.

The investor who believes he must be able to predict the future in order to make money searches for the "right" predictive method. The investor who falls under the spell of the Seventh Deadly Investment Sin thinks he already knows what the future will bring.

So when the mania eventually comes to its end, he loses most of his capital—and sometimes his house and his shirt as well.

Of all the Seven Deadly Investment Sins, coming to the market with a dogmatic belief is by far the most hazardous to your wealth.

Beliefs Are Not Always Enough

While the wrong beliefs will inevitably lead you astray, having the right beliefs isn't always enough.

For example, when I was researching the IceBreaker's strategy, one of my subjects was a charming Frenchman who was at ease talking to complete strangers. Like the IceBreaker, he believed that all people are interesting. Nevertheless, he still had to wait for a context, like being at a party or sitting at the same cafeteria table, before he felt able to start a conversation.

The moment I taught him the IceBreaker's mental strategy of hearing his own voice saying "Isn't he/she an interesting person," his need to wait for a context disappeared, and he began talking to every stranger who passed by.

So each element of the structure of a mental habit—the belief, the mental strategies, the sustaining emotion, and the associated skills—must be in place for any mental habit to become your own.

The Holy Grail of Investing

When I entered the investment arena in 1974, I knew nothing about mental habits and strategies, but I was a committed practitioner of all Seven Deadly Investment Sins.

As a publisher of the *World Money Analyst* and as a goldbug riding the inflationary waves of the 1970s I achieved minor guru status myself.

But I eventually discovered that . . .

- Of the dozens of fellow market gurus I got to know, none was any better at making predictions than I was.
- None of the fund managers I met was any good at making predictions either; and almost none of them consistently made money for their investors—or consistently beat the market, for that matter.

One of them partially let the cat out of the bag when I asked him why, since he was so good at making predictions (at least, according to his own marketing), he didn't just trade for himself rather than manage other people's money.

"No downside risk" was his answer. "When I manage money, I get 20 percent of the profits. But I don't share in the losses."

Another fund manager—hired at an enormous salary just after his fund tanked—completed the picture when his new employer stressed in an interview that the manager's "recent [dismal] fund performance wasn't nearly as important as his ability to pull new money into the funds he had overseen."[8]

- I'd met people who made their money *selling* investment and trading systems but who wouldn't dream of using those systems themselves. Every eighteen months or so they'd be back on the market with a *new* system—another one they didn't use.
- I'd developed my own system of making predictions (which I trumpeted in my marketing, of course) which worked for a while and then stopped working altogether when the era of free-floating currencies began.

I started to think that, perhaps, the search for some holy grail of investing was futile.

Paradoxically, it was only after I'd given up the search entirely that I came across the answer—and found that I'd been looking in the wrong place all along.

The problem wasn't ignorance. It wasn't something I didn't know. The problem was *me:* the poor mental habits I applied to my investment decisions.

Only when I changed my mental habits did I discover how easy it really is to consistently make money in the markets. That's what will happen to you when you adopt the Winning Investment Habits of Warren Buffett and George Soros.

When you first stepped into the investment arena you brought with you all the unexamined habits, beliefs, and mental strategies you'd built up over a lifetime. If they've been working for you, helping you make *and keep* money, then you're one of the lucky few.

For most of us, the mental habits we picked up somewhere— who knows where?—as we grew up have cost us, not made us, money.

And if we drifted into any of the Seven Deadly Investment Sins, we unknowingly picked up some extra bad habits to add to any we already had.

Changing your mental habits isn't always easy—just ask any smoker. But it can be done. And the first step is to discover the habits we should adopt.

Keep What You Have

"Rule No. 1: Never lose money.
Rule No. 2: Never forget Rule No. 1."

—WARREN BUFFETT

"Survive first and make money afterward."

—GEORGE SOROS[1]

"If you don't bet, you can't win.
If you lose all your chips, you can't bet."

—LARRY HITE[2]

GEORGE SOROS WAS BORN GYÖRGY Schwartz in Budapest, Hungary, in 1930. Fourteen years later, the Nazis invaded.

Strange as it may seem, Soros describes the twelve months of Nazi occupation as the happiest year of his life. Every day was a new and exciting—and risky—adventure. For a Jew in Nazi-occupied Hungary, there was only one penalty for discovery: death. Soros had just one aim: survival. An aim that has stayed

WINNING HABIT NO. 1:

PRESERVATION OF CAPITAL IS *ALWAYS* PRIORITY NO. 1

The Master Investor	The Losing Investor
Believes his first priority is *always* **preservation of capital,** which is the cornerstone of his investment strategy.	Has only one investment aim—"to make a lot of money." As a result, often fails to keep it.

with him for the rest of his life, and is the cornerstone of his investment style.

That the Soros family did not end up in one of the Nazis' death camps can be attributed to the survival instincts of Soros's father. Years later, Soros wrote in *The Alchemy of Finance:*

> When I was an adolescent, the Second World War gave me a lesson that I have never forgotten. I was fortunate enough to have a father who was highly skilled in the art of survival, having lived through the Russian Revolution as an escaped prisoner of war.[3]

Tivadar Soros had been captured by the Russians while fighting in the Austro-Hungarian army during the First World War and was sent to Siberia. He engineered a breakout from the prison camp, but the Russian revolution had led to civil war. Reds, Whites, bandit gangs, and roving units of foreign troops were killing each other—and any innocent bystanders who got in the way.

For the three dangerous years it took him to get back to Budapest, Tivadar Soros had only one objective: *survival.* And he did whatever he had to do to survive, no matter how abhorrent.

His stories of those times fascinated young George. As a child, George recalled, "I used to meet him after school, and we would go swimming. After swimming, he would tell me another installment of his life story. It was like a soap opera that I absorbed totally. His life experience became part of my life experience."[4]

At the beginning of 1944 it was clear that the Germans were going to lose the war. Russian troops were advancing from the east; the Allies had a foothold in Italy. In March, Hungary, which had been Hitler's ally since the beginning of the war, tried to find some way of coming to terms with the winning side. So the Nazis invaded to plug a potential hole in their Russian front.

Hungary's was one of the few remaining Jewish communities in Central Europe. But that began to change the day the Nazis arrived.

Like many other Jews in Europe, some of Hungary's Jews thought the Nazis would never invade; or they refused to believe the rumors of the Auschwitz death camps. And when the Nazis came, they thought "it couldn't happen here" or that the war would be over in just a few weeks anyway so it wouldn't matter.

Tivadar Soros thought differently.

He had shrewdly liquidated most of his property in the years before the Nazi invasion. That was a smart move, as the Nazis and their Hungarian collaborators quickly confiscated all Jewish assets. He bought false papers for his family; for the rest of the war George Soros became Sándor Kiss,[5] his elder brother Paul began "a new life under the name of József Balázs,"[6] and his mother was disguised as Julia Bessenyei.[7] By helping the Jewish wife of a Hungarian official, Tivadar arranged for George to pose as his godson, while he established different hiding places for each member of the family.

It was a harrowing year for the Soros family. But they all lived. "It was my father's finest hour," according to Soros,

> because he knew how to act. He understood the situation; he realized that the normal rules did not apply. Obeying the law became a dangerous addiction; flaunting it was the way to survive. . . . It had a formative effect on my life because I learned the art of survival from a grandmaster.[8]

Soros concluded: "That has a certain relevance to my investment career."[9]

What an understatement! In the markets, survival translates as Preservation of Capital. The very foundation of his investment success was laid in that year of the Nazi occupation of Hungary when Soros learned, from a grandmaster, how to survive in the face of the gravest possible risk.

Billions of dollars later, when it was clearly no longer an issue, "he talked all the time about survival," his son Robert recalled. "It was pretty confusing considering the way we were living."[10]

Soros admits he has "a bit of a phobia" about being penniless again—as he was at seventeen. "Why do you think I made so much money?" he asks. "I may not feel menaced now but there is a feeling in me that if I were in that position [penniless] again, or if I were in the position that my father was in in 1944, that I would not actually survive, that I am no longer in condition, no longer in training. I've gotten soft, you know."[11]

To Soros an investment loss, no matter how small, feels like a step on the road back to the "bottom" of his life, a threat to his survival. As a result, I conclude (though I cannot prove) that George Soros is even *more* risk-averse than Warren Buffett, hard as that may be to accept.

Warren Buffett was born halfway around the world from Budapest, in the sleepy—and peaceful—town of Omaha, Nebraska, in the same year as George Soros, 1930.

His father, Howard Buffett, was a securities salesman at Union Street Bank in Omaha. In August 1931—just two weeks before Buffett's first birthday—the bank collapsed. His father was jobless and broke, as all his savings disappeared along with the bank.

Howard Buffett quickly rebounded to open a securities firm. But the middle of the Great Depression was a tough time to sell stocks.

Just as the Nazi occupation of Hungary was a formative experience for the young George Soros, so those early years of hardship seem to have imprinted Warren Buffett with an abhorrence of parting with money.

He's lived in the same house since 1958, which he bought for $31,500. His only concession to his wealth is the addition of a few rooms and a racquetball court. His salary from Berkshire Hathaway is a mere $100,000 a year, making him the lowest-paid CEO of any Fortune 500 company. He would rather eat at McDonald's than Maxim's de Paris; and he buys his favorite drink, Cherry Coke, by the caseload—after scouring Omaha for the lowest price. Just like any housewife watching her budget.

Buffett has *saved* nearly every penny he's ever made . . . from the age of six when he started selling Cokes door to door, right up to today when the idea of selling even one of his shares in Berkshire Hathaway is unthinkable.

For Buffett, money once made is to be kept, never lost or spent. Capital preservation is the foundation of both his personality and his investment style.

"Never Lose Money"

Warren Buffett was a Depression baby. His young personality coalesced around a deep desire to become very, very rich.

In elementary school, as in high school, he would tell his classmates that he would be a millionaire before he was thirty-five. When he turned thirty-five, his net worth exceeded $6 million.

Once, when asked why he had this drive to make so much money, he replied: "It's not that I *want* money. It's the fun of making money and watching it grow."[12]

Buffett's attitude towards money is *future-oriented*. When he loses—or even spends—a dollar, he doesn't think of the dollar, but what the dollar could have *become*.

[Buffett's wife] Susie . . . was a virtuoso shopper. She dropped $15,000 on a home refurnishing, which "just about killed Warren," according to Bob Billig, one of his golfing pals. Buffett griped to Billig, "Do you know how much that is if you compound it over twenty years?"[13]

This attitude toward money permeates his investment thinking. For example, at the 1992 Berkshire annual meeting he said: "I guess my worst decision was that I went into a service station when I was twenty or twenty-one. And I lost 20 percent of my net worth. So that service station's cost me about $800 million now, I guess."[14]

Counting a Loss

When you or I lose money, we count the dollars we actually lost. Not Buffett. His loss is what those dollars could have been. Losing money, to him, is a gross violation of his underlying aim, which is to "watch money grow."

Preservation of capital is an investment rule propounded by many but practiced by few.

Why?

When I ask investors how it would feel to make preservation of capital their first priority, most report a sense of paralysis, a feeling that "I'd better not do anything because I might lose money."

This reaction reflects the Fifth Deadly Investment Sin: the belief that the only way to make big profits is to take big risks. It implies that the only way to preserve capital is to take *no* risk at all. So never taking a risk guarantees you'll never make any giant profits.

For people who take this view,

When Risk Equals Reward

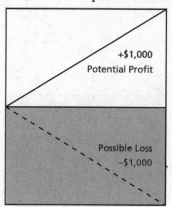

+$1,000
Potential Profit

Possible Loss
−$1,000

According to the conventional "wisdom," to have shot at making $1,000 you have to take the risk that you could lose $1,000.

profits and losses are related as if they were flip sides of the same coin: To have the chance of making a dollar you have to take the risk that you'll lose that dollar—and maybe more.

High-Probability Events

In the common view, the aim of capital preservation is to not lose money. It's seen as a restrictive strategy, one that limits your options.

But the Master Investor is focused on the long term. He does *not* view each investment he makes as a discrete, individual event. His focus is on the investment process, and the preservation of capital is the foundation of his process. It's built into his investment method; it underlies everything he does.

This doesn't mean that whenever the Master Investor considers an investment his first question is: How am I going to preserve my capital? Indeed, at the moment of decision, of making an investment, that question may not even occur to him.

A High Probability Event

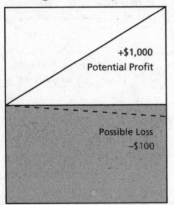

The Master Investor's system is built to find investments that look like this. That's why he KNOWS it's possible to make very big profits with little to even no risk of loss.

When you're driving, your focus is on getting from point A to point B, not on staying alive. That objective, however, underlies the *way* you drive. For example, I have a rule to keep a certain distance from the car in front, the distance varying with speed. Following the rule lets me brake to a stop if I need to without hitting the car in front, avoiding danger to life or limb. Following this rule means *survival*. But when I'm driving I don't think about all that. I just keep my distance.

In the same way, the Master Investor doesn't need to think about preservation of capital. By focusing on his investment rules he automatically preserves his capital, just as I stay alive by focusing on keeping my distance while I'm driving.

No matter what his personal style, the Master Investor's method is designed to find one thing only: what Buffett calls "high-probability events." He invests in nothing else.

When you invest in a high-probability event, you are almost certain to make money. The risk of loss is tiny—and sometimes nonexistent.

When capital preservation is built into your system, these are the only kinds of investments you will make. That's the Master Investor's secret.

"I Am Responsible"

The Master Investor accepts that he is responsible for his results. When he takes a loss he doesn't say, "The market went against me" or "My broker gave me bad advice." He says to himself, "I made a mistake." He accepts the result without recrimination and then analyzes what he did or didn't do so that he won't repeat the mistake. And moves on.

By taking responsibility for both his profits *and his losses* the Master Investor stays in command of himself. Like the expert surfer, he doesn't believe he commands the waves. But by being both experienced and in control of his own actions, he knows when to ride a wave and when to avoid it . . . and so rarely gets "dumped."

Can You Make It Back?

At many investment seminars I've asked the audience: "Who has lost money in the markets?" Just about everybody's hand goes up.

I then ask: "And how many of you made it back—in the markets?" Almost nobody's hand stays up.

To the average investor, investing is a sideline. When he takes a loss, he subsidizes his portfolio from his salary, pension fund, or other assets. He almost never makes it back in the markets.

To the Master Investor, investing is not a sideline. It's his life— so if he makes a loss, he is losing part of his life.

Here's why:

If you lose 50 percent of your investment capital, you have to double your money just to get back to where you started.

If you can average 12 percent a year return on your capital, it's going to take you six years to recover. It would take Buffett about three years and two months at his average return of 24.4 percent, while at 28.2 percent Soros could do it in "just" two-and-three-quarter years.

What a waste of time!

Wouldn't it have been simpler just to have avoided the loss in the first place?

You can see why Buffett and Soros would answer with a resounding yes. They know it's much easier to avoid losing money than it is to make it.

The Foundation of Wealth

Warren Buffett and George Soros are the world's most successful investors *because* they are both extremists at avoiding losses. As Buffett puts it, "It's much easier to stay out of trouble now than to get out of trouble later."

Preservation of capital isn't just the first Winning Investment Habit. It's the *foundation* of all the other practices the Master Investor brings to the investment marketplace, the cornerstone of his entire investment strategy.

As we'll see, every other habit inevitably traces back to Buffett's First Rule of Investing: Never lose money.

Wipeout!

What happens to investors who don't make preservation of capital their primary aim?

Often, they're wiped out completely. Well-known, high-profile investors who have been lauded by the media are not immune. Consider these recent examples:

	Long-Term Capital Management	Victor Niederhoffer
Collapse began	April 1998	October 27, 1997
Amount before collapse	$5 billion	$130 million
Time to make	4 years	20 years
Collapse over	October 1998	October 27, 1997
Amount left	$400 million	Nothing
Amount lost	$4.6 billion	$130 million
Time to lose	6 months	1 day

Both Long-Term Capital Management (LTCM) and Victor Niederhoffer followed investment systems that were fundamentally flawed. And they were flawed, as we'll see in chapter 18, because they were constructed around making money rather than keeping it.

Their implosions also illustrate how much easier it is to lose money than to make it.

4

George Soros Doesn't Take Risks?

"To survive in the financial markets sometimes means beating a hasty retreat."

—George Soros[1]

"It's not risky to buy securities at a fraction of what they are worth."

—Warren Buffett[2]

"What's your risk profile?" After discovering that Master Investors such as Warren Buffett and George Soros avoid risk like the plague, I hope this sounds like a pretty dumb question. Because it is.

But let's suspend disbelief for a moment to investigate what it means.

The average investment advisor's recommended portfolio will

WINNING HABIT NO. 2:

PASSIONATELY AVOID RISK

The Master Investor	The Losing Investor
As a result [of Habit No. 1], is **risk-averse**.	Thinks that big profits can only be made by taking big risks.

vary depending on his client's "appetite for risk." If the client wants to avoid risk, he will be offered a well-diversified portfolio of "safe" stocks and bonds that (theoretically) won't lose money—or make much, either.

If a client is willing to take risks, he'll probably be advised to invest in a portfolio full of so-called growth stocks, all with great promise but no guarantees.

This counsel makes sense to the advisor and the client who both believe it's impossible to make above-average profits without exposing yourself to the risk of loss . . . the Fifth Deadly Investment Sin.

When someone asks you, "What is your risk profile?" or "What's your appetite for risk?" what they're *really* asking you is: "How much money are you *willing to lose?*"

Fancy phraseology like "risk profile" merely disguises the belief that you must be willing to take the chance of losing a bundle of money in order to have the *chance* of making any.

Yet the practical application of making preservation of capital your first priority (Habit No. 1) is to be risk averse. If, like Buffett and Soros, you can be risk-averse *and* make far-above-average profits, there must be something severely wrong with the conventional wisdom.

Unsurprisingly, the Master Investor has a very different perspective on risk than the average investment professional. For example, Buffett puts "a heavy weight on certainty. If you do that, the whole idea of a risk factor *doesn't make any sense to me.*"[2]

To the Master Investor, risk is contextual, measurable, and manageable or avoidable.

Risk Is Contextual

Is the construction worker who walks along a plank sixty floors up in an unfinished skyscraper without a safety harness taking a risk? What about the expert skier who zooms down the almost vertical double black diamond slope at sixty miles an hour? Or the experienced rock climber, whose fingers are the only things holding him a hundred feet up a vertical cliff?

You would probably say, "Yes!" But what you really mean is: "Yes—if it was me."

Risk is related to knowledge, understanding, experience, and competence. Risk is *contextual*.

While we can't be certain that the construction worker, the skier, and the rock climber are taking *no* risks, intuitively we know they are taking less risk than we would, if we did what they did. The difference is *unconscious competence*.

Unconscious Competence

If you're an experienced driver, you have the ability to make instantaneous judgments—whether to slow down, speed up, turn right or left—to avoid a potential accident or a pothole in the road.

You can probably recall times when you have hit the brakes or swerved to avoid an accident—yet not been fully aware, *consciously*, of the nature of the danger until *after* you'd taken evasive action. The decision was made entirely at the subconscious level.

Such automatic reactions come as the result of years of experience.

Think about it for a moment and you'll realize that driving a car is quite a complicated activity. Think of all the things you're monitoring at the same time:

- Is that kid going to run onto the road?
- Is that idiot going to swerve in front of me?
- Is that car behind me too close?
- Will that car stop at the corner? [Has he had his brakes checked recently?]
- Is there enough space between me and the car in front in case he brakes hard—unexpectedly?

. . . and I'm barely scratching the surface of all the things you're monitoring as you drive. (Next time you get behind the wheel of a car, take a moment to become aware of all the things you're doing that you weren't consciously aware of doing.)

Even an apparently simple thing like changing lanes on the freeway is what's called a multibody problem in physics. You have to monitor your speed, the speed of the traffic, the speed of the cars behind you and in front of you on the lane you're in and the lane you want to move into, while maintaining awareness of traffic in the *other* lanes just in case. And you also have to make a judgment as to whether or not the drivers in the other lane are going to let you in.

And you do all this *at the same time*, almost instantaneously.

Multibody problems often stump the physicist. That's even though the physicist has a great advantage over you, the driver: the particles he's studying don't have free will. If they're moving in a certain direction at a certain speed, they don't suddenly swerve right or left or speed up or slow down. Nor do they drink and drive.

In a state of unconscious competence, you solve the multibody problem automatically—and just change lanes.

While your subconscious mind directs your driving, your conscious mind is free to carry on a conversation, be aware of the sights, or listen to the radio.

But for someone who has never driven before and has no experience or competence, just getting behind the wheel of a car is a high-risk, life-threatening activity. Like you . . . before you'd learned to drive.

The Four Stages of Learning

The Master Investor acts apparently effortlessly and instantaneously in a way that, to the outsider, seems risky—especially when the Master doesn't even seem to pause to think.

Warren Buffett can decide to buy a multimillion dollar company in ten minutes or less, doing all the calculations in his head. He doesn't even need the back of an envelope. What's more, most of the decisions he's made so quickly have proven to be the right ones.

That's only possible for someone who has gone through the four stages of learning:

- *Unconscious incompetence:* doesn't know that he doesn't know.
- *Conscious incompetence:* knows that he doesn't know.
- *Conscious competence:* knows what he knows and knows what he doesn't know.
- *Unconscious competence:* knows that he knows.

Unconscious incompetence is the state where you don't even know that you don't know: the state of mind so many young drivers are in when they begin to learn to drive. That's why young drivers have many more accidents than older, more experienced drivers: They fail (or refuse) to recognize their limited knowledge, skill, and experience.

People in *this* state are highly likely to take risks—expose themselves to danger or loss—for the simple reason they're totally unaware that that's what they're doing.

Investors who subscribe to any or all of the Seven Deadly Investment Sins are in this state. They *think* they know what they're doing, and they fail to recognize the reality of their ignorance.

Unconscious incompetence is also the reason why the worst thing that can happen to a novice investor is to make a pile of money on his very first investment. His success leads him to believe that he's found the secret of trading or investing and that he really knows what he's doing. So he repeats whatever he did the first time—only, much to his own surprise, to lose money hand over fist.

As futures trader Larry Hite explained to Jack Schwager in his book *Market Wizards*:

> I once worked for a firm where the company president, a very nice guy, hired an option trader who was brilliant, but not very stable. One day the option trader disappeared, leaving the firm stuck with a losing position. The president was not a trader, and he sought my advice.
>
> "Larry, what do you think I should do?"
>
> I told him, "Just get out of the position."
>
> Instead, he decided to hold on to the trade. The loss got a little worse, but then the market came back, and he liquidated the position at a small profit.
>
> After this incident, I told a friend who worked at the same firm, "Bob, we are going to have to find another job."
>
> "Why?" he asked.
>
> I answered, "We work for a man who has just found himself in the middle of a mine field, and what he did was close his eyes and walk through it. He now thinks that whenever you are in the middle of a mine field, the proper technique is to close your eyes and go forward."
>
> Less than one year later . . . this same man had gone through all of the firm's capital.[3]

Being in a state of unconscious incompetence can be highly hazardous to your wealth.

Conscious incompetence is the first step to mastering any subject. It's the conscious admission to yourself that you really don't know what to do, and the full acceptance of your own ignorance.

This may result in feelings of despair or futility or hopelessness—which stops some people from investing entirely. But it's the only way to realize that to master the subject requires a process of intensive learning.

Conscious competence is when you're beginning to have mastery of a subject, but your actions have yet to become automatic. In this stage of mastery, you have to take every action at the con-

> **The Four Levels of Wisdom**
>
> The man who knows and knows he knows is wise. Follow him.
> The man who knows and knows not he knows is asleep. Wake him.
> The man who knows not and knows he knows not is a student. Teach him.
> The man who knows not he knows not is a fool. Shun him.

scious level. While learning to drive, for example, you must be consciously aware about where your hands and feet are, think through each decision about whether to hit the brakes, turn the wheel, change gears . . . and as you do so, think consciously about *how* to do it.

In this stage, your reactions are far slower than the expert's.

This doesn't mean you *can't* do it: far from it. You *could* make the same investment decision as Warren Buffett. But what took Buffett ten minutes to decide might take you ten days . . . or even ten months: You have to think through every single aspect of the investment and consciously apply the tools of analysis (and acquire most of the knowledge) that Buffett has stored in his subconscious mind.

An amazing number of investors believe they can skip this stage of learning entirely. One way they attempt to do it is by adopting someone *else's* unconscious competence: following a guru or a set of procedures developed by a successful investor.

But people who've read a book on Gann triangles or Dow Theory, or whatever, and follow the steps outlined, or who adopt someone else's commodity trading system, sooner or later find that it doesn't work for them.

There's no shortcut to unconscious competence.

As your knowledge expands, as your skills develop, as you gain experience by applying them over and over again, they become more and more automated and move from your conscious mind into your subconscious.

You eventually reach the stage of . . .

Unconscious competence. This is the state of a Master, who just does it—and may not even know how, specifically, he does it.

When he acts from unconscious competence, the Master appears to make decisions effortlessly, and acts in ways that might scare you or me to death.

We interpret the Master's actions as being full of risk. But what we really mean is that they'd be full of risk to *us* if *we* took that same action. For example, as one visitor to Soros's office recalled thinking—as Soros interrupted the meeting to place orders worth hundreds of millions of dollars—"I would shake in my boots, I wouldn't sleep. He was playing with such high stakes. You had to have nerves of steel for that."[4]

Nerves of steel? Many people have made comments of that kind about Soros. What they mean is: *I* would have to have nerves of steel to do what Soros is doing.

Soros doesn't need nerves of steel: The Master knows what he is doing. We don't—until we learn what the Master has learned.

He knows what he is doing. Similarly, there's bound to be something you do in your life that, to an outsider, seems full of risk but to you is risk-free. That's because you have built up experience and achieved unconscious competence in that activity over the years. You know what you're doing—and you know what *not* to do.

To someone who doesn't have *your* knowledge and experience, what you do will seem full of risk.

It may be a sport—such as skiing, rock climbing, scuba diving, or car racing. It may be those instant, seemingly intuitive judgments you make in your business or profession.

Let me give you a personal example. Since it's in a field you probably know nothing about, I'll have to give you a little background first.

When I published *World Money Analyst,* profits from mailshots—solicitations to gain new subscribers—were a regular source of income for me. There were times when I spent hundreds of thousands of dollars I didn't have putting a promotion into the mail. Yet I never felt I was taking a risk.

Can You Walk and Talk?

Two examples of unconscious competence that almost every human being on the planet has mastered are walking and talking.

Do you realize that every time you take a step you're moving dozens of different muscles in your feet and legs? For just one step! You don't even know what muscles you're moving. If you tried to take just *one* step while consciously directing each muscle to contract or relax by the right amount in the right sequence, you'd fall right over.

To walk, you just decide consciously to go *there*, and your subconscious mind does the rest.

It's the same with speaking. You have mastery of your native language—and possibly others. Yet you couldn't explain to me any more than I could explain to you precisely *how* you store words, find them when you need them, and put them into grammatical (or at least understandable) sentences. Often, when you're talking, you don't know what specific word you'll say next. All you're aware of consciously is the meaning you want to communicate.

Unconscious competence is the brain's way of dealing with the limitations of consciousness. We can only hold seven bits of information (plus or minus two) in our conscious minds at the same time. When our subconscious mind takes over, it frees our conscious mind to focus on what's really important.

Practice makes permanent: Repetition and experience are the tools we use to delegate functions to our subconscious mind.

To send out a mailing, you have to pay for printing, lettershopping (putting everything into the envelopes), renting the mailing lists—and postage. Only the postage has to be paid up front; for everything else you can get thirty to ninety days' credit.

From records I'd kept of every mailing I'd ever done I knew that by the seventh day of response I would have received about half the total revenue I could expect. Since that was more than the postage, I could start paying the other bills as they came due.

Ah, you might ask, but how do you *know* that money is going to come in?

The level of response depends on three variables: the headline, the copy (the text of the advertisement), and the mailing list. When you create a new advertisement, you don't know for sure that it will work. So you test: You mail out 10,000 or 20,000 pieces to the best mailing lists available. Unless the copy is complete drivel, you're unlikely to lose very much money. (And if you lose the lot, it's only a couple of thousand dollars, so why worry?)

If the test mailing works (that is, if it's profitable), you "roll it out" to other mailing lists. Because I was mailing regularly, I knew which mailing lists worked, which didn't, and which worked sometimes. So I could select which mailing lists to roll out to, based on the profitability of the test. When the test was highly profitable, I could mail half a million pieces or more . . . if all I had to pay initially was the postage.

Still think I was taking unnecessary risks? I imagine you do. I'm not trying to convince you otherwise. But because I knew what I was doing, to *me* there was no risk at all.

Think about it for a while and I'm sure you'll find several similar examples where you feel you are taking little or no risk—but it's impossible to convince an outsider that there's no risk involved.

Risk declines with experience: There are many things you do today which you think of as risk-free. But at one time in your life, before you built up the necessary knowledge and experience, they were high-risk activities for you.

When George Soros shorted the pound sterling with $10 billion of leverage (as he did in 1992), was he taking a risk? To us, he was. But we tend to judge the level of risk by our own parameters or to think that risk is somehow absolute. On either of those measures, the risk was huge.

But Soros knew what he was doing. He was confident the level of risk was completely manageable. He'd calculated that the most he could lose was about 4 percent. "So there was really very little risk involved."[5]

As Warren Buffett says: *"Risk comes from not knowing what you are doing."*[6]

The highly successful investor simply walks (or more likely *runs*) away from any investment that is risky to *him*. But since risk is relative and contextual, the investment that Warren Buffett may shy away from can be the one that George Soros scoops up with both hands. And vice versa.

Risk Is Measurable

Restricting his investments to those where he has unconscious competence is one way the Master Investor can be risk-averse and, at the same time, make above-average profits. But how did he build that unconscious competence in the first place? By discovering that risk is *measurable*—and by learning *what* to measure.

The Master Investor thinks in terms of *certainty* and *uncertainty,* and his focus is on achieving certainty. He isn't really measuring risk at all. He is measuring the probability of profits in his continual search for, as Warren Buffett puts it, high-probability events. And he finds them by answering the question:

What Are You Measuring?

I once asked an investor what his aim was. He replied: "To make 10 percent a year."

"And what's your measure of whether you're achieving that?"

He answered: "By whether I made 10 percent or not."

This investor is rather like an architect who measures the quality of his building by whether or not it stands up when it's finished. Whatever result you are trying to achieve can only be the measure of whether you *have* achieved it, not the measure of whether you *will.*

A good architect knows that his building will stand up while it's still a blueprint. He knows this by measuring the strength of the materials, the loads they will have to bear, and the quality of the design and construction.

In the same way, the Master Investor knows, *before* he invests, whether he is likely to make a profit.

Profit (or loss) is a *residual:* the difference between income and expenditure. As a result, it's only measurable *with the benefit of hindsight.*

For example, a business does not make profits by aiming to make profits. It must focus on the activities that are measurable *in the present,* and later *result in* profits: in other words, activities that increase sales and income or cut costs. And by only undertaking activities where the managers are confident that income will exceed costs.

Investment Criteria

Master Investors focus their attention not on profits, but on the measures that will inevitably *lead to* profits: their investment criteria.

Warren Buffett doesn't buy a stock because he expects it to go up. He'll be the first to tell you the price could just as easily drop the moment after he's bought it.

He buys a stock (or the entire company) when it meets his investment criteria, because he knows from experience that he will ultimately be rewarded by either a higher stock price or (when he buys the whole company) rising business profits.

For example, in February 1973 Buffett began buying shares in the Washington Post Co. at $27 a share. As the price fell, Buffett bought more, and by October was the largest outside shareholder. To Buffett, the *Washington Post* was a $400 million business that was on sale for just $80 million. But that's not what Wall Street saw—even though most publishing analysts agreed with Buffett on the company's valuation.

Wall Street saw a collapsing market. The Dow was off 40 percent and the "Nifty Fifty" stocks such as IBM, Polaroid, and Xerox—which only a few years before Wall Street had been happy to buy at 80 times earnings—were off 80 percent or more. The economy was in recession and inflation was *rising*. That wasn't supposed to happen: Recession was supposed to send inflation down. To Wall Street, it looked like the "end of the world" might be coming. This was definitely not a time to buy stocks; and with inflation rising you couldn't even find safety in bonds.

When they looked at the Washington Post Co., investment professionals saw a stock that had fallen from $38 to $20 a share and which, like the market, could only go down. The "risk" of buying was far too high.

The irony is that the *Post* could have sold its newspaper and magazine businesses to another publisher for around $400 million—but Wall Street wouldn't buy it for $80 million!

To Buffett, when you can buy a sound, attractive business at an 80 percent discount to its value, there's no risk at all.

Buffett wasn't looking at the market—or the economy. He was using his investment criteria to measure the quality of the *Post*'s business. What he saw was a business that he understood: Due to its effective monopoly in the Washington area it had favorable economics that were sustainable (and because of its "monopoly" could raise prices in line with inflation and, so, was an inflation hedge); it wasn't capital-intensive; it was well managed—and, of course, it was available at a very attractive price.

While Wall Street was driven by fear of loss, and called it "risk," Buffett and other investors who knew what to measure were cleaning up. Intriguingly, often when the market is collapsing, investment professionals suddenly discover the importance of preserving capital and adopt a "wait-and-see" attitude—while investors who follow the first rule of investing, "Never lose money," are doing the exact opposite and jumping in with both feet.

After Buffett had made his investment, the price of the Washington Post Co. kept falling. Indeed, it was two years before the market came back to his original average purchase price of $22.75

per share. But Buffett didn't care about the share price; his focus was on his investment criteria, on measuring the quality of the business. And that quality—to judge by earnings alone—was improving.

In the investment marketplace, you are what you measure.

Risk Is Manageable

Soros achieves investment certainty in a very different way. Like Buffett, he measures his investments—all successful investors do—but Soros applies very different investment criteria.

The key to Soros's success is to actively manage risk, one of the four risk-avoidance strategies Master Investors use:

1. **Don't invest.**
2. **Reduce risk.**
3. **Actively manage risk.**
4. **Manage risk actuarially.**

There's a fifth risk-avoidance strategy that's highly recommended by the majority of investment advisors: diversification. But to Master Investors, diversification is for the birds (see chapter 7).

No successful investor restricts himself to just one of these four risk-avoidance strategies. Some—like Soros—use them all.

1. Don't Invest

This strategy is always an option: Put all your money in Treasury bills—the "risk-free" investment—and forget about it.

Surprising as it may seem, it is practiced by every successful investor: When they can't find an investment that meets their criteria, they don't invest at all.

Even this simple rule is violated by far too many professional fund managers. For example, in a bear market they'll shift their portfolio into "safe" stocks such as utilities, or bonds, on the theory they'll go down less than the average stock. After all, you can't appear on *Wall Street Week* and tell the waiting audience that you just don't know what to do at the moment.

2. Reduce Risk

This is the core of Warren Buffett's entire approach to investing.

Buffett, like all Master Investors, invests only in what he understands, where he has conscious and unconscious competence.

But he goes further: His method of avoiding risk is built into his investment criteria. He will only invest when he can buy at a price significantly below his estimate of the business's value. He calls this his "margin of safety."

Following this approach, almost all the work is done *before* an investment is made. (As Buffett puts it: "You make your profit when you *buy*.") This process of selection results in what Buffett calls "high-probability events": Investments that approach (if not exceed) Treasury bills in their certainty of return.

3. Actively Manage Risk

This is primarily a trader's approach—and a key to Soros's success.

Managing risk is very different from reducing risk. If you have reduced risk sufficiently, you can go home and go to sleep. Or take a long vacation.

Actively managing risk requires full-focused attention to constantly monitor the market (sometimes minute by minute) and the ability to act instantly with total dispassion when it's time to change course (when a mistake is recognized or when a current strategy is running its course).

Soros's ability to handle risk was "imprinted" on him during the Nazi occupation of Budapest, when the daily risk he faced was death.

His father, being a Master Survivor, taught him the three rules of risk which still guide him today:

1. It's okay to take risks.

2. When taking a risk, never bet the ranch.

3. Always be prepared to beat a hasty retreat.

Beating a Hasty Retreat

In 1987, Soros had positioned the Quantum Fund to profit from his hypothesis that a market crash was coming—in Japan—by shorting stocks in Tokyo and buying S&P futures in New York.

But on Black Monday, October 19, 1987, his scenario came apart at the seams. The Dow dropped a record 22.6 percent, which still stands as the largest one-day fall in history. Meanwhile, in Tokyo the government supported the market. Soros was bleeding at both ends of his strategy.

"He was on leverage and the very existence of the fund was threatened,"[7] according to Stanley Druckenmiller, who took over management of the Quantum Fund two years later.

Soros didn't hesitate. Following his third rule of risk management he got the hell out. But because his positions were so large, his selling drove down the price. He offered his 5,000 S&P futures contracts at 230, and there were no takers. Or at 220, 215, 205, or 200. Eventually he liquidated at between 195 and 210. Ironically, once he was out, the selling pressure was gone, and the market bounced back to close the day at 244.50.[8]

> Soros had lost his entire profit for the year. But that didn't faze him. He had admitted his mistake; realized he didn't know what was going on; and, as he always did whether the mistake was minor or, as in this case, threatening to his survival, he went into risk-control mode. The only difference this time was the size of his positions and the illiquidity of the market.

Survive first. Nothing else was important. He didn't freeze, doubt, stop to analyze, second-guess, or try to figure out whether he should hold on in case things turned around. He just got out.

Soros's investment method is to form a hypothesis about the market and then "listen" to the market to find out whether his hypothesis is right or wrong. In October 1987, the market was telling him he was wrong, dead wrong. As the market had shattered his hypothesis, he no longer had any reason to maintain his positions. Because he was losing money, his only choice was to beat a hasty retreat.

The crash of 1987 cast a cloud of doom and gloom over Wall Street that lasted for months. "Just about every manager I knew who was caught in that crash became almost comatose afterwards," said Druckenmiller. "They became nonfunctional, and I mean legendary names in our business."[9]

As prominent hedge fund manager Michael Steinhardt candidly admits: "I was so depressed that fall that I did not want to go on. I took the crash personally. The issue of timing haunted me. My prescient forewarnings [recommending caution] earlier in the year made the losses all the more painful. Maybe I was losing my judgment. Maybe I just was not as good as I used to be. My confidence was shaken. I felt alone."[10]

Not Soros. He had taken one of the biggest hits of all, but he was unaffected.

He was back in the market two weeks later heavily shorting the dollar. Because he knew how to handle risk, because he followed his rules, he immediately put the crash behind him. It was history. And the Quantum Fund ended *up* 14.5 percent for the year.

Emotional Disconnect

A mental strategy that sets Master Investors apart is that they can totally disconnect their emotions from the market. Regardless of what happens in the market, they are unaffected emotionally. Of course, they may feel happy or sad, angry or excited—but they have the ability to immediately put that emotion aside and clear their minds.

Being in a state where you are controlled by your emotions makes you vulnerable to risk. The investor who is overcome by his emotions—even if he knows full well, intellectually, what to do when things go wrong—often freezes up; agonizes endlessly over what to do; and ends up selling, usually at a loss, just to relieve the anxiety.

Buffett achieves the necessary emotional distance through his investment *method*. His focus is on the quality of the business. His only concern is whether his investments continue to meet his criteria. If they do, he's happy—regardless of how the market might be valuing them. If a stock he owns no longer meets his criteria, he'll sell it—regardless of how the market prices it.

Warren Buffett simply doesn't care what the market is doing. No wonder he often says he wouldn't mind if the stock market closed down for ten years.

"I Am Fallible"

Like Buffett, Soros's investment method helps distance him emotionally from the market. But his ultimate protection—aside from the self-confidence that he shares with Buffett—is that he "walks around telling whomever has the patience to listen that he is fallible."[11]

He bases an investment on a hypothesis he has developed about how and why a particular market will move. The use of the word "hypothesis" in itself signifies a very tentative stance, of someone unlikely to become "married to his position."

Yet, as his public prediction that the "Crash of '87" would start in Japan, not the United States, bears witness, there were times when he was *certain* of what "Mr. Market" would do next. When it didn't happen that way, he would be taken completely by surprise.

Overriding all the other beliefs Soros has is his conviction that he is fallible—the basis, as we will see, of his investment philosophy. So that when the market proves him wrong, he immediately realizes he's made a mistake. Unlike too many investors, he doesn't say "the market is wrong" and hang on to his position. He just gets out.

As a result, he can step back completely from his involvement, so appearing to others to be emotionless, a stoic.

4. Manage Risk Actuarially

The fourth way to manage risk is to act, in effect, like an insurance company.

An insurance company will write a life insurance policy without having any idea *when* it will have to pay out. It might be tomorrow; it might be a hundred years from now.

It doesn't matter (to the insurance company).

An insurance company makes no predictions about when you might die, when your neighbor's house might burn down or be burgled—or about any other specific item it has insured.

The insurance company controls risk by writing a large number of policies so that it can predict, with a high degree of certainty, the *average* amount of money it will have to pay out each year.

Dealing with averages, not individual events, it will set its premium from the *average expectancy* of the event. So the premium on your life insurance policy is based on the average life expectancy of a person of your sex and medical condition at the age you were when you took out the policy. The insurance company is making no judgment about *your* life expectancy.

The person who calculates insurance premiums and risks is called an actuary, which is why I call this method of risk control "managing risk *actuarially.*"

This approach is based on averages of what's called "risk expectancy."

Even though the Master Investor may use the same, commonly accepted terminology, what he's actually looking at is average *profit* expectancy.

For example, if you bet a dollar on heads coming up when you flip a coin, you have a 50:50 chance of winning or losing. Your average profit expectancy is 0. If you flipped a coin a thousand times and bet a dollar each time, you'd expect to end up with about the same amount of money you started with (provided, of course, that an unusual series of tails didn't wipe you out).

Fifty-fifty odds aren't at all exciting. Especially after you have paid transaction costs.

But if the odds are 55:45 in your favor, it's a different story. Your total winnings over a series of events will exceed your total losses since your average profit expectancy rises to 0.1—for each dollar you invest you can expect *on average* to get back $1.10.

Gambling, Investing, and Risk

gamble *n.* risky undertaking; any matter or thing involving risk
—*v.t.* risk much in the hope of great gain
—*v.i.* to stake or risk money on the outcome of something involving chance

Parallels are often drawn between investing and gambling—with good reason: In essence, the actuarial approach means playing the odds.

Another (but bad) reason is that far too many investors approach the markets with a gambling mentality: "in the *hope* of great gain." This is even more often the case with people entering the commodity markets for the first time.

To make the analogy clear, consider the difference between a gambler and a *professional* gambler.

A gambler plays games of chance for money—in the *hope* of making a great gain. Since he rarely comes out ahead, his primary reward is the excitement of playing the game. Such gamblers keep Las Vegas, Monte Carlo, Macau, and lotteries the world over in business.

The gambler throws himself the mercy of the "gods of chance." However benign these gods of chance may be, their representatives on earth live by the motto "Never give a sucker an even break." The result, in Warren Buffett's words:

> Las Vegas has been built upon the wealth transfers that occur when people engage in seemingly small disadvantageous capital transactions.[12]

A *professional* gambler, by contrast, understands the odds of the game he's playing and only makes bets when the odds are in his favor. Unlike the weekend gambler, he doesn't depend on one roll of the dice. He has calculated the odds of the game so that, *over time,* his winnings exceed his losses.

He approaches the game with the mentality of an insurance company when it writes a policy. His focus: average profit expectancy.

He has a system that he follows—just like the Master Investor. And part of the system, naturally enough, is to choose the game where it's statistically possible to win over time.

You can't eliminate chance from a game of poker, blackjack, or roulette. But you can learn to calculate the odds and decide whether it's possible to play that game with the average profit expectancy (the odds) in your favor.

If it's not, you don't play.

Sucker!

Professional gamblers do more than just calculate probabilities: They look for situations where the odds are *bound* to be in their favor.

A friend of mine, a member of Alcoholics Anonymous, lived a sixty-minute ferry ride away from town. When he took a late ferry home there were always a bunch of drunks at a table at the back of the ferry, continuing their binge with beers from the bar.

He'd pull up a chair, take a pack of cards from his bag and say, "Anyone feel like a round of poker?"

Professional gamblers never buy lottery tickets.

Professional gamblers don't actually gamble. They don't "risk much in the *hope* of great gain." They invest little, time after time, with the mathematical certainty that they will achieve a positive return on capital.

Investing isn't gambling. But professional gamblers act at the poker table in the same way Master Investors act in the investment marketplace: They both understand the mathematics of risk and only put serious money on the table when the odds are in their favor.

Actuarial Investing

When Warren Buffett started investing, his approach was very different from the one he follows today. He adopted the method of his mentor, Benjamin Graham, whose system was actuarially based.

Graham's aim was to purchase undervalued common stocks of secondary companies "when they can be bought at two-thirds or less of their indicated value."[13]

He determined value solely by analyzing publicly available information, his primary source of information being company financial statements.

A company's book value was his basic measure of intrinsic value. His ideal investment was a company that could be bought at a price significantly below its liquidation or break-up value.

But a stock may be cheap for a good reason. The industry may be in decline, the management may be incompetent, or a competitor may be selling a superior product that's taking away all the company's customers—to cite just a few possibilities. You're unlikely to find this kind of information in a company's annual report.

By just analyzing the numbers Graham could not know why the stock was cheap. So some of his purchases went bankrupt; some hardly moved from his purchase price; and some recovered to their intrinsic value and beyond. Graham rarely knew in advance which stock would fall into which category.

So how could he make money? He made sure he bought dozens of such stocks, so the profits on the stocks that went up far outweighed the losses on the others.

This is the actuarial approach to risk management. In the same way that an insurance company is willing to write fire insurance for all members of a particular class of risks, so Graham was willing to buy all members of a particular class of stocks.

An insurance company doesn't know, specifically, whose house is going to burn down, but it can be pretty certain how often it's going to have to pay for fire damage. In the same way, Graham didn't know *which* of his stocks would go up. But he knew that, on average, a predictable percentage of the stocks he bought would go up.

An insurance company can only make money by selling insurance at the right price. Similarly, Graham had to buy at the right price; if he paid too much, he would lose, not make, money.

The actuarial approach certainly lacks the romantic flavor of the stereotypical Master Investor who somehow, magically, only buys stocks that are going to go up. Yet it's probably used by more successful investors than any other method. For success, it depends on identifying a narrow class of investments that, taken together, have a positive average profit expectancy.

Buffett started out this way, and still follows this approach when he engages in arbitrage transactions. It also contributes to Soros's success. And it is the basis of most commodity trading systems.

Average profit expectancy is the investor's equivalent of the insurer's actuarial tables. Hundreds of successful investment and trading systems are built on the identification of a class of events which, when repeatedly purchased over time, have a positive average expectancy of profit.

Risk Versus Reward

Most investors believe that the more risk you take on, the greater the profit you can expect.

The Master Investor, on the contrary, does not believe that risk and reward are related. By investing only when his expectancy of profit is positive, he assumes little or no risk at all.

"The Market Is Always Wrong"

"Wealth is the product of man's capacity to think."
—AYN RAND[1]

"Most men would rather die than think. Many do."
—BERTRAND RUSSELL[2]

EVERY DECISION AN INVESTOR MAKES—to buy, sell, hold, or do nothing—results from his idea of what makes markets tick; that is, from his investment philosophy.

A philosophy is an explanation of how the world around us works and our means of understanding it. That understanding tells us what's right and what's wrong, what works and what doesn't. It's our guide to making choices, reaching decisions—and taking action.

Everyone has a philosophy of life—you cannot be human and *not* have one. Most people accept someone else's philosophy by default. Some consciously choose to adopt or modify someone else's. And a very few develop their own.

WINNING HABIT NO. 3:

Develop Your Own Unique Investment Philosophy

The Master Investor	The Losing Investor
Has developed his own investment philosophy, which is an expression of his personality, abilities, knowledge, tastes, and objectives. As a result, no two highly successful investors have the same investment philosophy.	Has no investment philosophy— or uses someone else's.

So it is in the investment arena.

An *investment philosophy* is a set of beliefs about:

- the nature of investment reality: how markets work and why prices move;
- a theory of value, including how value can be identified and what causes profits and losses; and
- the nature of a good investment.

Every investor has such a philosophy. As prominent investment psychologist Van Tharp says, you don't trade the market, you trade your beliefs about the market.[3] If you don't know what those beliefs are, how can you know what you are doing?

Most investors cling to a potpourri of beliefs, often self-contradictory, that they have absorbed from their environment. Because they haven't figured things out for themselves, they tend to change their investment beliefs along with the market's prevailing bias.

For example, in the 1990s it was widely believed that stocks will always go up in the long run, that you could get rich by doing nothing more than buying on dips.

In the dot-com boom, the majority of investors, analysts, advisors, and fund managers came to believe that the law of economic gravity ("What goes up must come down") had been repealed, that valuations and even profits didn't matter.

Not Warren Buffett and George Soros. Each devoted much time and thought to developing his own explicit and internally consistent investment philosophy, which doesn't change with the prevailing winds. The Master Investor's philosophy is his mental shield against the market's constant emotional chaos.

Whether the Master Investor has consciously adopted someone else's investment philosophy (as Buffett initially did Graham's) or independently developed his own (applies to both Buffett and Soros), he has consciously thought through each investment belief he holds; he is always fully aware of the why behind every investment action he takes.

The resulting clarity he brings to his investment decisions is a major key to his success.

Just as Buffett's and Soros's abilities, interests, skills, knowledge, and experiences are very different, so are their investment philosophies.

For example, Buffett was fascinated by money, business, and numbers from an early age. So it's hardly surprising that the focus of his investment philosophy is on his theory of value, which he applies to judge the quality of a business enterprise.

When Buffett comments on the nature of investment reality, he frames his remarks in terms of business value and how managers and investors often act on the basis of some erroneous concept of value.

Soros's main interest in life was and continues to be philosophy. He began his investment career in London arbitraging gold stocks between different international markets and made his name in New York as an expert in European stocks (which he described as "being one-eyed in the kingdom of the blind"). His radically different investment philosophy reflects these antecedents.

"Identifying Market Reality"

Buffett and Soros both view the same investment reality but draw totally different (if not opposite) conclusions about how to deal with it.

Their different rules for action stem from the differences in their psychology, character, history, interests, motives, goals, talents, and skills.

Yet their identification of investment reality is all but identical.

Buffett talks about the manic-depressive Mr. Market who will be wildly overexcited one day and deeply depressed the next.

Soros's initial premise about the nature of investment reality is that "The market is always wrong."

Buffett doesn't delve deeply into the reasons why the market is wrong; he just observes that it is and takes advantage of it. Soros, on the other hand, has developed a detailed theory of why the market is always wrong that is central to his way of profiting from it.

Both, then, vehemently reject investment philosophies like the efficient-market hypothesis (which can be restated as "The market is always right") and the random-walk theory which claim that above-average profits are either impossible or statistical discrepancies. To those theories, Buffett responds: "I'd be a bum on the street with a tin cup if the markets were always efficient."[4]

When you put Buffett's and Soros's investment philosophies together, you have an almost complete explanation of how investment markets work. Not the only one, to be sure—but wouldn't it be foolish to ignore the meeting of minds of the world's two greatest investors?

Appointment with Destiny

What brought everything together for Buffett—what gave him
the investment philosophy he was searching for—was Benjamin
Graham's book, *The Intelligent Investor.*

> For Buffett, reading the book was an epiphany.
> "It was like Paul on the road to Damascus. I read the first
> edition of the book early in 1950, when I was nineteen. I
> thought then that it was by far the best book about invest-
> ing ever written. I still think it is."[5]

Benjamin Graham revolutionized investing with the publication
of *Security Analysis* in 1934. Known today as the "Father of Value
Investing," Graham gave a mathematically based method of finding certainty in a field dominated then (as now) by approaches
such as momentum investing, chart reading, Gann triangles, and
Elliot Waves; in an arena where investors behave, more often than
not, like lemmings rather than the rational beings humans are supposed to be.

Graham's methodology spoke directly to Buffett's mathematical bent and changed his investment behavior forever.

Meet Mr. Market

The foundation of both Benjamin Graham's and Warren Buffett's
investment philosophies is a view of the nature of investment
markets that Graham personified in Mr. Market.

In one of his letters to Berkshire Hathaway shareholders, Warren Buffett describes Graham's Mr. Market in this way:

> Ben Graham, my friend and teacher, long ago described the
> mental attitude toward market fluctuations that I believe to

be most conducive to investment success. He said that you should imagine market quotations as coming from a re- markably accommodating fellow named Mr. Market who is your partner in a private business. Without fail, Mr. Market appears daily and names a price at which he will either buy your interest or sell you his.

Even though the business that the two of you own may have economic characteristics that are stable, Mr. Market's quotations will be anything but. For, sad to say, the poor fel- low has incurable emotional problems. At times he falls eu- phoric and can see only the favorable factors affecting the business. When in that mood, he names a very high buy-sell price because he fears that you will snap up his interest and rob him of imminent gains. At other times he is depressed and can see nothing but trouble ahead for both the business and the world. On these occasions he will name a very low price, since he is terrified that you will unload your interest to him.

Mr. Market has another endearing characteristic: He doesn't mind being ignored. If his quotation is uninteresting to you today, he will be back with a new one tomorrow. Transactions are strictly at your option. Under these condi- tions, the more manic-depressive his behavior, the better for you.

But, like Cinderella at the ball, you must heed one warn- ing or everything will turn into pumpkins and mice: Mr. Market is there to serve you, not to guide you. It is his pock- etbook, not his wisdom, that you will find useful. If he shows up someday in a particularly foolish mood, you are free to either ignore him or to take advantage of him, but it will be disastrous if you fall under his influence. Indeed, if you aren't certain that you understand and can value your business far better than Mr. Market, you don't belong in the game. As they say in poker, "if you've been in the game 30 minutes and you don't know who the patsy is, *you're* the patsy."[6]

Underlying this Graham-Buffett view of the market are several important beliefs about the nature of investment markets and the attitude to them that investors should adopt if they want to be successful.

First is the belief that *the market is always* (or often) *wrong*.

Second, embedded in this view of the market is Graham's and Buffett's strategy for investment profits. If Mr. Market is subject to psychotic mood swings, then, inevitably, there will be times when he'll offer a price for a stock that is insanely cheap and other times when he'll be willing to buy the same security at a price that's ridiculously high.

But it's impossible to predict *when* Mr. Market's mood swings will occur or to know in advance how depressed or euphoric he will get.

In other words, it's impossible to predict the future course of market prices. So prediction plays no part in a Graham–Buffett-style investment strategy.

Third, as Buffett points out, "Mr. Market is there to serve you, not to guide you. . . . It will be disastrous if you fall under his influence."

So if it's a mistake to seek guidance from Mr. Market or from people who are under his spell, if it's imperative to avoid getting swept up in Mr. Market's mood swings, what is your basis for making investment decisions?

Graham's and Buffett's answer is to use their own, independently derived standard of value for determining when a stock is cheap or expensive.

With their determination of value based on their own judgment, their attitude to Mr. Market's manic-depressive behavior is basically one of *indifference*. They *ignore him*. They merely take note of the price Mr. Market offers: If it accords with their own, independently derived judgment of value, they will act; if it doesn't, they will happily wait until Mr. Market changes his mind, confident that sooner or later he will.

Buffett and Graham accept market fluctuations as a given. They don't have a detailed theory of *why* markets fluctuate—and their investment approach doesn't need one. The focus of their investment philosophies is on determining value and the characteristics of a sound investment.

Buffett Changes Course

In 1956, Buffett started managing other people's money, forming a series of partnerships that were eventually amalgamated into one: the Buffett Partnership.

He continued to follow a pure Benjamin Graham approach, as he had since 1950. But Buffett was not Graham.

Though successful as an investor, Graham was primarily a scholar, a theoretician. Buffett—though he did lecture at the University of Omaha, and still loves to teach—is primarily a businessman.

Though Graham had written, in *Security Analysis* in 1934:

It is an almost unbelievable fact that Wall Street never asks: "How much is the *business* selling for?" Yet this should be the first question in considering a stock purchase.[7]

he didn't *view* a company as a business; and wasn't particularly interested in a company's management or products. He focused only on the numbers.

But the question Graham asked in 1934—"How much is the *business* selling for?"—was to become the foundation of Buffett's own, personal style of investing.

The first indication that he might be departing from Graham was when he invested one-fifth of his partnership assets in a 70 percent controlling interest in Dempster Mill Manufacturing Co., a company that made windmills and farm implements. But its business was static and turning it around just wasn't Buffett's cup of tea. It wasn't long before he put the company up for sale.

But he did not question the Graham-like premise that had led to its *purchase*. In fact, Graham's influence permeated the partnerships. Aside from Dempster, the money was sprinkled among forty stocks—cigar butts, arbitrages, workouts (such as liquidations)—all from the Graham-Newman playbook.[8]

In 1963 Buffett began accumulating the first stock he bought that Graham definitely would *not* buy: American Express. Again, he bought big, putting twenty-five percent of the partnership's assets into the company.

Buffett adhered then—as he does today—to Graham's fundamental principle that you only buy value you can see at a price which gives you a significant margin of safety. In American Express, Buffett saw both value *and* a margin of safety. But what he was "seeing" and how he calculated value was changing.

An American Express subsidiary operated a warehouse that stored tanks of vegetable oil. In return, it issued receipts to its customers. Unfortunately, one of them—Allied Crude Vegetable Oil and Refining—was run by a crook. Allied's credit rating was zero. But it discovered it could turn vegetable oil into American Express receipts, which were bankable.

When Allied went bankrupt, its creditors came knocking on American Express's door for their receipts—or their money instead. Only then was the scam uncovered: The tanks Allied had in storage were mainly seawater, with just enough vegetable oil floating on top so to make them appear full. American Express was facing a $60 million loss—"more than we had," in the words of CEO Howard Clark.[9]

From $60 a share in November 1963, before the salad oil scandal broke, American Express's stock sank to $35 in early 1964.

Would American Express survive? Wall Street was advising "sell"—in effect, answering no.

Buffett saw the problem as a one-off event *that did not affect American Express's main business:* the American Express card and its traveler's checks.

But how to value the company?

For Graham the company—even at $35 a share—was a no-no. It still cost far more than the value of its tangible assets—its book value.

What American Express had was *in*tangible: its customer base, the world's leading credit card (this was before VISA and Master-Card), and hundreds of millions of dollars in "float" on traveler's checks issued but not yet cashed.

Buffett saw an ongoing business with a valuable, irreplaceable business franchise generating steady earnings—and those earnings could be had at a bargain price.

Buffett's question became: "Has American Express's *business franchise* been affected?" Not the sort of question you can find an answer to in the annual report.

He became a detective. He spent an evening standing behind the cash register at his favorite steakhouse in Omaha and discovered that people were still charging their American Express cards—it was business as usual. From banks, travel agents, supermarkets, and drugstores he found there had been no decline in sales of American Express traveler's checks and money orders. He called on competitors and found that the American Express card was as strong as ever.

He concluded that American Express would survive. And once he had reached that conclusion, he scooped up American Express shares with both hands.

The "Four Dimensional" Investor

While Benjamin Graham was developing what came to be called value investing in New York, another now-famous investor, Philip Fisher, who wrote *Common Stocks and Uncommon Profits*, was creating what was later called growth investing a continent away in San Francisco.

It was Fisher's influence that led Buffett to his purchase of American Express. Indeed, today Buffett's investment approach seems to have more in common with Fisher's than Graham's.

Where Graham's method of valuation was quantitative, Fisher's was qualitative. Graham relied solely on the numbers from companies' financial statements. To Fisher, by contrast, "reading the printed financial records about a company is never enough to justify an investment."[10] According to Fisher:

> What really counts in determining whether a stock is cheap or overpriced is not its ratio to the current year's earnings, but its ratio to the earnings a few years ahead. . . . [This is] the key to avoiding losses and making magnificent profits.[11]

Like Graham, Fisher was looking for cheap stocks. He also had "an intense dislike for losing money."[12]

But determining a company's earnings "a few years ahead" is clearly a very different proposition from figuring out its book or liquidation value from an annual report. As you would expect, Fisher's investment criteria were very different from Graham's.

He could estimate, with confidence, a company's future earnings *only by understanding the company's business.* So his first rule was to stay within his "circle of competence" at all times. Like Buffett does today, he only invested in industries he understood.

Within that "circle of competence," he looked for companies that met all of his "Four Dimensions":

1. They must have a decided edge on their competition by being the lowest-cost producer in the industry, or have superior production, financial, research, and marketing skills.

2. They must have outstanding management, which he saw as the underlying cause of outstanding results.

3. The economic characteristics of the business must all but ensure that the company's current above-industry-average

profits, return on assets, profit margin, and growth of sales will continue for an extended period of time.

4. The price must be attractive.

How did Fisher do it?

By talking to people.

Of course, a lot can be discovered from annual reports and other available company information. Mostly they will tell you which companies to avoid. For example, you can often determine the honesty—or lack thereof—of the management simply by reading a few past years' annual reports.

But for Fisher, there was no substitute for first-hand information.

When possible, he would talk to the company, of course, and get to know its executives. But no matter how honest and forthcoming company officials are, their perspective is necessarily incomplete.

One of Fisher's favorite sources of information was scuttlebutt: what people were saying about the company and its products. He would talk to people who dealt with the company—customers, consumers, and suppliers; to former employees; and, especially, to competitors. An executive may be reluctant to give you too much detail about his own company. But he'll happily tell you everything he knows about his competition.

In his first foray into this kind of analysis—while he was working in the investment department of a bank in San Francisco in 1928—Fisher talked to buyers in the radio department of several San Francisco stores.

I asked them their opinions of the three major competitors in this industry. I was given surprisingly similar opinions from each of them . . . . One company, Philco, which from my standpoint unfortunately was privately-owned so that it represented no stock market opportunity, had developed models which had especial market appeal. As a result, they were getting market share at a beautiful profit to themselves because they were highly efficient manufacturers. RCA was just about holding its own market share, whereas another company which was a stock market favorite of the day was slipping dramatically and showing signs of getting into trouble . . . . Nowhere in material from Wall Street firms who were talking about these "hot" radio issues could I find a single word about the troubles that were obviously developing for this speculative favorite.[13]

Fisher watched the stock he had singled out for trouble sink while the stock market climbed to new highs.

It was my first lesson in what later was to become part of my basic investment philosophy: reading the printed financial records about a company is never enough to justify an investment. One of the major steps in prudent investment must be to find out about a company's affairs from those who have some direct familiarity with them.[14]

Having discovered an outstanding company that met all his criteria, Fisher would invest a large percentage of his portfolio in it.

Fisher preferred to own just a few outstanding companies, not a large number of average businesses. He rarely owned more than ten stocks, and usually three or four companies accounted for three-quarters of his equity.

Once he had bought a company he would keep it for years—sometimes decades. He described his average holding period as "20 years, and [I] held one stock for 53 years."[15]

When, according to Fisher, was the best time to sell?

If the job has been correctly done when a common stock is purchased, the time to sell it is—almost never.[16]

He said there were only three times to sell a stock. The first was when you found you'd made a mistake, and the company didn't meet the criteria after all. The second time was when the company ceased to meet the criteria: For example, a less able management assumed control; or the company had grown so big it could no longer grow faster than the industry as a whole. And the third was when you came across a fantastic opportunity and the only way you could buy it was to sell something first.

Fisher also had his equivalent of Graham's Mr. Market—his philosophy about the nature of the market—which, like Mr. Market, showed him the best time to buy.

He believed (rather like George Soros) that market prices were determined more by perceptions (and *mis*perceptions) than by the facts. In short, he believed that Wall Street focuses on the short term and ignores the long term. And that can present magnificent investment opportunities.

For example, when a company makes a mistake, Wall Street punishes it severely.

> When [a mistake] happens and the current year's earnings drop sharply below previous estimates as the costs of the failure are added up, time and again the investment community's immediate consensus is to downgrade the quality of the management. As a result, the immediate year's lower earnings produce a lower than the historic price earnings ratio to magnify the effect of the reduced earnings. The shares often reach truly bargain prices. Yet if this is the same management that in other years has been so successful, the chances are the same ratio of average success to average failure will continue on in the future. For this reason, the shares of companies run by abnormally capable people can be tremendous bargains at the time one particular bad mistake comes to light.[17]

Fisher could have been describing American Express at the time Buffett invested.

Charlie Munger: Buffett's Alter Ego

At the same time as he was investing in American Express, Buffett continued to buy cheap companies (which he later termed "cigar butts"—they have just a few puffs left but the price is right) like Berkshire Hathaway. And despite the success of his investment in American Express, most of his investments continued to be classic Graham.

That began to change as his friendship with Charlie Munger—whom he met in 1959—deepened.

A lawyer by training, Munger managed an investment partnership from 1962 to 1975, achieving an annual return of 19.8 percent (compared to 5.0 percent for the Dow over the same period). Eventually he and Buffett merged their interests under the single roof of Berkshire Hathaway, with Munger as vice chairman.

> It was Charlie Munger who was most responsible for moving Buffett towards Fisher's thinking. Charlie, in a sense, was the embodiment of Fisher's qualitative theories. Charlie had a deep appreciation of the value of a better business. Both See's Candy Shops and Buffalo News were tangible examples of good businesses available at reasonable prices. Charlie educated Buffett about the wisdom of paying up for a good business.[18]

In 1971, Blue Chip Stamps (a company controlled by Buffett and Munger) was offered See's Candies for $30 million. Unimpressed by the book value of the company (though it included $10 million in cash), they offered $25 million.

Luckily for them, Mr. See phoned back the next day and accepted. Now wholly owned by Berkshire, since 1984 See's has made *over* $25 million in pretax profits *every year*. See's was just the first of the many noninsurance companies Berkshire now owns outright.

These purchases represented a dramatic departure from Graham's style of investing. Like See's (and American Express), their book value was usually far *lower* than the price Buffett paid. And Buffett took management control, buying 80–100% of the shares depending on whether or not the owners wanted to retain a stake.

The method of valuation was primarily Fisher—constrained by Graham; but taking control was pure Buffett. He was returning to his original incarnation as a businessman.

Buffett describes himself today as "85% Graham, 15% Fisher." Whatever the actual mix—and I suspect Fisher's influence is far higher than 15 percent—he has combined the two with his own experience and insights into his own, personal style of investing, which is 100 percent Buffett.

Like American Express and See's Candies, most of the investments he makes today are in companies that Graham wouldn't buy—but Fisher might.

Reading the Mind of Mr. Market

Unlike Buffett, George Soros never set out to be an investor or businessman. Indeed, as a teenager he had fancied himself as some kind of economic reformer like John Maynard Keynes. Or even a scientist like Einstein.

So in 1949—having escaped from Soviet-occupied Hungary two years before—he enrolled at the London School of Economics to study economics and international politics. The LSE was a hotbed of socialism, no different from most other universities at the time, except that Harold Laski, one of the most influential Keynesians, taught there. (Laski was the model for Ayn Rand's antihero Ellsworth Toohey, in her best-selling novel *The Fountainhead*.)

But the LSE was also home to two very unfashionable thinkers, free market economist Friedrich von Hayek and philosopher Karl Popper. Soros learnt from both, but Popper became his mentor and a major intellectual influence on his life.

I finished my degree course, which was supposed to take three years, in two. I had to spend an extra year as a registered student to qualify for the degree, and I was allowed to select a tutor. I chose him [Popper] because I was very much taken by his philosophy. I had lived through Nazi persecution and Soviet occupation. Popper's book, *Open Society and Its Enemies,* struck me with the force of revelation—it showed that fascism and communism have a lot in common, and they both stand in opposition to a different principle of social organization, the principle of open society. I was even more influenced by Popper's ideas on scientific method.[19]

Popper provided Soros with the intellectual framework that, later, evolved into both Soros's investment philosophy and his investment *method.*

Soros has acknowledged Popper's influence by naming his charitable organizations Open Society Foundations.

But that was later. In his student days, his aim was still to become an academic, a philosopher of some kind. He began writing a book he called *The Burden of Consciousness.* When he realized he was merely regurgitating Popper's philosophy, he put it aside and turned to a financial career. Ever since, he has viewed the financial markets as a laboratory where he could test his philosophical ideas.

"Our Views of the World Are Flawed or Distorted"

While struggling with philosophical questions, Soros made what he considered to be a major intellectual discovery:

I came to the conclusion that basically all our views of the world are somehow flawed or distorted, and then I concentrated on the importance of this distortion in shaping events.[20]

Applying that discovery to himself, Soros concluded: "I am fallible." This was not just an observation; it became his operational principle and overriding belief.

Most people agree that other people make mistakes. Most will admit to having made mistakes—in the past. But who will openly acknowledge that they are fallible *while* making a decision?

Very few, as Soros implies in his comment about his former partner, Jimmy Rogers (fund manager and author of *The Investment Biker*):

> The big difference between Jim Rogers and me was that Jim thought that the prevailing view was always wrong, whereas I thought that we may be wrong also.[21]

When Soros acts in the investment arena, he remains aware that he can be wrong, and is critical of his own thought processes. This gives him unparalleled mental flexibility and agility.

Beliefs and Consequences

If, as Soros believed, *everybody's* view of the world is "somehow flawed or distorted," then our understanding of the world is necessarily imperfect and often wrong.

To take an extreme example: When Christopher Columbus set sail across the Atlantic Ocean for India, everybody "knew" the earth was flat and he would fall off the edge of the world.

This belief made it very difficult for him to find a backer—and even harder to crew his ships. After all, his backers weren't going along for the ride.

While European sailors hugged the shoreline, Polynesians,

who had no such belief, sailed their dugout canoes over the track-less Pacific to tiny islands as far apart as Fiji and Hawaii. That's a feat of navigation that will probably never be surpassed.

Soros turned his realization that people's understanding of reality is imperfect into a powerful investment tool. On those occasions when he could see what others could not—because they were blinded, for example, by their beliefs—he came into his element.

When he started the Quantum Fund (originally named the Double Eagle Fund) he tested his theory by searching for developing market trends or sudden changes about to happen that nobody else had noticed.

He found one such trend change in the banking industry.

Heavily regulated since the 1930s, banks were seen as staid, steady, conservative, and, most of all, boring investments. There was no future for a hotshot Wall Street analyst in the banking business.

Soros sensed this was about to change. He had discovered that the old-style managers were retiring and being replaced by new, aggressive youngsters with MBAs. This new management, he felt, would focus on the bottom line and shake up the industry.

In 1972, Soros published a report titled "The Case for Growth Banks," forecasting that bank shares were about to take off. "He recommended some of the better-managed banks. In time, bank stocks began to rise, and Soros garnered a 50 percent profit."[22]

Where Buffett seeks to buy $1 for 40 or 50 cents, Soros is happy to pay $1, or even more, for $1 when he can see a change coming that will drive that dollar up to $2 or $3.

How Beliefs Alter Facts

To Soros, our distorted perceptions are a factor in shaping events. As he puts it, "what beliefs do is alter facts"[23] in a process he calls reflexivity, which he outlined in his book *The Alchemy of Finance*.

For some, like the trader Paul Tudor Jones, the book was "revolutionary"; it clarified events "that appeared so complex and so overwhelming,"[24] as he wrote in the foreword of the 1994 paperback edition. Through the book Soros also met Stanley Druckenmiller, who sought him out after reading it and eventually took over from Soros as manager of the Quantum Fund.

To most others, however, the book was impenetrable, even unreadable, and few people grasped the idea of reflexivity Soros was attempting to convey. Indeed, as Soros wrote in the preface to the paperback edition,

> Judging by the public reaction . . . I have not been successful in demonstrating the significance of reflexivity. Only the first part of my argument—that the prevailing bias affects market prices—seems to have registered. The second part—that the prevailing bias can in certain circumstances also affect the so-called fundamentals and changes in market prices cause changes in market prices—seems to have gone unnoticed.[25]

Changes in market prices cause changes in market prices? Sounds ridiculous.

But it's not. To give just one example, as stock prices go up, investors feel wealthier and spend more money. Company sales and profits rise as a result. Wall Street analysts point to these "improving fundamentals," and urge investors to buy. That sends stocks up further, making investors even wealthier, so they spend even more. And so on it goes. This is what Soros calls a "reflexive process"—a feedback loop: a change in stock prices has caused a change in company fundamentals, which, in turn, justifies a further rise in stock prices. And so on.

You have no doubt heard of this particular reflexive process. Academics have written about it; even the Federal Reserve has issued a paper on it. It's known as "the wealth effect."

Reflexivity is a feedback loop: Perceptions change facts; and facts change perceptions. As happened when the Thai baht collapsed in 1997.

In July 1997 the Central Bank of Thailand let its currency float. The bank expected a devaluation of around 20 percent, but by December the baht had collapsed from 26 to the US dollar to over 50, a fall of more than 50 percent.

The bank had figured out that the baht was "really worth" around 32 to the dollar. Which it may well have been according to the theoretical models of currency valuation. What the bank failed to take into account was that floating the baht set in motion a self-reinforcing process of reflexivity that sent the currency into free fall.

Thailand was one of the Asian Tigers, a country that was developing rapidly, and was seen to be following in Japan's footsteps. Fixed by the government to the US dollar, the Thai baht was considered a stable currency. So international bankers were happy to lend Thai companies billions of US dollars. And the Thais were happy to borrow them because US dollar interest rates were lower.

When the currency collapsed, the value of the US dollar debts companies had to repay suddenly exploded . . . when measured in baht. The fundamentals had changed.

Seeing this, investors dumped their Thai stocks. As they exited, foreigners converted their baht into dollars and took them home. The baht crumbled some more. More and more Thai companies looked like they would never be able to repay their debts. Both Thais and foreigners kept selling.

Thai companies cut back and sacked workers. Unemployment skyrocketed; workers had less to spend—and those who still had money to spend held onto it from fear of uncertainty. The Thai economy tanked—and the outlook for many large Thai companies, *even those with no significant dollar debts,* began to look more and more precarious.

As the baht fell, the Thai economy imploded—and the baht fell some more. A change in market prices had caused a change in market prices.

Applied Reflexivity

For Soros, reflexivity is the key to understanding the cycle of boom followed by bust. Indeed, he writes, "A boom/bust process occurs only when market prices . . . influence the so-called fundamentals that are supposed to be reflected in market prices."[26]

His method is to look for situations where Mr. Market's perceptions diverge widely from the underlying reality. On those occasions when Soros can see a reflexive process taking hold of the market, he can be confident that the developing trend will continue for longer, and prices will move far higher (or lower) than most people using a standard analytical framework expect.

Soros applies his philosophy to identifying a market trend in its early stages and positioning himself before the crowd catches on.

In 1969 a new financial vehicle, real estate investment trusts (REITs), attracted his attention. He wrote an analysis—widely circulated at the time—in which he predicted a "Four Act" reflexive boom/bust process that would send these new securities sky-high—before they collapsed.

Act I: As bank interest rates were high, REITs offered an attractive alternative to traditional sources of mortgage finance. As they caught on, Soros foresaw a rapid expansion of the number of REITs coming to market.

Act II: Soros expected that the creation of new REITs, and expansion of existing ones, would pour floods of new money into the mortgage market, causing a housing boom. That would, in turn, increase the profitability of REITs and send the price of their trust units skyrocketing.

Act III: To quote from his report, "The self-reinforcing process will continue until mortgage trusts have captured a significant part of the construction loan market."[27] As the housing boom slackened, real estate prices would fall, REITs would hold an increasing number of uncollectible mortgages—"and the banks will panic and demand that their lines of credit be paid off."[28]

Act IV: As REIT earnings fall, there would be a shakeout in the industry—a collapse.

Since "the shakeout is a long time away," Soros advised there was plenty of time to profit from the boom part of the cycle. The only real danger he foresaw "is that the self-reinforcing process [Act II] would not get under way at all."[29]

The cycle unfolded just as Soros had expected, and he made handsome profits as the boom progressed. Over a year later, after REITs had already begun to decline, he came across his original report and "I decided to sell the group short more or less indiscriminately."[30] His fund took another million dollars in profits out of the market.

Soros had applied reflexivity to make money on the way up *and* the way down.

To some, Soros's method may appear similar to trend following. But trend followers (especially chartists) normally wait for a trend to be confirmed before investing. When the trend followers pile in (as in "Act II" of the REIT cycle) *Soros is already there.* Sometimes he would add to his positions as the trend-following behavior of the market increased the certainty of his convictions about the trend.

But how do you know when the trend is coming to an end? The average trend follower can never be sure. Some get nervous as their profits build, often bailing out on a bull market correction. Others wait until a change in trend is confirmed—which only happens when prices have passed their highs and the bear market is under way.

But Soros's investment philosophy provides a framework for analyzing how events will unfold. So he can stay with the trend longer and take far greater profits from it than most other investors. And, as in the REIT example, profit from both the boom and the bust.

Buffett, by contrast, merely notes that Mr. Market is psychotic. Or, to quote Benjamin Graham, "In the short run, the market is a voting machine—reflecting a voter-registration test that requires only money, not intelligence or emotional stability—but in the long run, the market is a weighing machine."[31]

Why Women's Skirts Go Up—and Down

To a mere male such as myself—especially one who wears something comfortable until it literally falls apart—there has never been any logical reason why women's fashions should change so dramatically from one season to the next. Yet a new women's fashion trend can spread like wildfire. Whether inspired by a Paris designer or by something a movie star or teenagers in California, Brooklyn, or Tokyo wore, somehow the new style becomes the in thing to be seen in, and in no time at all you see it everywhere.

Why becomes clear when you view the fashion business through the lens of reflexivity: Behind each new fashion trend is a new *belief* about what looks good. The profitability of billion-dollar companies isn't just shaped by but is *based on* ever-changing beliefs.

If a company is caught with an inventory of clothes that are suddenly out of fashion, it has to write them off. To avoid that, lead times between ordering, production, and sale are continually tightened. Today clothes are made in small batches in China or Mauritius or Bangladesh and air-freighted to retailers around the world. So if a retailer or manufacturer guesses wrong, his loss is small.

Women's fashion buyers are like Wall Street gurus trying to ride the next trend. How well they read the opinion of the market determines their company's profits. And (as on Wall Street) there is never a guarantee that someone who got it right today will repeat their success tomorrow.

The only constant in the women's fashion industry is that what women like to wear this season they probably won't want to be seen dead in a year from now.

Consumers, buyers, retailers, designers, and manufacturers are engaged in a circular and never-ending guessing game of who'll be wearing what when and what will be in and out. The result: a constant state of change, of disequilibrium—the natural state of an industry that is purely reflexive in nature, *ruled entirely by beliefs or opinions.*

Soros's theory of reflexivity is his *explanation* for Mr. Market's manic-depressive mood swings. In Soros's hands it becomes a method for identifying when the mood of the market is about to change, for enabling him to "read the mind of the market."

The Master Investor's Edge

The Master Investor's investment philosophy explains investment reality, how markets work, how to determine value, and why prices change; it is his guide to taking action.

His philosophy makes his investment criteria clear and allows him to identify "high probability events" with reasonable certainty.

To a large degree, investing is a cerebral process, and if there's one single factor that sets the Master Investor apart, it is *the amount of thinking he's done.*

Buffett and Soros have both developed highly detailed and unique investment philosophies.

Every action that they take is an expression of the extent and depth of their *previous* thinking. And they continue to think deeply about every investment they make before they invest a dime.

The Master Investor's investment philosophy also gives him a powerful psychological edge: It's what enables him to keep his head while all those around him are losing theirs.

"I Deserve to Make Money"

Your investment philosophy reflects your beliefs about the external world: the nature of investment reality.

Just as important are the beliefs you have about yourself as an investor. Both Buffett and Soros share certain beliefs about themselves that are an essential component of their success.

- They believe that they deserve to succeed and make money.
- They believe that they are responsible for their own financial destiny; that they, not the markets or some external force, cause their profits or losses; that they are in control.

These beliefs are held *subconsciously,* and are behind the self-confidence the Master Investor exhibits in applying his investment philosophy.

Someone who adopts a proven investment philosophy may still end up being unsuccessful if his subconscious beliefs about himself get in his way.

Psychologists' offices are filled with people who have become successful—yet are now unhappy because, subconsciously, they have a fear of success or feel deep down that they don't deserve to succeed; with people whose subconscious belief that "I'm not lovable" is destroying their relationships; and with investors who inexplicably "give back" some of their profits because deep down they don't feel they deserve to make money.

An integral part of Buffett's and Soros's success is that neither is held back by such self-limiting beliefs.

It's easy to see why such beliefs are so crucially important.

If you don't believe that you deserve to make money, then investment success will make you anxious. Inevitably, your emotions will cloud your judgment, and you'll make some mistake and give the money back.

Similarly, only by taking responsibility for your own results can you be in control of your actions. This doesn't mean that you can control outside events, but you can define what is within your control and stay there.

Investors who act on some broker's tip, who do what their friends are doing, or whose main source of investment wisdom is the daily newspaper are like corks bobbing on the ocean waves. They let others control their actions, so it's never *their* fault when they lose money. As a consequence, they never learn.

BEWARE! Mixing Religion with Markets
Can Be Hazardous to Your Wealth

One important factor to keep in mind while you think through
your own investment philosophy is what happens to investors
who bring a religious- or fundamentalist-style theory to the
marketplace. Putting on a set of these blinders will hide
investment reality, not reveal it.

When I started my investment newsletter in 1974, I was a gold
bug. I *believed* in gold. I believed that inflation would inevitably
rise until the dollar disappeared in a South American–style
hyperinflation.

Back then, gold bugs made money. Lots of it. Inflation was
rising, and commodities was where the action was. For gold bugs,
the stock market was dullsville.

When gold bugs congregated at investment seminars like the
annual one in New Orleans, attended by over 3,000 investors in
its heyday, there was a tone of religious fervor in the air. Among
the speakers and attendees alike.

As one prominent investment advisor whispered to me,
commenting on the current speaker. "But he doesn't *believe* in gold!"

If a surfer who is riding a wonderful wave gets to thinking he's
invulnerable, he inevitably gets into trouble when the wave
breaks. As it always does.

If he has been making fistfuls of money while riding that wave,
the comedown will be traumatic. Following a religious theory
about the markets is fine while the theory is working. Once the
wave is over, though, it's a guaranteed road to the poorhouse . . .
as too many gold bugs discovered.

As a gold bug, I was blind to any evidence that the gold wave
had broken. Luckily for me, it only took a couple of years for
reality to tear the blinders off my eyes.

6

You Are What You Measure

"I believe that systems tend to be more useful or successful for the originator than for someone else. It's important that an approach be personalized; otherwise, you won't have the confidence to follow it."

—GIL BLAKE[1]

"The [secret] is for a trader to develop a system with which he is compatible."

—ED SEYKOTA[2]

"Virtually every successful trader I know ultimately ended up with a trading style suited to his personality."

—RANDY MCKAY[3]

JUST AS EVERY MASTER INVESTOR's philosophy is unique, so are his investment *criteria* and his investment *method*.

His criteria describe the kind of investment he is looking for.

WINNING HABIT NO. 4:

DEVELOP YOUR OWN, *PERSONAL* SYSTEM FOR SELECTING, BUYING, *AND SELLING* INVESTMENTS

The Master Investor

Has developed—and *tested*—his own **personal system** for selecting, buying, *and selling* investments.

The Losing Investor

Has no system. Or has adopted someone else's without testing and adapting it to his own personality. (When such a system doesn't work for him, he adopts another one—which doesn't work for him either.)

His method is a set of rules about what to do once he has identified an investment that matches his criteria.

The unifying factor is the answer to the question *What are you measuring?*

What the Master Investor is measuring against, of course, is his investment criteria. His investment criteria tell him what kind of investment to buy and its specific nature, when he should buy it, and when he should sell it. His criteria also define how he goes about searching for investments that meet them.

Buffett aims to buy a dollar of value at a bargain price. His criteria for investing can be summed up as "a quality business at the right price." And the quality of the business is what he measures.

Soros aims to profit from a change in Mr. Market's mood. He bases his investment decisions on a hypothesis about the coming course of events. What he measures is the quality of his hypothesis and the progress of events.

To apply his criteria each Master Investor has developed his own, personalized investment system. Though their approaches are very different, each Master Investor's system is built from the same twelve critical elements:

	BUFFETT MEASURES: QUALITY OF BUSINESS	SOROS MEASURES: QUALITY OF HYPOTHESIS
1. What to buy	All or part of a business that he understands—and that meets his criteria.	Assets that will change in price if his hypothesis is valid.
2. When to buy it	When the price is right.	At the right time—which he determines by testing his hypothesis.
3. What price to pay	A price that gives him a margin of safety (i.e., a discount to the business's estimated value).	The current price.
4. How to buy it	Pay cash.	Futures, forward contracts, margin, with borrowed money.
5. How much to buy as a percentage of portfolio	As much as he can. Limits: How much cash he has available, how much stock is on the market—and for how long it's available at the right price.	As much as he can. Limits: Rarely exceeds 50% margin (on a total portfolio basis).
6. Monitoring progress of investments	Does the business *still* meet his criteria?	Is the hypothesis *still* valid? Is it progressing as expected? Has it run its course?
7. When to sell	Stock: When the business no longer meets his criteria. Wholly-owned business: When it's "broken and we can't fix it."[4]	When hypothesis has run its course or is no longer valid.
8. Portfolio structure and leverage	No target structure. Leverage only through insurance float, or borrowing when interest rates are low.	The base is stocks, fully owned, which becomes security for leverage.

	BUFFETT MEASURES: QUALITY OF BUSINESS	SOROS MEASURES: QUALITY OF HYPOTHESIS
9. Search strategy	Reads lots of annual reports; answers the phone.	Monitors political, economic, industry, currency, interest rate, and other trends. Looks for linkages between disparate, unfolding events.
10. Protection against systematic shocks such as market crashes	Only buys quality businesses he understands at a price that gives him a substantial margin of safety. Buffett-style businesses often expand market share when their competitors are in trouble, so becoming more profitable in the long run.	1. Judicious use of leverage ("never bets the farm"). 2. Beats a hasty retreat.
11. Handling mistakes	Gets out (stock market investment). Admits, accepts, and analyzes mistakes to avoid repeating them. Also considers "sins of omission" mistakes.	Gets the hell out. Has a detailed strategy for analyzing mistakes so he doesn't make the same mistake again.
12. What to do when the system doesn't work	Stops (e.g., closed Buffett Partnership in 1969); seeks flaw in method (e.g., adopting Fisher's methodology). Continually reviews system to see if it can be improved.	Stops. Continually reviews system to see if it can be improved.

Listening to the Market

Soros's investment process begins with framing a hypothesis. As one of his understudies at the Quantum Fund recalled: "George always used to say, '*Invest first and investigate later.*'"[5] His method is to form a hypothesis, dip his toe in the market with a small position to test it, and see whether he'll be proven right or wrong.

Why does Soros then test his hypothesis? Because he may not be certain it's valid or because he's uncertain about the timing.

Once he has a toehold, he "listens to the market" to learn what he should do next. If his test makes money, the market is telling him he is right, and he buys (or shorts) more to build his position.

If he loses money, the market is telling him he's wrong. So he gets straight out. He may test the same hypothesis again, later; or he may revise it or discard it altogether.

When I explained Soros's approach to a friend of mine, his reaction was: "You could go broke doing that!"

And if you lost big money on test after test, so you would.

After all, anyone can frame a hypothesis about the future. Indeed we all do, all the time.

If Soros's hypotheses were not of a much higher quality than random conjecture, he, too, would consistently lose money, not make it.

But Soros only tests when he has a hypothesis *worth* testing. What makes the difference is his deep understanding of markets and the actors on the stage, and little-noticed linkages between seemingly unconnected events. It was this depth of understanding that led to the investment that made him famous as "The Man Who Broke the Bank of England."

"The Bundesbank Calls the Tune"

In 1987, Britain became a member of the European Exchange Rate Mechanism, or ERM—a group of Common Market currencies colloquially known as "the snake"—anchored by the Deutsche Mark.

Investors came to believe that sterling, now linked to the Deutsche Mark, was as good as the mark. But as British interest rates were higher, money poured into sterling. In a reflexive, self-fulfilling prophecy, this increase in demand for sterling helped keep it stable against the mark . . . and set the scene for its subsequent fall.

Then the Berlin Wall was torn down, the Soviet Union collapsed, Germany was reunified, and the system, said Soros, "was thrown into a state of dynamic disequilibrium."[6]

The Deutsche Mark was now to become the currency of East as well as West Germany, which precipitated a bitter battle between the Bundesbank and Chancellor Helmut Kohl.

The fight was over the rate at which East Germany's currency, the Ostmark, should be exchanged for Deutsche Marks. The Ostmark, which had been almost worthless, rose in value to about four Ostmarks to one Deutsche Mark.

With his eye on his party's popularity in the coming election, when the "Ossies" would vote for first time, Kohl wanted a higher rate. To the Bundesbank, the economic and monetary effects of a higher rate were horrifying. The East German economy was a shambles, and it was debatable that its factories and businesses were worth buying even at 4:1. The higher the rate, the more Deutsche Marks everything in the East would cost, from the massive investment needed to westernize its economy to the social spending that would balloon as West German government benefits were extended eastward. The higher the rate, the harder it would be to persuade private businesses to invest there.

At a rate higher than 4:1, the Bundesbank foresaw a massive increase in government spending, an exploding deficit, high unemployment in the East . . . and most dangerous of all, the prospect of inflation.

Kohl won the dispute, and Ostmarks were exchanged at the incredibly overvalued rate of 1:1 for the first 4,000, and 2:1 thereafter.

But the Bundesbank was right. Kohl's overvaluation became a drag on the German economy for years, even requiring a special income tax hike to pay for his "generosity."

That, as Soros saw it, set the scene for the collapse of the "snake."

According to my theory, every exchange rate regime is flawed. There was a latent flaw in the ERM as well, but it became blatant only as a consequence of the reunification. The flaw was that the Bundesbank played a dual role in the system: It was both the anchor of the ERM and the constitutional protector of the stability of the German currency. During the near-equilibrium period, the Bundesbank could fill both roles without any problems, but the reunification of Germany, which caused the exchange of the East German currency for the Deutschemark at a very high, excessive rate, created a conflict between the two roles of the Bundesbank: its constitutional role and its role as an anchor of the ERM. . . .

The tremendous injection of capital from West Germany into East Germany set up strong inflationary pressures within the German economy. The Bundesbank was duty-bound—by the constitution, not just by law—to counteract it by pushing up interest rates and it did so with considerable vigor. This was at a time when Europe in general, and Britain in particular, were in the depths of a recession. The high German interest rate policy was totally inappropriate to the conditions that prevailed in England. A conflict arose between the two roles of the Bundesbank—and, under the constitution, there was no doubt which role would take precedence. Pursuing a resolutely tight monetary policy at a time when the rest of Europe was in recession disqualified the Bundesbank from serving as the anchor of the ERM. That threw the ERM, which had been operating near-equilibrium, into dynamic disequilibrium.[7]

To make sure the other members of the Common Market accepted the reunification of Germany—which, of course, instantly incorporated East Germany in the Common Market—Kohl proposed to French president François Mitterrand a strengthening of European institutions. Which set the framework for, among other things, what eventually became the euro.

[This] was the death knell of the Bundesbank, because the Bundesbank was going to be superseded by a European Central Bank. One might say that the European Central Bank was the spiritual successor to the Bundesbank, but that is scant consolation for an institution that is extremely powerful and enjoys its power. . . . [The] Treaty endangered the very existence of the Bundesbank.

So there was a conflict over these three issues: one, that Germany needed a different monetary policy than the rest of Europe; two, that the Bundesbank advocated a different fiscal policy for Germany than the one that Chancellor Kohl actually adopted; and three, that the Bundesbank was fighting for its institutional survival. In my view, of the three conflicts the third was the least understood and the most decisive.[8]

With "the Bundesbank calling the tune," as he put it, Soros figured it was only a matter of time before the strain of tight money in Germany shook the weak currencies out of the "snake." But the change that Soros had identified, from equilibrium to disequilibrium, began in 1989 with German reunification. *When* would it be time to actually put money on the table?

Not until 1992 was the timing right. . . .

I got my first hint [that a breakdown was in the offing] from Bundesbank President Schlesinger in a speech he gave. . . .

He said that he thought investors were making a mistake when they thought of the ECU (European Currency Unit) as a fixed basket of currencies. He was alluding particularly to the Italian lira as a currency that was not too sound. I asked him after the speech whether he liked the ECU as a currency, and he said that he liked it as a concept but he didn't like the name. He would have preferred it if it were called the mark.

I got the message.[9]

With the Bundesbank president effectively confirming the core of his hypothesis, Soros began testing it in the market. The Quantum Fund shorted the Italian lira, and the lira was soon forced out of the "snake." This confirmed his expectation that the Bundesbank was happy to see the "snake" fall apart, and the profit on the lira trade became a cushion for his much bigger position in a much bigger target: sterling.

Soros was not alone in shorting sterling—or the lira. Hundreds, possibly thousands of other traders saw the signs. Most currency traders are aware that the finance minister usually announces he's NOT going to devalue the currency the day before he does so.

But thanks to his depth of thinking, Soros had a far clearer understanding of *why* sterling would fall. This gave him the confidence to build up a $10 billion position against sterling at a time when the Quantum Fund's total assets were only $7 billion.

Ironically, he said later, "We planned to sell more than that.

"In fact, when [Britain's Chancellor of the Exchequer] Norman Lamont said that just before the devaluation he would borrow nearly $15 billion to defend sterling we were amused because that was about how much we wanted to sell. But things moved faster than we expected and we didn't manage to build up to the full position."[10]

Soros shorted $7 billion worth of sterling. But he also saw the collapse of sterling having a cascade effect on other European currency and stock and bond markets. In an example of the linkages he sees between different markets, he also sold other weak European currencies short, went long $6 billion in Deutsche Marks and also went long the French franc, bought $500 million of British stocks (on the hypothesis that they'd rise after the currency's fall), went long German and French bonds, and shorted German and French equities.

This was all financed with borrowings of £5 billion.

The pound had been tied to the mark at a central rate of 2.95. Sterling collapsed on Black Wednesday, September 16, 1992. By the end of that month, one pound was worth only 2.5 Deutsche Marks.

Altogether, the Quantum Fund took home profits of $2 billion when the Bank of England gave up the ghost.

Shooting Fish in a Barrel

Throughout, Soros is measuring the quality of his hypothesis— and even refining it to include the effect of sterling's collapse on other European markets.

His understanding of events and the clarity with which he saw the linkages between them gave Soros enormous confidence in his hypothesis. Always willing to buy as much as he could, his confidence that sterling would collapse led him to relax his normal rule of leveraging only $1 for every dollar of equity. He was willing to go as high as two for one.

He also judged what would happen if sterling was *not* forced out of the "snake": not much. It was almost impossible for the pound to go up. In the worst case, he would have had to unwind his positions at a loss he calculated as no more than 4 percent. Soros never bets the farm.

What is widely perceived as his most speculative bet was, to Soros, like "shooting fish in a barrel"—one with little risk.

Both Buffett and Soros agree with Mae West when she said: "Too much of a good thing can be wonderful." The size of a position they're willing to take is limited only by the resources at their disposal.

When to Sell

Soros takes profits when his hypothesis has run its course. His sterling hypothesis was event-related, so the time to sell was as soon as sterling was ejected from the ERM.

The beginnings and ends of currency trends are not always so clear-cut.

In 1985 Soros shorted the dollar heavily. The US dollar had been rising inexorably since Reagan became president. Imports were pouring into America, its exports were falling, and American industrialists were beating on the doors of the White House desperate to get a cheaper dollar.

On the weekend of September 22, 1985, the finance ministers of the United States, Britain, France, West Germany, and Japan got together at the Plaza Hotel in New York—and agreed to drive the dollar down. Soros got wind of this over the weekend and spent Sunday night in New York adding to his long positions in the yen and the mark in Tokyo, where it was already Monday morning.

When Soros came into the office the following morning, he'd made $40 million overnight. Some of his traders were already banking those profits. As Stanley Druckenmiller said later:

"Supposedly, George came bolting out of the door, directing the other traders to stop selling the yen. . . . The government had just told him that the dollar was going to go down for the next year, so why shouldn't he be a pig and buy more [yen]?"[11]

While most traders saw this fall in the dollar as a onetime event, Soros saw it as just the *beginning* of a trend. And with all the world's biggest central banks "on your side," how could you go wrong?

The dollar's decline eventually petered out. Soros made $150 million from the dollar's fall by not selling until the currency's weakness had run its course.

"Price Is What You Pay, Value Is What You Get"

Warren Buffett's investment trademark is the purchase of whole businesses, such as See's Candies, or huge equity investments in companies, such as Coca-Cola.

To Buffett, the difference between partial or complete ownership of a business makes no difference: His focus is always on the same thing, the *quality of the business.*

Central to his investment method is determining a business's value. To judge that value he applies a clear set of criteria, his first screen being:

"Do I Understand This Business?"

If Buffett can't understand a business, he has no way to measure its quality or its future—so he can't value it.

To Buffett, a company's value is the present worth of its future earnings. So he wants to be able to judge a business's earnings ten to twenty years into the future. And you can't do that if you don't understand the business.

He has often been criticized for avoiding high-tech companies—

especially during the dot-com boom when the technophiles glee-fully told anyone who'd listen "he'd lost his touch." But as he wrote:

> A business that must deal with fast-moving technology is not going to lend itself to reliable evaluations of its long-term economics. Did we foresee thirty years ago what would transpire in the television-manufacturing or computer in-dustries? Of course not. (Nor did most investors and corpo-rate managers who enthusiastically entered those industries.) Why, then, should Charlie and I now think we can predict the future of other rapidly-evolving businesses? We'll stick instead with the easy cases. Why search for a needle buried in a haystack when one is sitting in plain sight?[12]

Through the technology boom Buffett stuck to his system, as he always does. Telling Berkshire shareholders about recent acquisi-tions, in the 2001 annual report he wrote: "We have embraced the 21st century by entering such cutting-edge industries as brick, car-pet, insulation, and paint. Try to control your excitement."[13]

Focusing on "businesses I understand" also determines Buffett's "circle of competence." And as long as he stays within that circle, he can invest with minimal risk.

One of the simplest of Buffett's investments to understand is Coca-Cola. In 1988 he bought 113 million shares in Coca-Cola at an average price of $5.22 each. Since—as he has said himself—the nature of Coke's business has hardly changed since it was founded in 1886, why didn't he buy it before?

One reason: It hadn't met his other criteria.

Does Management Allocate Capital *Rationally?*

In the 1970s, under the leadership of CEO J. Paul Austin, Coke had accumulated a huge pile of cash—over $300 million. Austin didn't really know what to do with it and went on a spending spree, buying "an assortment of unrelated enterprises, including inland shrimp farms, private-label coffee, and factories that made plastic straws, moist towelettes, and carpet shampoos."[14] The company's annual return on capital was a miserable one percent.

To Buffett, a CEO's most important job is to allocate capital *rationally:* to run the business so that it earns the highest possible return for its owners—the shareholders. When a company cannot invest surplus cash profitably, if it's acting rationally it will return that money to the owners by hiking dividends or buying back shares. Coke was doing neither; it was squandering the money on businesses of dubious profitability.

Do I Want to Buy This Business with Its *Existing* Management?

A company's future results depend primarily on the quality of its management. A poor management can ruin a good business—as Austin had been doing to Coke.

In 1981, Robert Goizueta took the helm from Austin. As one of his first actions was to buy a movie company, it didn't look like much was going to change.

But as Goizueta dug into the nooks and crannies of the company, he discovered that even its cola business was poorly run. "In many countries the company was warehousing more than a year's worth of inventory—bottle caps, ingredients, and other items."[15] This alone was costing Coke $22 million a day. He came to realize that Coke was a goldmine. He dumped the movie company, the shrimp farm, and all the other "cats and dogs" (as he called them) and refocused Coke on Coke.

Goizueta revamped management and inventory systems, overhauled Coke's marketing, dramatically improved the company's relationship with its bottlers, and introduced a new product, Diet Coke, which became a smash hit.

Now refocused on soft drinks, Coke had a management team that Buffett would be happy to work with.

Does the Business Have Favorable Economics (and Are They Sustainable)?

Buffett distinguishes between two kinds of businesses: Those that have a franchise of some kind, and commodity businesses that don't.

Agriculture is the classic example of a commodity business. Farmers have absolutely no influence over the price of their product. Airlines, steel, and personal computeer manufacturing are also businesses with little or no pricing power. Profits from these businesses fluctuate unpredictably as the market dictates price. These businesses have highly *un*favorable economics. As Buffett says, "In a business selling a commodity-type product, it's impossible to be a lot smarter than your dumbest competitor."[19]

Buffett is only interested in the other kind of business, those with some of "moat" that keeps competitors at bay. Like the *Washingtom Post* with its effective monopoly of the Washington-area newspaper market; American Express with its dominant position of the high end of the credit card market; or Coke, with its powerful brand name. Companies that focus on making their

Buffett's Investment Criteria

Do I understand this business?
Says he only understands "simple" businesses such as candies, newspapers, soft drinks, shoes, and bricks. Clearly defines his "circle of competence" and never strays beyond it.

He wants to be able to see "what can happen 5-10-15 years from now to affect or change the economics of the business. If we can't see that we don't even look at it."[16]

Does it have favorable economics?
Avoids regulated industries in which the government, not the company, sets prices or the return on equity.

Avoids capital-intensive industries; invests in companies that can finance their capital requirements from cash flow, profits, or *very* modest borrowings. By the same token, avoids companies with heavy debt loads.

Avoids commodity businesses that have no pricing power.

Seeks businesses that have what he calls a "franchise," "moat," or "tollgate." Examples: companies with the lowest costs in their industry (Nebraska Furniture Mart), a powerful brand name (Coke), premium-priced, high-quality products (See's Candies), market dominance (the Washington Post Co.)

Are those favorable economics sustainable?
Consistent history of a management that works to continually widen its "moat."

Businesses where demand will continue to grow (e.g., razor blades and Gillette).

Checks for any developments likely to upset a business's franchise (e.g., he liked TV networks a lot better "when there were only three networks").

Does management allocate capital rationally?
Wants managers who think and act like owners, and who avoid the "institutional imperative" (ego-boosting takeovers, etc.).

When the management cannot reinvest $1 to create *at least* $1 of value, they should return capital to the owners by increasing dividends or share buybacks.

Do I want to own this business with its *existing* management?
He will only invest in a company "operated by honest and
competent people, managers for whom he can feel admiration
and trust."[17]

Wants managers who have integrity, are honest and candid,
who tell shareholders the bad news and don't try to hide or gloss
over it. "We want managers who tell the truth and tell *themselves*
the truth—which is more important."[18]

Likes cost-conscious and frugal managers.

Does it have an above-average return on equity?
The higher its return on equity, the more profitably the company
can reinvest its earnings. The higher its return on equity, the
faster its value increases from one year to the next.

Do I like the price?
He will only invest when he sees a "margin of safety"; when he
can invest at a discount to his estimate of the company's value. If
a company meets all his other criteria but the price is too high,
he'll pass.

moats wider and deeper, and fill them with piranhas, crocodiles,
and fire-breathing dragons, are what Buffett is after.

The power of Coke's brand was demonstrated by the New
Coke fiasco.

Stung by the Pepsi Challenge—a series of ads featuring blind
tasting which showed that even Coke drinkers preferred Pepsi—
Coke revamped its secret formula and rolled out New Coke.

But in an astounding demonstration of brand loyalty, the
market rejected it. Coke had misappraised the power of its own
brand, and New Coke was soon withdrawn from supermarket
shelves. Coke had an unbeatable business franchise. As Buffett
put it later:

> If you gave me $100 billion and said take away the soft
> drink leadership of Coca-Cola in the world, I'd give it back
> to you and say it can't be done.[20]

Buffett was impressed with the way Goizueta had slimmed down Coke into a focused company that sold a syrup which cost next to nothing to make at a premium price. He had even restructured Coke to off-load all the capital-intensive distribution businesses— and associated debt—on to independent bottling companies. Yet the biggest chunk of the profit on every bottle of Coke sold continued to go the Coca-Cola Company, Inc.

When Goizueta took over, Coke's cola profits were derived about evenly from the US market and the rest of the world. By 1987, not only had foreign sales risen and profit margins increased, but nearly three-quarters of Coke's income was coming from overseas.

Coke's US sales weren't rising much faster than the economy was growing. In the rest of the world, where Coke sold 25 to 100 servings per capita each year, compared to around 250 in the US, it was a different story. Buffett could see that there was ample room for growth and that Coke's favorable economics were sustainable.

Above-Average Return on Equity

The changes under Goizueta proved so effective that Coke's return on equity rose from the microscopic 1 percent of the 1970s to a stunning 33 percent.

The significance of this becomes clear when you compare a company with a 33 percent return on equity with one that's got just 8 percent:

PRESENT VALUE OF TWO COMPANIES
WITH DIFFERING RETURNS ON EQUITY

Year	Company A: 8% return on equity, all profits reinvested		Company B: 33% return on equity, all profits reinvested	
	Equity	PV*	Equity	PV*
Starting equity:	$10,000	$10,000	$10,000	$10,000
1	$10,800	$9,818	$13,300	$12,091
2	$11,664	$9,640	$17,689	$14,619
3	$12,597	$9,464	$23,526	$17,676
4	$13,605	$9,292	$31,290	$21,372
5	$14,693	$9,123	$41,616	$25,840
6	$15,869	$8,957	$55,349	$31,243
7	$17,138	$8,795	$73,614	$37,776
8	$18,509	$8,635	$97,907	$45,674
9	$19,990	$8,478	$130,216	$55,224
10	$21,589	$8,324	$173,187	$66,771

*PV: Present value of equity, discounted at 10%.

The difference is stunning: After ten years, Company B is worth eight times as much. And Company A, with an 8 percent ROE, has a *declining* present value.

That's why Buffett says he would "rather have a $10 million business making 15 percent than a $100 million business making 5 percent."[21]

Goizueta had not only turned Coke around, he was even grading his managers by return on capital and using some of its higher profits to buy back shares. Goizueta was looking better and better.

Do I Like the Price?

To Buffett, the value of a business isn't what it might be worth on the stock market tomorrow, but its future stream of earnings.

When he can apply his investment criteria—in a business he understands—he can judge with reasonable confidence the cash that a business is going to throw off over the next ten or more years. He is then willing to buy those earnings, but *only at a discount to their present value.*

Following Graham, he calls this discount his margin of safety.

Buffett's Purchase of Coke

When Berkshire Hathaway bought shares in Coca-Cola in 1988, Coke's earnings were 36 cents a share. These earnings were generated using equity of $1.07 per share. So Coke's return on equity was 33.6 percent. What's more, its return on equity had been around this level for several years.

Coke had been reinvesting 58 percent of its earnings in its operations and paid the rest as dividends.

Assuming Coke achieved the same return on equity, and paid out the same ratio of profits as dividends, then its earnings in ten years' time would grow to $2.13 a share.

At the time of Buffett's purchase, Coke's P/E ratio ranged from 10.7 to 13.2 times earnings. At those same multiples, Coke's share price would be somewhere between $22 and $28 ten years in the future.

Buffett aimed for a 15 percent return on the capital *he* invested. Buffett's average purchase price was $5.22, which at a 15 percent annual return would grow to $21.18 in ten years.

What if Coke's stock tanked? Buffett was buying a share of a business. If the business is healthy, stock market fluctuations wouldn't matter. Coke would still throw off the same earnings. And those earnings would still grow. And Coke would continue to pay dividends. Indeed, he could estimate pocketing close to $5 per share in dividends in the following ten years.

As it turned out, at the end 1998 Coke's P/E ratio was 46.5, and the stock closed the year at $66.07 per share. On his purchase price of $5.22, that gave Buffett an annual compound return of 28.9 percent. Plus dividends.

"I've Never Seen Him Do One"

Applying their investment system is second nature to Buffett and Soros. Like every Master of his art who has built unconscious competence through repetition and experience, they no longer have to think through every step consciously.

Buffett, for example, often talks about discounting the estimated future earnings of a company to determine its present value, using the current rate of interest on long-term Treasury bonds.

But is that what he actually does?

Not according to his partner, Charlie Munger, who once quipped at a Berkshire Hathaway annual meeting: "I've never seen him do one."

That's because Buffett does it *subconsciously*.

When he looks at a company he understands, thanks to decades of experience in figuring out what a business is worth, his subconscious generates a mental picture of what the company should look like in ten to twenty years. He can simply compare two mental images—the company as it is now, and the company as it's likely to be—and decide then and there whether or not he wants to buy it.

The supermarket shopper who spies her favorite soap on sale at 50% off doesn't need to do a complex mental calculation to know a bargain when she sees one.

Nor does Buffett when he sees a company on sale at a bargain price. To him, an investment either looks like a bargain or it doesn't.

While Buffett's subconscious communicates in Technicolor, Soros's signals kinesthetically. At times, he feels uncomfortable about a position—literally. "When I'm short and the market acts a certain way," says Soros. "I get very nervous. I get a backache and then I cover my short and suddenly the backache goes away. I feel better."[22]

When the subconscious has done its work, it usually presents the conscious mind with just the *conclusion*. The answer appears as the sudden "flash of insight," as a picture, as a phrase that pops into the mind, as if from nowhere—or as a "gut feeling."

"Invest First, Investigate Later"

Buffett does all his measuring up front, before he invests a dime. Soros often follows a strategy that's exactly the opposite: "Invest first, investigate later."

This may seem crazy. But it's partly a matter of personality.

For example, in my own investing I follow a Graham/Buffett style. Yet until I own a few shares of a stock I'm thinking of buying, I just don't feel involved. Only when I've put money on the table, even if it's only a few pennies, do I get serious.

Second, Soros is a trader trying to "read the mind of the market." So at times actually entering the market can be part of his investigation.

> Soros would say, "I want to buy $300 million of bonds, so start by selling $50 million."
>
> "I want to *buy* $300 million," Marquez [a Soros protégé] would remind Soros.
>
> "Yes," Soros would reply, "but I want to see *what the market feels like first.*" [emphasis added][23]

If the bonds are easy to sell, you know there are lots of buyers in the market. But if they're hard to sell—or can only be sold at a lower price—the market is telling you that the buying power to drive prices higher isn't there.

A shopkeeper wondering whether to add a new product to his shelves may follow the same process. Before buying a large inventory, he'll test the market by offering a few for sale. He'll place a large order only if the first lot flies off the shelf.

Buy More When It Goes Up—or Down?

If Coke had gone down after Buffett started buying it, what would he have done? If he thought it was a bargain at $5.22, it's even more of a bargain at $3.75, and he probably would have bought a lot more.

Soros's methodology is exactly the opposite. If something he has bought goes down, the market is telling him he is wrong—and he gets out. If it goes up he buys more—because the market is confirming his hypothesis.

These strategies, while polar opposites, make perfect sense in the context of Buffett's and Soros's own personal investment systems.

Buffett's aim is to buy a quality business at a discount to its value. As the stock price has no effect on the value of the business, according to Buffett, a falling share price just means he's getting a bigger discount, a greater margin of safety.

Soros's aim is to profit from an expected change in Mr. Market's mind. His buying strategy is first to test his hypothesis with a small amount of his capital. His next action depends on whether Mr. Market confirms or falsifies the hypothesis. He may test again if he thinks it's just a matter of getting his timing right.

Both Soros's and Buffett's buying strategies are consistent with their particular investment philosophy—as is their use of leverage.

The "Rocket Fuel" of Leverage

Leverage is a powerful component of both Soros's and Buffett's success. But—as you'd expect—the forms of leverage they use are different.

Soros uses leverage in two ways. He will borrow to invest; and he will use leveraged investment instruments such as futures and forward contracts. This is what most people think of when you talk about financial leverage.

People associate highly leveraged investments with the name George Soros. But, in reality, his use of leverage is quite conservative, rarely exceeding one dollar of leverage for every dollar of equity. If you followed this strategy in buying a house, you'd put down 50% of the purchase price.

By contrast, Buffett's use of leverage is disconnected from any particular investment he might make. He will occasionally borrow money—but only when interest rates are very low. At such times, he probably sees no investment opportunities at all on the horizon. He's just salting away some extra cash for the day that a bargain appears.

But his most innovative form of leverage is insurance "float," which he calls "rocket fuel."[24]

The first company Berkshire Hathaway bought with Warren Buffett in the driver's seat, in 1967, was National Indemnity, an insurance company. With the takeover of General Re in 1999, insurance now dominates Berkshire Hathaway's balance sheet. That's how much Buffett likes "float."

An insurance company takes in premiums today in return for the promise to pay claims tomorrow—or next decade. Until the money is paid out in claims, it's Buffett's to invest. At the end of 2003, Berkshire Hathaway had $44.2 *billion*[25] in reserves against future claims—or "float."

Thanks to the conservative way Buffett's insurance companies are run, in most years they take in more in premiums than the combined cost of paying out claims and running the business. On average, this float has cost Berkshire Hathaway next to nothing:

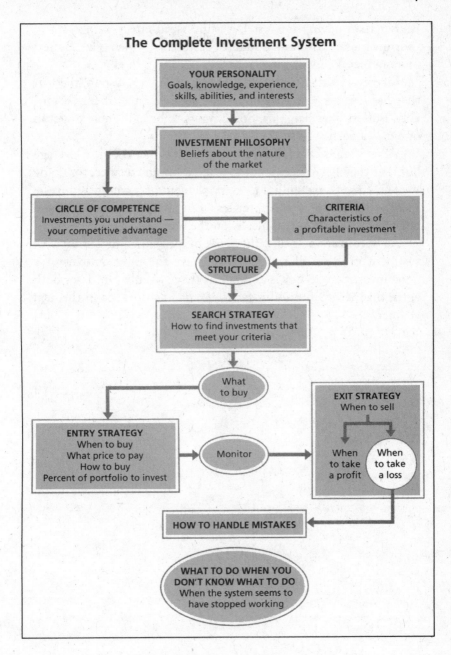

The Complete Investment System

YOUR PERSONALITY
Goals, knowledge, experience,
skills, abilities, and interests

INVESTMENT PHILOSOPHY
Beliefs about the nature
of the market

CIRCLE OF COMPETENCE
Investments you understand —
your competitive advantage

CRITERIA
Characteristics of
a profitable investment

PORTFOLIO STRUCTURE

SEARCH STRATEGY
How to find investments that
meet your criteria

What to buy

EXIT STRATEGY
When to sell

ENTRY STRATEGY
When to buy
What price to pay
How to buy
Percent of portfolio to invest

Monitor

When to take a profit

When to take a loss

HOW TO HANDLE MISTAKES

WHAT TO DO WHEN YOU DON'T KNOW WHAT TO DO
When the system seems to
have stopped working

Rather than paying interest Berkshire is, in effect, *being paid* to "borrow money" from its insurance customers, which gives Buffett more money to invest.

Like every other aspect of a Master Investor's system, the *way* they use leverage—if they do—matches their investment personality. Buffett likes bargains; Soros wants to be agile, able to get in or out in a flash.

What's important is not how or even whether they use leverage but that they have specific rules, worked out in advance, for doing so. The same thing applies to every element of a complete investment system, each of which relates to an investor's philosophy and personality as shown graphically on the previous page.

As Soros's coup against the Bank of England and Buffett's investment in Coke illustrate, both believe the right amount of a good investment to buy is as much as they possibly can. They both agree that "diversification is for the birds," as we'll see in the next chapter.

7

"You Call *That* a *Position*?"

"Too much of a good thing can be wonderful."

—MAE WEST

"[Soros taught me] it's not whether you're right or wrong that's important, but how much money you make when you're right and how much you lose when you're wrong."

—STANLEY DRUCKENMILLER[1]

"Diversification is a protection against ignorance. [It] makes very little sense for those who know what they're doing."

—WARREN BUFFETT[2]

SOON AFTER HE TOOK OVER the Quantum Fund from Soros, Stanley Druckenmiller shorted the dollar against the German mark. The trade was showing a profit when Soros asked him, "How big a position do you have?"

WINNING HABIT NO. 5:

Buy As Much As You Can

The Master Investor	The Losing Investor
Does not believe in diversification; always buys as much as he can of an investment that meets his criteria.	Lacks the confidence to take a huge position on any one investment.

"One billion dollars," Druckenmiller answered.

"You call that a position?" Soros said, a question that has become a part of Wall Street folklore.[3]

Soros prompted him to double his position.

"Soros has taught me," noted Druckenmiller, "that when you have tremendous conviction on a trade, you have to go for the jugular. It takes courage to be a pig. It takes courage to ride a profit with huge leverage. As far as Soros is concerned, when you're right on something, you can't own enough."[4]

"You can't own enough" isn't something you'll hear from your Wall Street investment advisor. He's more likely to follow the conventional wisdom, which states:

1. your money should be divided among stocks, bonds, and cash; and

2. your stock portfolio should have a broad range of stocks, preferably diversified among a variety of industries and even different countries.

Yet the exact opposite of diversification—*concentration* in a small number of investments—is central to both Buffett's and Soros's success.

As *Fortune* once put it: "One of the fictions of investing is that diversification is a key to attaining great wealth. Not true. Diversification can prevent you from losing money, but no one ever joined the billionaire's club through a great diversification strategy."[5] To understand why, let's translate the conventional wisdom into another arena entirely.

The Investment Advisor and Bill Gates

Imagine that this same advice were to be given to businessmen instead of investors. Businessmen like Bill Gates.

The investment advisor turned business consultant would tell the young Gates something along the following lines:

> Mr. Gates, you're making a fundamental mistake focusing all your energies on the software business. Diversify, diversify, diversify . . . that's the secret of success.
>
> Right now, as you're starting your business, it's the time to set a sound course that will ensure your ultimate success and prosperity.
>
> With DOS, you're a single-product company. All your eggs are in one basket. Very dangerous.
>
> Instead of just making software, why not make computers as well? But give serious consideration to balancing the high-risk business you're in with some other business ventures that will be more stable and countercyclical. Utilities, for example, are very stable businesses.

And what if the same advisor were asked to make career recommendations to the young Pavarotti?

> Opera singing is all very well, but after all the returns to be had aren't all that great.

Sure, I know you really love opera. And I'm certainly not going to advise you to give it up. Far from it.

But I urge you to consider the virtues of diversifying your repertoire into rock and other more popular types of music. After all, you've got to think about paying the rent.

In any event, the career you've chosen is exceedingly risky. So few people achieve fame and fortune as opera singers—or rock singers, for that matter.

Do you have any other, nonmusical interests?

Good. Cooking is much safer, sounder field. Why not get some training in that part-time so you'll always have something to fall back on?

When put like this, it sounds ridiculous doesn't it? You immediately grasp that this is foolish advice to give to a Gates or a Pavarotti—or anyone else, genius or not.

Yet that's *exactly* what most investment advisors counsel.

Every successful person, regardless of the field, is single-minded in the pursuit of his goal. They do NOT diversify their energies into a variety of fields.

"Pavarocky"

Drawn by Jhomar Cruz

The result of such single-minded devotion to the achievement of one goal is Mastery.

Like the diversified investor, the jack-of-all-trades is master of *none;* so he is rarely as successful as the person who devotes his entire energy to the single-minded pursuit of a single goal.

The reason is simple—and obvious in any field except investing:

- Your time and energy are limited. The more widely you spread your energies, the less you can spend on any one activity.

To quote from the legendary investor Bernard Baruch (who sold all his stocks before the crash of 1929):

> *"It is unwise to spread one's funds over too many different securities*. Time and energy are required to keep abreast of the forces that may change the value of a security. While one can know all there is to know about a few issues, one cannot possibly know all one needs to know about a great many issues."[6] [Emphasis added.]

Diversification—or concentration—of an investment portfolio directly correlates with the amount of time and energy put into making the selections. The more diversification, the less time for each decision.

Diversification and Fear of Risk

The conventional wisdom is like an empty litany that has been repeated so often everyone assumes it to be true. You'll hear it from just about every stockbroker or investment analyst. But ask him to *justify* diversification, and what you'll find at the bottom of this school of money management is the *fear* of risk.

Fear of risk is a legitimate fear—it's the fear of losing money (and so breaking the First Rule of Investing).

But Master Investors don't *fear* risk, because they passionately and actively avoid it. Fear results from uncertainty about the outcome, and the Master Investor only makes an investment when he has strong reasons to believe he'll achieve the result he wants.

Unlike the Master Investor, those who follow the conventional advice to diversify simply don't understand the nature of risk, and they don't believe it is possible to avoid risk *and* make money at the same time.

Worse, while diversification is certainly a method for minimizing risk, it has one unfortunate side effect: It also minimizes profit!

How Diversification Suffocates Your Profits

Compare two portfolios. The first is diversified among one hundred different stocks; the second is concentrated, with just five.

If one of the stocks in the diversified portfolio doubles in price, the value of the *entire* portfolio rises just 1 percent. The same stock in the concentrated portfolio pushes the investor's net worth up 20 percent.

For the diversified investor to achieve the same result, twenty of the stocks in his portfolio must double—or one of them has to go up 2,000%. Now, what do you think is easier to do:

- identify *one* stock that's likely to double in price; or
- identify *twenty* stocks that are likely to double?

No contest, right?

Of course, on the other side of the coin, if one of the diversified investor's stocks drops in half, his net worth only declines 0.5 percent. If the same thing happens in the second portfolio, the concentrated investor sees his wealth drop 10 percent.

But let me ask you the same question again . . . which is easier to do:

- identify 100 stocks that are *unlikely* to fall in price; or
- identify five stocks that are *unlikely* to fall in price?

Same answer: no contest.

And here we have the key to one difference between the average investor and the Master Investor: Because the Master Investor's portfolio is concentrated, he focuses his energies far more intensely—and far more effectively—on identifying the right investments.

However, concentration is the effect, not the cause. The Master Investor doesn't set out deliberately to hold only a few investments. Concentration stems from the *way* the Master Investor selects his investments.

He spends his time and energy searching for high probability events that meet his criteria. When he finds one, he knows the risk of losing money is low. There's no fear of risk to hold him back.

Second, high probability events are hard to discover. Who knows when he'll find the next one? What's the point in sitting on a pile of cash waiting for an opportunity that may be a long time coming when, right now, he can see piles of money sitting on the table, begging to be scooped up?

When Buffett and Soros buy, they buy big.

There's a Wall Street saying: "Bears make money, bulls make money, but pigs get slaughtered." It should be amended to read "pigs *who don't know what they're doing* get slaughtered."

"Go for the Jugular"

Buffett's and Soros's portfolios clearly don't follow any simple rule of position sizing, such as an equal percentage in each investment.

Neither's portfolio gives any clue as to how it was assembled.

That's because they buy good investments as they discover them. Whatever opportunities they saw, they took—and that's why their portfolios look the way they do today.

The only rule they follow is one you'll never learn from your stockbroker: expectancy of gain. The higher their expectancy of profit, the greater the percentage of their portfolio they'll devote to that investment.

Expectancy of gain is something that can and should be measured or estimated. For example: Buffett is looking at two companies. One is returning 15 percent on capital and the other 25 percent on capital. The shares of both are available at prices he's willing to pay. He would clearly prefer to put more money into the second company.

With the river of cash that Berkshire Hathaway's investments and insurance operations are throwing off every year, Buffett's main problem now is finding enough high probability events to invest in. So he would probably buy both.

But if you or I, with our somewhat more limited resources, were following Buffett's approach, we'd buy stock only in the *second* company. We'd ignore the first one completely. And if we already owned it, we'd probably sell it to put more into the stock that has the far higher expectancy of gain.

So the Master Investor doesn't set out with the *aim* of devising a concentrated portfolio.

Rather, concentration *results from* the way he approaches investing. When Buffett and Soros are certain they're going to make money, their only limit is how much they can buy.

They don't give damn how their portfolio "looks." They just want to make money.

The Investment That Makes a Difference

Over lunch one afternoon my companions—mostly Asian stockbrokers—began reminiscing about the killings they'd made when the Asian markets crashed in 1997. They talked about the blue chip stocks they'd bought at a quarter or a tenth of their current prices.

Whenever investors get together, reminiscing about past successes like this is the kind of talk you'll expect to hear.

But what percentage of their assets had they put into these bargain-basement blue chips in 1997? Since, by and large, they'd focused on the prices they'd paid, not the profits they'd made, I just didn't have the heart to ask. I'm sure their answers would have turned an enjoyable lunch into a wake for all the profits they'd missed.

At such times Buffett, by comparison, loads up to the gills with bargains. He says he feels like an oversexed guy in a whorehouse, and his main complaint is that he doesn't have *enough* money to buy *all* the bargains he can see.

At other times, when he sees a stock he really likes (like Coke), he'll simply buy as much as he can.

Soros has a similar attitude. In 1985, convinced that Jaguar was turning around and the car would become a hot seller in the United States, the Quantum Fund had put $20 million, nearly 5% of its assets, in the stock—a huge position for most funds.

Allan Raphael, who'd initiated the investment, told Soros that it was panning out just as he'd thought and that he was happy with the position. So he was stunned when Soros's reaction was to immediately tell his traders: "Buy another quarter of a million shares of Jaguar. . . .

"*If the stock goes up, you buy more.* You don't care how big the position gets as part of your portfolio. If you get it right, then build."[7]

To Soros, investment success comes from "preservation of capital *and home runs.*"[8]

Likewise, Buffett wants investments that are "large enough to have a worthwhile impact on Berkshire's"[9] net worth.

Neither of them buys piddling amounts. When the opportunity presents itself, *they buy enough to make a real difference to their wealth.*

> "[The trustees] wanted me to diversify. Bugger that."
> —Jim Millner[10]

A Penny Saved Is a Dollar Earned

"The really good manager does not wake up in the morning and say, 'This is the day I'm going to cut costs,' anymore than he wakes up and decides to practice breathing."

—WARREN BUFFETT[1]

"What is the most powerful force in the universe? . . . Compound interest."

—ALBERT EINSTEIN

"I don't know what the seven wonders of the world are, but I do know the eighth—compound interest."

—BARON ROTHSCHILD

SINCE WARREN BUFFETT ASSUMED CONTROL of Berkshire Hathaway the company has paid dividends in just one year; and Buffett quips, "I must have been in the bathroom at the time."[2]

WINNING HABIT NO. 6:

Focus on *After*-tax Return

The Master Investor	The Losing Investor
Hates to pay taxes (and other transaction costs) and arranges his affairs to legally minimize his tax bill.	Overlooks or neglects the burden that taxes and transaction costs place on long-term investment performance.

Berkshire doesn't pay dividends, and Buffett doesn't like them. Why?

Taxes.

When dividends are paid, income is taxed twice. First, the company pays income tax; then the shareholder pays tax on his dividends. A dollar of company profits becomes 65 cents after corporate tax. When paid out in dividends, just 55 cents is left after federal income tax; and if you live in New York or California you end up with just 44 to 45 cents after you have paid state income tax as well.

If a company pays no dividends, the money is taxed only once; and the company can then compound those retained earnings at its return on equity. If it's a Buffett-style company, it can compound that 65 cents of retained earnings at 15 percent or more per year.

For the shareholder to get the same return on the 44 to 55 cents he has left from his dividend check, he must find a company with a 20 percent return on equity.

Buffett doesn't like paying dividends because he doesn't want his shareholders (especially himself) to have their net worth cut by double taxation. He doesn't want to receive dividends either because he knows he'll be better off with them left to compound in the businesses he's already bought.

The Rip Van Winkle Investor

Buffett doesn't like paying capital gains taxes, either. That's one reason his favorite holding period is "forever": capital gains taxes are deferred indefinitely.

In his 1989 Letter to Shareholders, he explained why he likes the "Rip Van Winkle" style of investing:

> Imagine that Berkshire had only $1, which we put in a security that doubled by year end and was then sold. Imagine further that we used the after-tax proceeds to repeat this process in each of the next 19 years, scoring a double each time. At the end of 20 years, the 34% capital gains tax that we would have paid on the profits from each sale would have delivered about $13,000 to the government and we would be left with about $25,250. Not bad. If, however, we made a single fantastic investment that itself doubled 20 times during the 20 years, our dollar would grow to $1,048,576. Were we then to cash out, we would pay a 34% tax of roughly $356,500 and be left with $692,000.
>
> The sole reason for this staggering difference in results would be the timing of tax payments. Interestingly, the government would gain from Scenario 2 in exactly the same 27:1 ratio as we—taking in taxes of $356,5000 vs. $13,000—though admittedly, it would have to wait for its money.[3]

Buffett wants to reduce his tax bill to maximize the annual rate at which his money compounds in value.

The average investor, by contrast, is focused on the profits he hopes to make from his next investment. Buffett wants to "watch his money grow" over the long term. His time horizon isn't his next investment, it's the next decade, even two.

One way to increase the speed at which his money compounds is to cut taxes and other transaction costs. Small amounts saved today can have a large effect on your net worth in the long run, thanks to the magic of compound interest. Buffett magnifies that effect by feeding all these savings into his investment system, to increase the rate of compounding.

George Soros thinks exactly the same way. "I am interested in the overall performance of the [Quantum] Fund *over the long term*,"[4] he writes. "If you keep making 30 to 40 percent per annum for 25 years, you make an awful lot of money even if you start with very little. So the amount of money I have amassed is truly awesome."[5] But Soros's method of neutralizing the drag of taxation is much simpler than Buffett's: He just incorporated the Quantum Fund in a tax haven, the Netherlands Antilles, so it can compound its profits tax-free. If subject to American taxes, the Quantum Fund's annual compound rate of return would have fallen from 28.2 percent to under 20 percent. Instead of being number 54 on the Forbes 2004 list of the world's richest people, with $7 billion, Soros wouldn't have made the list at all. He wouldn't have been poor, but would have had "only" around $500 million.

No wonder the Master Investor is focused on his total return. No wonder he takes into account *all* factors that will either increase or decrease that return.

Shaving Brokerage Fees

Tax isn't the only transaction cost that can kill your return.

Consider a commodity trader following an actuarial investment approach. For simplicity's sake, let's assume that his system produces one winning trade out of every seven he makes (not an unusual situation).

But to keep the math simple, we'll also make the highly *un*realistic assumption of mechanical regularity: each winning trade gives him a profit of 65 percent; and on each losing trade he loses 5 percent. Let's also say that he can make seven trades every two months—or 42 trades per year—and puts an equal portion of his portfolio into each position (another unrealistic assumption).

If he starts with $7,000 and puts $1,000 into each trade, at the end of two months he has a profit of $650 on one, and losses of $50 on each of the six others. Overall, he has made $350—5 percent.

At the end of the year he has $9,380—an annual of return 34.0 percent.

What's the simplest way he could increase his return?

Most investors look for some way to increase the profit on their winning trades—or to increase the number of winning trades they can make.

But to do that you have to revise your system.

It is much easier, as the seasoned investor does, to *first* focus on cutting costs.

Say this trader can cut the brokerage fee or other transaction costs he pays by a mere 5 percent per trade. That reduces each of his losses from $50 to $47.50.

His annual return jumps to 35.9 percent.

"I *Like* to Pay Lots of Tax"

A successful investor once surprised me by stating: "I *like* to pay lots of tax."

Why? Because he only paid lots of tax when he had made lots of money. To quote Vinod Khosla, cofounder of Sun Microsystems: "One correct move is far better than all the tax savings you can do in a lifetime."[6]

The tax regime you face should definitely be a factor in your investment strategy. But it's a mistake to make "Never Pay Taxes" your primary aim. After all, the simplest way of never paying taxes is to have no income or profit at all. Not recommended.

Return on investment is the ultimate measure. Return on investment means the *after-tax return*. The Master Investor takes into account everything, including taxes and other transaction costs, that will affect his net worth. You should, too.

That's a nice boost. But taken over ten years this tiny savings of just 5 percent per transaction has an enormous effect on his net worth.

Before the change, his initial $7,000 would have grown to $130,700 in ten years. That's an annual compound rate of 34 percent—nothing to sneeze at.

But by shaving his loss on each trade through lower commissions, ten years later he has $150,800. The savings alone added $20,100 to his net worth—*triple* what he started with.

The Master Investor knows that a penny saved can grow into a dollar through the power of compound interest.

9

Stick to the Knitting

"Know what you are doing."

—Benjamin Graham[1]

"The market, like the Lord, helps those who help themselves. Unlike the Lord, the market does not forgive those who know not what they do."

—Warren Buffett[2]

"Don't do anything until you know what you are doing."

—Jimmy Rogers[3]

At a dinner one night, I met an investor named Larry who is basically a one-man venture capital fund. He doesn't even have a secretary.

Larry arrived in New York penniless at the age of twenty, landed a job on Wall Street, and two years later had $50,000 in

WINNING HABIT NO. 7:

ONLY INVEST IN WHAT YOU UNDERSTAND

The Master Investor

Only invests in what he understands.

The Losing Investor

Doesn't realize that a deep understanding of what he is doing is an essential prerequisite to success. Rarely realizes that profitable opportunities exist (and quite probably abound) within his own area of expertise.

---

profits from his investing. A couple of years after that, he quit his day job and began investing full-time for himself.

Now a multimillionaire, he specializes in getting in on the ground floor of promising biotech start-ups.

The secret of Larry's success is that he has found his market niche. He is fascinated by the biological sciences. He has a powerful underlying motivation: he wants to live a very long life. He's an avid reader of *Nature* and other science journals. His research starts with the science, not the companies. He lives and breathes biotech.

So when, during the dinner, he was asked a question about investing, he proceeded to tell us all why the greatest profits were to be had in biotech.

The woman I was sitting next to, Mary, said to me: "I've been thinking I should do something on the stock market. Maybe I should look into biotech."

I could tell from the one of her voice that she was far from convinced. So I asked her: "What have you invested in before? Tell me about the profits you have made."

A few years ago, she told me, she had bought two condominiums, which had since more than doubled in price. All her friends, and everyone she knew in the real estate business, had urged her not to buy them. The condominium association that ran this building was involved in litigation, internal disputes, was running out of money—a hornet's nest, she was advised by all and sundry, that she should stay away from.

As proof, they pointed to the low prices these condos were selling at. "Obviously," they would only go lower.

Mary, who had been in the real estate business for many years, knew differently. To her, these condos were a steal. She knew that eventually the association problems that had depressed the prices of these apartments would be sorted out, one way or another. At worst, their prices would come back to the market level.

I said to her: "Why do you want to know about biotech? Why should you even look at the stock market? You already know how to invest and make money. Why not do what you already know?"

The Penny Drops

For a moment, she sat there in a kind of stunned silence. And her face, her whole demeanor changed. It was like a blinding lightbulb had gone on in her mind. For her, the penny had dropped.

Mary is the exact opposite of Warren Buffett, who once said: "Why should I buy real estate when the stock market is so easy?"[4] For Mary, it's "Why should I buy stocks when real estate is so easy?"

Mary already knew her investment niche. She just didn't know that she knew. Awed by the success of people like Larry, she discounted her own knowledge and expertise in real estate as being worthless. Under the virtually universal notion that the grass is always greener on the other side, she looked for the secret to investment success everywhere except the one place she was sure to find it: in her own backyard.

What's His Niche?

Every successful person has a clearly defined niche. For example, I'll bet you can name, instantly, what John McEnroe, Michael Jordan, Babe Ruth, and Tiger Woods are famous for—even if, like me, you have almost no interest in sports whatsoever.

And you know intuitively that John McEnroe on a basketball court or Babe Ruth at Wimbledon would flounder around like fish out of water.

In exactly the same way, every successful investor has his own niche. If you have been in the investment arena for even a short while, chances are you can also associate each of these investors . . .

Benjamin Graham
Warren Buffett
George Soros
Peter Lynch
John Templeton
Jimmy Rogers
Jesse Livermore

with an investment specialty or a certain investment style.

It may seem strange to say that investment "whales" like Warren Buffett and George Soros occupy a tiny niche. Yet even Buffett's Berkshire Hathaway, with $77.6 billion in net assets, is only a medium-sized fish in the $32.3 *trillion* pond of all the world's listed companies.[5]

Different species of whale occupy specialized environments and rarely cross paths with each other. Similarly, Buffett and Soros inhabit different ecological niches in the investment ocean. And just as the whale's ecological niche is related to the food it can eat, the investor's market niche is determined by the kind of investments he *understands*.

"I Want to Double My Money"

Unfortunately, I've met hundreds of investors who simply refuse to believe that the investment world is no exception to the general rule that specialization and success go hand in hand. For example, many years ago I asked an attendee at one of my investment seminars why he had come.

"I want to learn how I can double my money in the next twelve months," he replied.

This man had built a multimillion dollar fortune by spending twenty years putting in twenty-four-hour days to build his business. He knew what it took to make money, yet he didn't believe me when I said he would need to put in the same kind of effort to invest profitably.

Too many investors believe, thanks in part to the marketing put out by investment newsletters and mutual funds, that to make money by investing is easy, rather like buying a lottery ticket but getting a winner every time.

That was certainly my attitude when I bought my first stock. I was about nineteen, and I rushed out to buy some stock that a broker I'd met at a party the night before was touting. While I can't recall the name of the company, I do remember that I bought it within a few cents of its all-time high.

To this day, I have no idea whether the broker believed what he was saying or was simply trying to dump his own shares. Whichever was the truth, it doesn't matter. What does matter is that this same scenario is repeated daily in brokers' offices around the world.

The belief that investing is easy underlies every one of the Seven Deadly Investment Sins. Consider the time and energy devoted to just the first of these sins: that prediction is the key to investment success.

By turning to the stock market page of your daily newspaper, or tuning your TV to a financial program you'll immediately notice that the underlying theme is: *What is the market going to do next?*

Even most investment professionals are devotees of the first Deadly Investment Sin.

And then there are the myriad ways people have attempted to codify this belief. The search for chart patterns, or indicators such as relative strength, moving averages, and momentum that, it is hoped, will help forecast the market's direction. There are cycle theories like the Elliott and Kondratieff Waves, each based on the idea that there's some regularity in the markets that, once detected, will ensure profits effortlessly. All these cycle theories have one thing in common: blurry vision and 20/20 hindsight.

I even know one investor who's *certain* that astrology is the secret to investment success. His only problem, one that's dogged him for nigh on twenty years, is that every astrologer he's tried has cost him money. But that hasn't dented his faith, and I'm sure his search will continue to the day he dies or goes broke—whichever comes first.*

The investor who believes that investing is easy will dismiss out of hand the idea that *understanding* is the real secret. The getting of understanding is hard, he might respond. It takes time and effort . . . overlooking the time and effort, not to mention the money he's lost trying to find the shortcut to easy street.

Circle of Competence

It's no accident that every successful investor narrows his focus to a small segment of all possible investments and specializes in those and those alone.

The very act of developing his investment philosophy defines the kinds of investments the Master Investor understands. This becomes his circle of competence, and as long as he invests within

---

*On second thought, even going broke will only hinder, not halt his quest.

"Understanding" versus "Knowledge"

You can put knowledge in a bottle (or a book) and sell it like candies. But not understanding.

To understand is to combine knowledge with *experience*. Not someone else's experience: your own. Experience only comes from doing, not from reading about what someone else did (though that can add to your knowledge).

As the word "knowledge" (or "know") is often used in the sense of "understand," it pays to grasp what both words really mean:

Knowledge *n.* **1 a** awareness or familiarity (of or with a person or thing) *(have no knowledge of that)* **b** person's range of information.
2 a understanding of a subject *(good knowledge of Greek)* **b** sum of what is known *(every branch of knowledge)*.

Understand 1 *v.* perceive the meaning of (words, a person, a language, a subject, etc.) *(understood you perfectly; cannot understand algebra)*.
2 perceive the significance or cause of *(do not understand why he came)*.

The meanings of these two statements . . .

"Marion has a good knowledge of Greek"
"Peter understands Greek"

. . . are clearly different.

Does Marion speak Greek well? Or can she only read Greek? Or does she just know a lot about Greek (for example, its grammar, history, word derivations, linguistics, and so on)? It's hard to say.

By comparison, it's safe to assume that Peter speaks Greek pretty well, if not fluently.

Similarly, if you say "she knows a lot" maybe all you mean is she's good at Trivial Pursuit. "She understands nuclear physics" is, qualitatively, a very different statement.

Knowledge usually means a collection of facts—a "person's range of information" or the "sum of what is known." But "understanding" implies *Mastery*—the ability to apply information and get the *desired* results.

that circle he has a competitive advantage that enables him to do better than the market as a whole.

That competitive advantage is his ability to *measure* whether an investment has a positive average profit expectancy. The moment he looks at any other kind of investment, his "tools of measurement" no longer work. Unable to measure it, his ability to know whether such an investment is likely to be profitable is no different from the average investor's.

The Master Investor doesn't set out to occupy a particular "ecological" market niche. That's just a natural result of what he understands and what he does not understand; and the distinction between the two is crystal-clear in his own mind.

In Warren Buffett's words: "The most important thing in terms of your circle of competence is not how large the area of it is, but how well you've defined the perimeter."[6]

By viewing the investment world through the lens of his investment criteria, he literally only sees those investments he can understand.

10

If You Don't Know When to Say Yes, *Always* Say No

"If you don't understand it, don't do it."

—Warren Buffett[1]

"We know that we don't know."

—Larry Hite[2]

I ONCE ASKED A FRIEND of mine, Andrew, one of my favorite questions: "How different would your net worth be today if you'd never made any investments at all, if instead you'd put all your money in the bank and let the interest pile up?"

"Oh, *much* worse off," he replied. This puzzled me since I knew that in the previous three or four years he had lost money on every one of his forays into the stock market.

Andrew's wealth came from two sources: the various businesses

WINNING HABIT NO. 8:

REFUSE TO MAKE INVESTMENTS THAT DO *NOT* MEET YOUR CRITERIA

The Master Investor	The Losing Investor
Refuses to make investments that do *not* meet his criteria. Can effortlessly say no to everything else.	Has no criteria; or adopts someone else's. Can't say no to his own greed.

he had established, and real estate. So I asked him: "How different would your net worth be today if you'd only invested in your businesses or real estate?"

Without hesitation he replied: "*Much* better off."

In real estate Andrew knew what he was doing. He had a simple rule: a return of 1% per month or he would walk.

Andrew made a common mistake. He assumed that because he was successful in real estate he could be successful in every investment market.

Although he had clearly defined his criteria for real estate investments, he did not realize that the key to investment success is to *have* criteria.

He deluded himself for four years until his staggering pile of losses forced him to admit that he didn't understand the stock market at all. Only when, so to speak, he went back to investment kindergarten did he start making money in stocks.

When you enter an unfamiliar arena, regardless of your knowledge and skills you are in a state of unconscious *in*competence. Mental habits that underlie success in one area can be so embedded in your subconscious that they lead to failure in another.

If you're a good tennis player you have built up a repertoire of habitual ways of holding the tennis racquet, swinging it, serving, returning the ball, and so on.

The moment you move onto a squash, racquetball, or badminton court, nearly all these habits get in your way. You have to *un*learn your good tennis habits and learn a whole new set of habits to succeed at any of these superficially similar, but in fact very different, games.

Andrew did not have a well-thought-out investment philosophy. He failed to clarify what he did and did not understand. He had not defined his circle of competence. So he didn't know when to say yes and when to say no.

As Warren Buffett puts it, "What counts for most people in investing is not how much they know, but rather how realistically they define *what they don't know*."[3]

The Master Investor is very clear about what he does and doesn't understand. So, when confronted with an investment he doesn't understand, he's simply not interested.

His attitude of indifference contrasts starkly with the behavior of the average investor, who lets his emotions color his judgment.

The Grass Is Always Greener

Investors who don't have the mental anchor of a consistent investment philosophy often end up making investments against their better judgment. This always happens in manias like the dot-com boom.

In the early stages of such a boom, most investors are skeptics. They point out that companies such as Amazon.com, which projected losses as far as the eye can see, had no fundamental value whatsoever. Some of them even shorted such stocks, much to their later regret.

As the so-called New Economy party became more frenzied, the investment mantra became "profits don't matter" and valuations became irrelevant. The prices of the dot-coms kept skyrocketing, while the Old Economy value stocks fell out of favor.

This confused the hell out of the skeptics. Sitting on the sidelines, all the evidence they could see—the rising prices, the profits that people around them were making—contradicted every investment rule they had applied successfully in the past.

Unable to make sense out of what was going on, they began to doubt and question their own investment beliefs, lost confidence in themselves, and, one by one, threw in the towel and joined the party. At the end of the mania, only the true "heretics"—those investors like Buffett with a firm philosophy all their own—stayed out of the fire.

As a result, sad to say, the skeptics are always among the biggest losers from a mania. Having held out till near the very end, they buy just before the bubble bursts . . . and lose their shirts.

This is an extreme example of the belief that the grass is always greener on the other side. Investors who see other people making money while they are not often succumb to self-doubt and pursue a mirage. Others, like Mary, discount their own knowledge and expertise as being worthless and seek their pot of gold on some other rainbow, totally unaware they're already sitting on the right one.

The common denominator of this behavior is the failure to understand when to say yes and when to say no.

Contrast this with Warren Buffett, who at the height of a bull market in 1969 closed down the Buffett Partnership, writing to his investors:

> I am not attuned to this market environment, and I don't want to spoil a decent record by trying to play a game I don't understand just so I can go out a hero.[4]

False Understanding

Even worse than succumbing to temptation and investing in things you don't understand is to believe, falsely, that you do know what you're doing. This is the state of the teenage driver who, even before he's got his learner's license, is convinced that driving is a piece of cake. Despite what he thinks, he's in a state of unconscious *in*competence.

In 1998 a friend of mine, Stewart, opened a brokerage account with $400,000 and proceeded to buy stocks such as Amazon.com, AOL, Yahoo!, eBay, and Cisco Systems. By the end of 1999, the value of his account had grown to $2 million, of which $800,000 was margin money.

Whenever I spoke to Stewart, as I did frequently, it was impossible to shake his belief in all the New Economy myths. "Warren Buffett has lost his touch," he told me repeatedly. As his profits grew, his conviction that he knew exactly what he was doing became stronger and stronger.

Nevertheless, as the year 2000 dawned, he began to get nervous. He took a few profits, and shorted a few stocks as a "hedge." Unfortunately, the market kept rising and he had to meet his first margin call.

By the end of the year, the value of the stocks in his portfolio had fallen back to his opening balance of $400,000—but he still had $200,000 of margin, and had to meet yet another margin call. Sad to say, the collapse hadn't shaken his belief that the future of his dot-com stocks still glowed. And although everyone advised him not to, he paid his margin down with $200,000 from his savings. Today, with his portfolio down to about $200,000, it's not advisable to ask Stewart about his investments.

His self-delusion that he was an expert on dot-com stocks led him to turn $600,000 of his savings into $200,000, so violating Investment Rule No. 1: "Never lose money." (And its corollary: "Never meet a margin call.")

That's exactly why the Master Investor always says no to any investment he does not understand. By putting his capital at risk outside his circle of competence, he would be threatening the very foundation of his investment success: preservation of capital.

Defining Your Circle of Competence

The Master Investor is indifferent to investments he doesn't understand because he knows his own limitations. And he knows his limitations because he has defined his circle of competence.

He has also proven to himself that he can make money easily when he stays within that circle. The grass may be greener somewhere outside his circle—but he's not interested. His proven style of investing *fits his personality*. To do something else would be like wearing a suit that doesn't fit. An Armani suit that's too big or too small is worse than a cheap suit that's your exact size.

Buffett and Soros built their circle of competence by answering these three questions:

- What am I interested in?
- What do I know now?
- What would I like to know about, and be willing to learn?

One other important consideration is whether it's possible to make money in an area that intrigues you. For example, I've always been fascinated by airlines. But with one or two possible exceptions, the airline industry is an investment black hole requiring endless amounts of capital which usually ends up going to the pilots' union.

Only by answering these three questions, as the Master Investor has done, can you find *your* investment niche and be crystal-clear about your own limitations. Only then will it be easy for you to walk away from investment "opportunities" that fail to meet your criteria—and stop losing money and start making it.

11

"Start with the A's"

"If I'm interested in a company, I'll buy 100 shares of all its competitors to get their annual reports."

—WARREN BUFFETT[1]

"Discovery consists of seeing what everybody has seen and thinking what nobody has thought."

—ALBERT SZENT-GYÖRGYI VON NAGYRAPOLT[2]

EVERYBODY WANTS TO KNOW HOW Master Investors like Warren Buffett and George Soros find the investments that make them rich.

The simple answer is: on their own.

Buffett's favorite source of investment ideas is available to anyone, usually free for the asking: company annual reports. In an interview with "Adam Smith" (author of *Supermoney*) Buffett advised novice investors "to do exactly what I did forty-odd years ago, which is to learn about every company in the United States that has publicly traded securities, and that bank of knowledge will do him or her terrific good over time."

WINNING HABIT NO. 9:

DO YOUR OWN RESEARCH

The Master Investor

Is continually searching for
new investment opportunities
that meet his criteria and
actively engages in his own
research. Likely to listen only
to other investors or analysts
whom he has profound reasons
to respect.

The Losing Investor

Is looking for the thousand-to-one
shot that will put him on easy
street. As a result, often follows the
"hot tip of the month." Always
listening to anyone styled as an
"expert." Rarely makes a deep study
of any investment before buying.
His research consists of getting the
latest "hot" tip from a broker, an
advisor—or yesterday's newspaper.

"But there are twenty-seven thousand public companies," Smith responded.

"Well," replied Buffett, "start with the A's."[3]

Buffett has been reading annual reports since 1950, when he first read Benjamin Graham's book *The Intelligent Investor*. Today, in Buffett's office, there are no quote machines, but in the file room are 188 drawers filled with annual reports. Buffett's only "research assistant" is the person who files them. "I have spent my life," he says, "looking at companies, starting with Abbott Labs and going through to Zenith."[4]

As a result, Buffett has an incredible amount of information about all major American companies stored in his long-term memory. Which he continues to update . . . with the latest corporate reports.

When something he wants to know isn't in the annual report he'll go out and dig up the information. As he did in 1965, when . . .

Buffett says he spent the better part of a month counting tank cars in a Kansas City railroad yard. He was not, however, considering buying railroad stocks. He was interested

---

It Pays to Advertise

Buffett began buying stocks, but today he prefers to buy entire companies. He quips that his strategy for finding them is "very scientific. We just sit around and wait for the phone to ring. Sometimes it's a wrong number."[5]

It's true that the first contact is usually made by the prospective seller rather than by Buffett. But Buffett actively encourages people to give him that call.

From his comments to shareholders in Berkshire's annual reports, referrals from his happy sellers, to even the occasional ad in the *Wall Street Journal,* Warren Buffett knows that it pays to advertise.

---

in the old Studebaker Corp., because of STP, a highly successful gasoline additive. The company wouldn't tell him how the product was doing. But he knew that the basic ingredient came from Union Carbide, and he knew how much it took to produce one can of STP. Hence the tank-car counting. When shipments rose, he bought Studebaker stock, which subsequently went from 18 to 30.[6]

In this case, thanks to his fieldwork, Buffett could invest with conviction. He had learned something that nobody else outside the company knew. Others who might have had the same idea didn't "go the distance" to confirm it.

The Master Investor's secret is not so much seeing things that other people don't see, but the way he interprets what he sees. And then being willing to "walk the extra mile" to back up his initial estimate.

Buffett and Soros view the investment world through the filters of their investment criteria. They don't care what other people think. Not only that, what other people think or say is of little or no value to them. Buffett even says, "You have to think for yourself. It always amazes me how high-IQ people mindlessly imitate. *I never get good ideas talking to people.*"[7]

It only makes sense to a Master Investor to depend on other

people who share his investment philosophy and use the exact same filters just as successfully as he does—such as Buffett's partner Charlie Munger and Soros's successor at the Quantum Fund, Stanley Druckenmiller.

In the Kingdom of the Blind

Like Buffett, George Soros has always done his own research. He has always looked at the market differently from his investment peers, even before he founded the Quantum Fund.

When he first arrived in New York in 1956 he discovered he had a competitive advantage. In London, experts on European stocks were a dime a dozen, but in New York they were as scarce as hen's teeth. That led to his first big breakthrough on Wall Street in 1959, when European stocks began to boom.

> It started with the formation of the Coal and Steel Community, which eventually became the Common Market. There was a massive interest in European securities among United States banks and institutional investors who thought they were getting in on the ground floor of a United States of Europe. . . . I became one of the leaders of the European investment boom. It made me a one-eyed king among the blind. I had institutions like Dreyfus Fund and J. P. Morgan practically eating out of my hands because they needed the information. They were investing very large amounts of money; I was at the center of it. It was the first big breakthrough of my career.[8]

Some analysts with the same edge would simply sit in New York and enjoy being the resident "expert." Not Soros. Like his ideas, his research was original and firsthand. Fluent in German and French, as well as English and Hungarian, he would delve into tax returns to unveil the hidden assets of European companies. And he visited the management—something almost unheard of in those days.

His independent research led to his first big coup in 1960. He discovered that the stock portfolios of the German banks were worth significantly more than their total market value. Turning to the German insurance industry, he found one group of insurance companies, Aachener-Muenchner, whose intricate cross holdings between the various group members meant some of those stocks could be had at an enormous discount to their real value.

> Just before Christmas I went to J. P. Morgan, showed them the chart of these 50 interconnected companies, and told them my conclusion. I said that I was going to write it up during the Christmas holidays. They gave me an order to start buying immediately, before I completed the memo, because they thought that those stocks could double or triple on the basis of my recommendation.[9]

Today, Soros is known for his leveraged investments in futures and forward markets. But in 1969, when he and his then partner, Jimmy Rogers, established the Quantum Fund, futures contracts were only available for agricultural commodities such as wheat and coffee and metals such as silver and copper. The explosion of derivative contracts on currencies, bonds, and market indexes only began in the 1970s. Nevertheless, Soros applied the same principles before the advent of financial futures as he does now, seeking emerging *industry* trends that he could capitalize on by buying—or shorting—individual companies' stocks.

How did Soros and Rogers find such stocks? They read. Intensely. Trade publications like *Fertilizer Solutions* and *Textile Week*. Popular magazines, looking for social or cultural trends that might affect the market. They pored through annual reports. And when they thought they had spotted a trend, they went out and visited company managements.

In 1978 or 1979, Soros recalled, Jimmy Rogers had the idea that the world was going to switch from analog to digital.

Jim and I went out to the AEA (American Electronics Association) conference in Monterey—it was called WEMA then—and we met with eight or ten managements a day for the entire week. We got our arms around this whole difficult field of technology. We selected the five most promising areas of growth and picked one or more stocks in each area. This was our finest hour as a team. We lived off the fruits of our labor for the next year or two. The Fund performed better than ever before.[10]

The growth of futures markets gave Soros a whole new arena to apply his philosophy of reflexivity. These highly liquid markets were ideal for the Quantum Fund. Soros could establish enormous positions far faster than he could in the stock market—and with little danger that his buying or selling would affect the price.

Soros switched his attention to monitoring political, economic, industry, currency, interest rate, and other trends, always on the lookout for linkages between disparate, unfolding events. His method hadn't changed, merely his focus.

He also talked to people. He'd built up an enormous Rolodex of contacts in the markets around the world. He would sometimes call them to help him determine what Mr. Market was thinking.

Always highly self-critical, Soros was constantly refining his ideas. And if one of his staff really liked an idea, Soros would tell them to rethink their idea—and then think again. He'd also urge them to test it by talking to someone with the opposite point of view to see if their thinking measured up.

Both Soros and Buffett follow a rigorous, systematic approach to uncovering investments that meet their criteria. Personally in control of the process, they are willing to take every step necessary to ensure that they have found an investment with a high positive profit expectancy.

Compare this to the search process of the typical individual investor. He bases his investment decisions largely on second-hand information gained haphazardly from his broker, analyst write-ups, investment newsletters, financial TV programs, and newspa-

pers and magazines. Only occasionally will he even bother to read
a company's annual report before buying its stock—let alone, as
Buffett does, those of all its competitors.

Even fewer individual investors will go out and dig up firsthand
information by talking to people involved with the company in one
way or another, such as employees, customers, or competitors.

Even when he does follow a rigorous search strategy, he will often overlook one of the most crucial components of the Master
Investor's success: carefully monitoring, in a process just as rigorous as his search strategy, all the investments he has already made.

There's No Such Thing As a
One-Decision Stock

My own most vivid lesson in the importance of monitoring came
from Harold, an investor I met when I was much younger than I
am today. He was in his seventies when I first met him (so if he's
still alive now he's well past the century mark). Harold began investing as a hobby, using the *Value Line Investment Survey* to find
undervalued companies. He was having so much fun (and making
so much money) that he quit his job when he was forty to invest
fulltime.

He told me about his investment in a company I'll call Paper
Forms, Inc., which he had bought, in the late 1970s, at between $2
and $3 a share and finally sold at $21.

Paper Forms was in the business of making all manner of business forms. It had twenty factories and warehouses scattered all
over the United States. What caught Harold's eye was that all its
premises had been leased for twenty years in the 1950s, with an
option to buy at the end of the lease. The exercise prices of the options were set at levels that no doubt seemed high in the preinfla-
tion era of the late 1950s, but were ludicrously cheap in the era of
double-digit inflation at the end of the 1970s.

Finding Baby Oak Trees

"You shouldn't pay too much attention to what the market thinks. You should do your own research and decide what you think a stock is worth. You can often find some real acorns [i.e., that will grow into oak trees] there that everyone else, for all sorts of reasons, thinks are dangerous.

—Robert Maple-Brown[11]

The company was generating steady if unspectacular profits, so the only compelling reason to buy the stock was for the hidden value of the real estate options.

And buy it Harold did, accumulating a sizable stake at between $2 and $2.50 a share, becoming the biggest shareholder after the founder's family.

If anything sounds like a stock you could buy and forget, surely this one does. But if Harold had taken that view, he would never have made a dime in Paper Forms. Because soon after he had started buying, the founder and controlling shareholder of the company died.

His shares ended up in the hands of a bank trust department. Control of the company now rested with the bank's bean counters.

You'd think that even the dumbest member of the trust department wouldn't pass over a windfall like the opportunity to buy real estate in the late 1970s at 1950s prices.

But to the bankers, options were dangerous derivatives. Exercising them would put Paper Forms in the risky business of real estate development. Better, in their view, that the company stick to its knitting. After all, what banker was ever criticized for taking the safe, conservative route?

The fact that the founder had died and the bank was now in control of the company was readily available, public information. But Harold knew from experience that with a change in management anything, even the ridiculous, could happen.

As Harold's sole reason for buying stock in Paper Forms was

those options, it was crucial that he know their fate. So by repeatedly phoning the company's head office—and getting to know some of the middle managers in the process—he made sure he knew what the company was going to do. When he learned that in its wisdom the bank's trust department had decided NOT to exercise the company's options, he made an appointment to see the bank's president.

When they met, he asked the bank's president if it was true that his trust department had decided not to exercise Paper Form's options. The bank president said he knew nothing about it, so Harold filled him in. Then he asked:

"How would you like to be the target of a class-action lawsuit on behalf of the minority shareholders for failing to maximize this company's value?"

"Are you buying shares?" the president asked.

"You bet. And I'm going to keep buying."

Thanks to Harold's activism, the bank trust department changed its mind.

Harold continued to buy shares up to $3. Soon after, Paper Forms became the object of a takeover bid. The initial offer price was $18, but again Harold stuck to his guns and he wound up being bought out for $21 per share. If Harold had not actively monitored his investment, his entire profit of $18+ per share would never have come about.

Monitoring is a continual process. It's a continuation of the search process, not to find an investment but so you know that all is well, or that it's time to take a profit, liquidate the investment or, like Harold, take some other action to protect your capital.

Only the *frequency* of monitoring differs from one Master Investor to another. Buffett, for example, can safely review his investments on a monthly or even quarterly basis, while keeping his eye out for any news or development that might impact one of his companies in some way.

For Soros, the frequency of monitoring is far more intense, sometimes minute by minute rather than once every month or so.

And while, for Buffett, the distinction between searching and

monitoring is clear-cut, in Soros's investment style the two processes can merge together.

For example, Soros will first test his hypothesis by dipping his
toe in the market. Monitoring that position helps him judge the
quality of his hypothesis. His tests are also a component of his
search strategy—searching for the right *timing;* the right moment
to pull the trigger.

Monitoring his test helps him get a "feel for the market"; and
the failure of a test may lead him to revise his hypothesis, so refining his search.

Despite the differences in their styles, both Buffett and Soros
are personally on the lookout for new investments that meet their
criteria at all times. And constantly measuring the investments
they already own against their criteria to judge whether and
when some further action is needed, whether to take a profit, a
loss, or, like Harold, threatening a bank president with a class-
action suit.

12

"When There's Nothing to Do, Do Nothing"

"The trick is, when there's nothing to do, do nothing."

—WARREN BUFFETT[1]

"To be successful, you need leisure. You need time hanging heavily on your hands."

—GEORGE SOROS[2]

"What was Soros's secret . . . ? Infinite patience, to start with."

—ROBERT SLATER[3]

BOTH BUFFETT AND SOROS KNOW, and have accepted, that by sticking to their investment criteria there will be times, possibly extended periods, when they cannot find anything to invest in. Both have the patience to wait indefinitely. As Buffett quips,

WINNING HABIT NO. 10:

Have Infinite Patience

The Master Investor	The Losing Investor
Has the patience when he can't find an investment that meets his criteria to wait indefinitely until he finds one that does.	Feels that he has to be doing something in the market at all times.

"Lethargy bordering on sloth remains the cornerstone of our investment style."[4]

At Berkshire Hathaway's 1998 annual meeting he told shareholders:

> We haven't found anything to speak of in equities in a good many months. As for how *long* we'll wait, we'll wait *indefinitely*. We're not going to buy anything just to buy it. We will only buy something if we think we're getting something attractive . . . We have no time frame. If the money piles up, then it piles up. And when we see something that makes sense, we're willing to act very *fast* and very *big*. But we're not going to act on anything if it doesn't check out.
>
> You don't get paid for *activity*. You only get paid for being *right*.[5]

For Soros, periods of inactivity are far from frustrating. Indeed, he views them as essential. As he puts it, "To be successful, you need leisure. You need time hanging heavily on your hands." Why? To have time to think. "I insist on formulating a thesis before I take a position," he says. "But it *takes time* to discover a rationale for a perceived trend in the market."[6]

And even when Soros has a solid investment hypothesis, he may have to wait quite a while before the time is right to pull the trigger. For example, when Britain joined the European "snake" in 1987, Soros knew that it would one day fall apart. It wasn't until

the reunification of Germany three years later that he could for-
mulate a specific investment hypothesis, namely that the pound
sterling would be thrown out. But two more years had to pass before it was time to go for the jugular. All in all, Soros had to wait
five years before he could implement his investment idea. So, his
profit of $2 billion was equivalent to $400 million for each year he
waited. For the Master Investor, waiting pays off.

Buffett is perfectly happy to wait almost as long. "All I want is
one good idea every year," he says. "If you really push me, I will set-
tle for one good idea every two years."[7]

Getting Paid for Activity

The Master Investor's incorporation of waiting into his investment system is a strategy that won't fly on Wall Street. It's a myth
that the investment professional is paid for making you money.
He's actually paid to turn up every day and "do" something.

Analysts earn their keep by writing reports even when there's
no real reason for one to be written. Market commentators are
paid to have an opinion, even on days when they have to invent
one. Fund managers are paid to invest, not sit on piles of cash—
even at those times when cash is king. Investment newsletter
writers have to make a recommendation because a publishing
deadline is looming, not necessarily because they've got a great
stock to recommend.

The Master Investor is different.

As Soros once told his friend Byron Wien, Morgan Stanley's
US investment strategist:

> "The trouble with you, Byron, is that you go to work every
> day [and think] you should do something. I don't. . . . I only
> go to work on the days that make sense to go to work. . . .

And I really do something on that day. But you go to work and you do something every day and you don't realize when it's a special day."[8]

Master Investors like Buffett and Soros don't suffer from these same constraints. There is no institutional imperative that forces them to act when their investment system dictates there's nothing sensible to do. Unlike a typical fund manager, they don't buy "defensive" stocks (i.e., stocks that will lose *less* money in a declining market than the market as a whole) when it makes more sense to just sit on a pile of cash.

Nor do they have to go to the office when there's nothing to be done. Buffett learnt from Graham that "there would periodically be times when you couldn't find good values, and it's a good idea to go to the beach."[9]

Or as Soros's former partner Jimmy Rogers put it: "One of the best rules anybody can learn about investing is to do nothing, absolutely nothing, unless there is something to do."[10]

Prospecting for Gold

The investor whose criteria are incomplete (or, more often, nonexistent) feels he must be in the market at all times. Waiting is alien to his mentality because, without criteria, he has no idea what to wait for. When he's not regularly calling his broker saying, "Buy this, sell that," he doesn't feel he's investing.

By contrast, the Master Investor is like a gold prospector. He knows exactly what he's looking for; he has a general idea of where to find it; he's got *all* the right tools; and he keeps searching until he discovers gold. And after he's found one deposit and developed it, he gathers his tools and starts looking all over again.

In this sense, the Master Investor never waits. His time be-

tween strikes is filled with his daily activity of hunting for new opportunities. It's a continual, never-ending process.

His only distraction from his search is the necessity to park his
cash somewhere. Somewhere safe, so it's immediately available the
minute his investment system says it's time for him to act.

13

Pull the Trigger

"When we see something that makes sense, we're willing to act very fast and very big."

—WARREN BUFFETT[1]

"Time and tide wait for no man."

—OLD ENGLISH PROVERB

"He who hesitates is a damn fool."

—MAE WEST

ONCE THE MASTER INVESTOR HAS made a decision to buy or sell, he acts immediately.

What could hold him back? He has found an investment that he understands; it meets all his investment criteria; he knows how much he wants to buy or sell at what price and has the resources available; his cumulative experience and the thinking he has done have proven to him the validity of both his investment philosophy and his investment system. There is nothing else for him to think about.

Buying or selling becomes no more than a routine matter.

WINNING HABIT NO. 11:

ACT *INSTANTLY*

The Master Investor	The Losing Investor
Acts instantly when he has made a decision.	Procrastinates.

You can probably easily relate to the Master Investor's state of mind—in noninvestment activities. In fact, I'm sure you act dispassionately and routinely many times a day.

For example, imagine you have decided to go to a particular restaurant. You just pick up the phone and make a reservation. You *don't* hesitate; you *don't* have an internal debate about the wisdom of going to this restaurant—or think about other restaurants that might be better; you *don't* wonder if you're doing the right thing, feel unsure about whether you should spend so much money, or wonder if the food might be better tomorrow (or regret not going there yesterday). Your mind is on other matters—perhaps the pleasure of meeting your friends or the anticipation of a pleasant evening—and the act of making the reservation is purely mechanical.

Buffett and Soros call their brokers with the same lack of emotion you exhibit when you make dinner, theater, or airline reservations. Why do so many investors procrastinate about buying or selling, with the feeling that pulling the trigger is like pulling teeth? What are they not doing that Buffett and Soros are doing?

The investor who hasn't clarified his investment criteria has no way of measuring the worth of any investment idea he may have. Even if he has researched an investment intensely and decided to buy, without criteria he cannot be sure. One way he can "test" his thinking is by asking a friend, or even his broker, for an opinion, substituting somebody else's view for the criteria he doesn't have. It's hardly surprising that when he calls the broker, deep down he's still wondering: *Am I doing the right thing?*

The investor who has no criteria is always plagued by self-

The What-If Game

There is an endless supply of what-ifs that can prey on an investor's mind. What if a better investment comes along next week? What if I sell A so that I can buy B, and A turns out to be better? What if I'm making a mistake? What if interest rates go down—or up—or the chairman of the Federal Reserve gets out of the wrong side of the bed tomorrow morning? What if the market tanks? What if the price goes down, giving me a better entry point tomorrow—or next week?

The doubt, "What if I'm wrong?" often causes an investor to buy far less than he intended. Say he's convinced himself to buy 10,000 shares and feels comfortable about that—until he calls his broker. Now that it's time to put real money on the line, he begins to doubt his own judgment. "Perhaps," he tells himself, "I'll just buy 2,000 first. See what happens. And buy the rest later." And never does.

Such questions never enter the Master Investor's mind. For him, calling the broker is a mechanical act of completion. His mind is already moving on to some other topic; perhaps another investment idea he is pondering . . . or what's on TV tonight.

Another common constraint is a felt lack of resources. Perhaps the investor has no cash available because he is fully invested, so he thinks he simply can't afford to buy it. This is a restraint the Master Investor also faces, especially in his early years. But since his criteria are clear, he is able to judge whether his latest investment idea is or isn't superior to one or more of the investments he currently owns. If he faces such a constraint, when he pulls the trigger he has already decided what investment he is going to sell to be able to do so.

Or, in another example I'm aware of, the investor has the money to act—but it's in some other account. As he thinks about all the steps he has to go through to make the money available quickly, his self-doubt grabs that as a lever to stop him in his tracks. Any delay gives him plenty of time to more fully develop the thinking behind all of his doubts and worries.

doubt. There can be no finality to his decision-making process. He can *never* be certain he is doing the right thing.

Instant Decisions

The Master Investor doesn't only act instantly; he can also decide very quickly whether to make an investment. Sometimes it's almost impossible to distinguish decision from action.

Once, Soros was in the middle of a tennis game when the phone rang. It was 1974, and the Watergate scandal was threatening President Richard Nixon's survival.

On the line was a broker from Tokyo. He'd called to tell Soros that Watergate was giving Japanese markets the jitters. Soros had millions of dollars in Japanese stocks, and he had to decide what to do.

He didn't hesitate. In just a fraction of a second he told the broker to get him out.

Warren Buffett can make up his mind just as quickly. He "can say 'no' in 10 seconds or so" to most of the investment proposals that come his way "simply because we have these filters."[2]

His filters are his investment criteria. They enable him to choose between suitable and unsuitable investments with lightning speed, as when he bought Borsheim's, America's second-largest retailer of jewelry after Tiffany's.

When Buffett was looking at a ring while Christmas shopping at Borsheim's in 1988, [co-owner Donald] Yale yelled out, "Don't sell Warren the ring, sell him the store!"

After the first of the year, Buffett called and asked if a sale were possible. A short time later Buffett bought the store from Ike Friedman, Borsheim's president, after a brief meeting at Friedman's house with Friedman and Yale.

"The substantive part of the talk was 10 minutes," Yale said. "He asked us five questions and Ike had a price. The three of us later met at Buffett's office and Ike and Warren shook hands on the sale."[3]

Buffett isn't joking when he can promise—as he did in the 1982 annual report to Berkshire shareholders—"to respond to any offers quickly, 'customarily within five minutes.'"[4]

To Buffett and Soros, making an investment decision is like choosing between black and white. There are no shades of gray: Either the investment meets their criteria or it doesn't. When it does, they pounce.

Know When to Sell *Before* You Buy

"I know where I'm getting out before I get in."
—Bruce Kovner[1]

"Sell when the company no longer meets your buying criteria."
—T. Rowe Price[2]

No matter how much time, effort, energy, and money you put into making an investment, it will all come to naught if you don't have a predetermined exit strategy.

That's why the Master Investor never makes an investment without, first, knowing when he is going to sell.

Exit strategies vary from investor to investor depending on their method and system. But every successful investor has a selling strategy that's compatible with his system.

Both Warren Buffett's and George Soros's exit strategies stem from their buying criteria.

Buffett continually measures the quality of the businesses he's invested in with the same criteria that he used to invest in the first

WINNING HABIT NO. 12:

Hold a Winning Investment Until There's a *Predetermined* Reason to Sell

The Master Investor	The Losing Investor
Holds a winning investment until a predetermined reason to exit arises.	Rarely has a predetermined rule for taking profits. Often scared that a small profit will turn into a loss, so he cashes it in—and regularly misses giant gains.

place. Though his favorite holding period is "forever," he will sell a stock market investment when any of those criteria have been broken; for example, the business's economic characteristics have changed, the management loses its focus, or the company has lost its "moat."

In 2000, Berkshire's filings with the SEC revealed that it had sold the bulk of its shares in Disney. Buffett was asked why he had sold this stock by a shareholder at the 2002 Berkshire annual meeting.

His policy is to never comment on his investments, so he answered the question obliquely by saying: "We had one view of the competitive characteristics of the company and that changed."[3]

There's no question that Disney had lost its focus. It was no longer the same company that made timeless family classics such as *Snow White and the Seven Dwarfs*. Disney's CEO, Michael Eisner, had awarded himself options with a gusto that must have made Buffett squirm. They'd frittered money away in the dot-com boom, poured capital into Web sites such as search engine Goto.com, and bought other money losers such as InfoSeek. It's easy to see why, in 2000, Disney no longer met Buffett's criteria.

Buffett will also sell an investment when he needs the capital to fund an even better investment opportunity. But this isn't something he has had to do since his early days, when he had more ideas than money. With the cash generated by Berkshire's insurance float, his problem is now the opposite: He has more money than ideas.

His third rule for selling is when he realizes he's made a mistake and should never have made the investment in the first place, the subject of chapter 16.

Like Buffett, George Soros has clear rules on when to liquidate an investment. And like Buffett, they are directly related to his criteria for making the investment.

He will take profits when his hypothesis has run its course, as in his coup against the pound sterling in 1992. He will take a loss when the market proves that his hypothesis is no longer valid.

And Soros will always beat a hasty retreat whenever his capital is jeopardized. The prime example of that is the way he dumped his long positions in S&P 500 futures during the crash of 1987—an extreme case of the market proving him wrong.

Regardless of his method, like Buffett and Soros every successful investor knows *at the time he invests* what will cause him to take either a profit or a loss. And he knows *when* to do so by continually measuring the progress of his investments against his criteria.

Exit Strategies

When they sell, Buffett, Soros and other successful investors all employ one or more of six possible exit strategies:

1. **When Criteria Are Broken,** as in the example of Buffett selling Disney.

2. **When an Event Anticipated by their System Occurs.** Some investments are made in anticipation of a particular event taking place. Soros's hypothesis that the pound sterling would be devalued is one example; the time to exit was when the pound was kicked out of the European Exchange Rate Mechanism.

   When Buffett engages in takeover arbitrage, the time for him to exit is when the takeover is consummated—or when the deal falls apart.

In either case, the occurrence of a particular event determines when the investor takes his profit or loss.

3. **When a System-Generated Target Is Met.** Some investment systems generate a target price for an investment, which becomes the exit strategy. This is a characteristic of Benjamin Graham's method, which was to buy stocks well below their intrinsic value and sell them when they rose to that value—or in two to three years if they did not.

4. **When an Investor's System Generates a Sell Signal.** This is a method used primarily by technical traders whose sell signals may be generated by a particular chart pattern, volume or volatility indicator, or some other technical indicator.

5. **When a Mechanical Rule Triggers Action,** such as a stop loss set 10 percent below the entry point, or the use of a trailing stop (a stop that rises as the price goes up, but is not moved if the price goes down) to lock in profits. Mechanical rules are most often used by successful investors or traders who follow an actuarial approach, the rules being generated by the investor's risk control and money management strategy.

One intriguing example of such a mechanical exit strategy was used by the grandfather of a friend of mine. His rule was to sell whenever a stock he owned went up *or* down by 10 percent. By following this rule, he survived the crash of 1929 with his capital intact.

6. **When the Investor Realizes He Has Made a Mistake.** Recognizing and correcting mistakes is essential to investment success, as we'll see in chapter 17.

The investor with incomplete or nonexistent criteria is clearly unable to use the first exit strategy. And neither will he know when he's made a mistake.

An investor without a system cannot have any system-generated targets or sell signals either.

His best bet is to follow a mechanical exit strategy. This will at least limit his losses. But it gives him no guarantee that he'll ever make any profits because he has not done what the Master Investor has done: first identified a class of investments with a positive average profit expectancy and built a successful system around it.

"Cut Your Losses, Let Your Profits Run"

All these exit strategies have one thing in common: For the Master Investor, they take the emotion out of selling.

His focus isn't on the profit or loss he might have made in this investment; it's on following his system, of which his exit strategy is merely one part.

A successful exit strategy cannot be created in isolation. It can only be successful when it's a direct consequence of the investor's investment criteria and investment system.

This is why the typical investor has such difficulty in realizing profits and taking losses. He has heard from every source that investment success depends on "cutting your losses and letting your profits run." The Master Investor will agree with this—which is precisely why he has a system that allows him to successfully implement this rule.

Without such a system, the typical investor has nothing to tell him when a losing investment should be sold, or how long a winning investment should be held. How can he decide what to do?

Typically, both profits and losses cause him anxiety. When an investment shows a profit, he begins to fear that the profit might evaporate. To relieve that anxiety, he sells. After all, don't the experts say "You can never go broke taking a profit"?

And of course he feels good when he banks a profit, even if it's only 10 percent or 20 percent.

Faced with a loss, he might tell himself that it's only a paper loss—as long as he doesn't realize it. And he is ever hopeful that

> ### Getting Out of a Boom
>
> "The lessons I've learnt are if you are participating in a boom, realize you are speculating not investing, always take your profits, cut your losses and when the boom ends if you have any speculative stocks left, sell them.... When the boom ends the bust is equally incredible in terms of the levels stocks can get to."
> —Anton Tagliaferro[4]

this is just a "temporary" correction and the price will soon turn around.

If the loss grows, he might tell himself that he'll sell out when the price goes back to what he paid for it.

If the price continues to drop, eventually the hope that it will rise is replaced with fear that it will continue to fall. So he finally sells out, often near the ultimate bottom.

The overall result is that he ends up with a series of small profits which are more than offset by a string of much larger losses, the exact opposite of Soros's recipe for success: capital preservation and home runs.

Without criteria, the question of whether to take a profit or a loss is dominated by anxiety. At each step along the way he finds himself reinventing all the reasons why the stock might be a good investment, convincing himself to hold on and so avoiding the issue.

Most people feel anxious when they are confused but must act regardless. An investor can procrastinate indefinitely about making an investment. But he cannot escape the decision to take a profit or a loss. He can only rid himself of this anxiety by clarifying his investment philosophy and criteria.

15

Never Second-Guess Your System

"I still go through periods of thinking I can outperform my own system, but such excursions are often self-correcting through the process of losing money."

—ED SEYKOTA[1]

"For me, it's important to be loyal to my system. When I'm not . . . I've made a mistake."

—GIL BLAKE[2]

"Over the long run, I think my performance is best served by following my systems unquestioningly."

—TOM BASSO[3]

WINNING HABIT NO. 13:

FOLLOW YOUR SYSTEM *RELIGIOUSLY*

The Master Investor	The Losing Investor
Follows his own system *religiously*.	Continually "second-guesses" his system—if he has one. Shifts criteria and "goalposts" to justify his actions.

JOEL IS A STOCK TRADER I met a few years ago through a mutual friend. He uses a technical system based on computer-generated buy and sell signals.

Even though he had been using his system successfully for over five years, he told me, he still had trouble selling stocks when the system told him to do so.

"I used to second-guess my sell signals all the time," he said. "I could always think of a reason why the stock was going to keep going up. Then one day, a couple of years ago, I sat down and analyzed all the stocks I'd sold or should have sold. I found that second-guessing my system had cost me a hell of a lot of money."

"So now," I asked him, "you follow every sell signal religiously?"

"Yes, but I still have to literally force myself to. It's like I close my eyes and call the broker."

So why did Joel have a problem taking his system's sell signals?

When given a buy signal, he would investigate the company and only take those buy signals when the company's fundamentals stacked up.

When it came time to sell, nine times out of ten, the company's fundamentals didn't seem to have changed. Everything he knew about the company, everything he could see, conflicted with the computer-generated sell signal, so he was very reluctant to execute it. He was shifting his criteria in midstream, from the technical sell signals that he knew worked to fundamental ones that "felt" better but were irrelevant to the system.

Having realized how much it was costing him, now, when the computer says sell, he has disciplined himself to simply not look at any fundamental data.

Which is working—most of the time. But because his natural inclination is to also use fundamentals, he still occasionally second-guesses his system. Like most people, he can't help but hear the siren call of temptation. Unlike most people, he can usually resist it.

He will always have this problem as long as he uses this system, because it doesn't perfectly fit his personality. Joel's Analyst tendencies (see box) get in his way.

Many successful investors are just like Joel: They have a system, they've tested it so they know it works, but they have trouble following it because some aspect of the system doesn't fit their makeup.

A person who's impatient and impetuous and who wants to see instant results would never feel comfortable with a Graham-style investment strategy that requires him to wait two or three years for a stock to get back to its intrinsic value.

Similarly, someone who likes to quietly study and think through all the implications before acting simply doesn't have the temperament for, say, foreign exchange trading, which requires instant judgment, gut feel, continual action, and constant connection to the markets.

A person who is only comfortable buying something tangible, something where he can see and even feel the value, would never be able to follow a system that invests in technology or biotech start-ups. If the products are only ideas, not even at the developmental, let alone testing stage, only potential value exists. There is nothing concrete or tangible for him to latch on to.

It's easy to see, in these three admittedly extreme examples, that the investor will fail miserably if he adopts a system that is totally alien to *his* personality—even though it works perfectly for somebody else.

As Joel's example shows, following a system that almost, but not quite, fits your personality can be profitable. Indeed, Joel is doing

The Analyst, the Trader, and the Actuary

I have identified three different investor archetypes: the Analyst, the Trader, and the Actuary. Each takes an entirely different approach to the market, depending on his investment personality.

The Analyst is personified by Warren Buffett. He carefully thinks through all the implications of an investment before putting a single dime on the table.

The Trader acts primarily from unconscious competence. This archetype, epitomized by George Soros, needs to have a "feel" for the market. He acts decisively, often on incomplete information, trusting his "gut feel," supremely confident that he can always beat a hasty retreat.

The Actuary deals in numbers and probabilities. Like an insurance company, he is focused on the overall outcome, totally unconcerned with any single event. The actuarial investment strategy is, perhaps, best characterized by Nassim Nicholas Taleb, author of *Fooled by Randomness*. Originally a mathematician, he now manages a hedge fund and is willing to suffer hundreds of tiny losses while waiting for his next profitable trade, which he knows, actuarially, will repay his losses many times over.

Like all such characterizations, these three investor archetypes are mental constructs illustrating extreme tendencies. No individual is ever a perfect example of any single one. Indeed, the Master Investor has mastered the talents of all three.

Yet, like everyone else, he has a natural affinity with one of the three archetypes and will tend to operate primarily from that perspective.

better than 99% of all investors. But Joel will always be fighting, and occasionally giving in to, the temptation to second-guess his system.

In the words of commodity trader William Eckhardt, "If you find yourself overriding [your system] routinely, it's a sure sign that there's something that you want in the system that hasn't been included."[4]

The difference between the merely successful investor and Master Investors like Buffett and Soros is that the Master Investor always follows his system religiously.

And unlike Joel, they never have to force themselves to do so. They can effortlessly follow their system 100 percent of the time because every aspect of their system fits them like a tailor-made glove.

Each has built his investment method himself, from the foundation of his investment philosophy to how he selects investments and his detailed rules for buying and selling. So he's never even tempted to second-guess his system.

But that doesn't mean he never makes a mistake.

16

Admit Your Mistakes

"Where I do think I excel is in recognizing my mistakes . . . that is the secret to my success."

—GEORGE SOROS[1]

"An investor needs to do very few things as long as he or she avoids big mistakes."

—WARREN BUFFETT[2]

"Quickly identify mistakes and take action."

—CHARLIE MUNGER[3]

SUCCESSFUL PEOPLE FOCUS ON AVOIDING mistakes, and correcting them the moment they become evident. Sometimes, success can come from focusing *solely* on avoiding mistakes.

This is how Jonah Barrington became British and world squash champion in the 1960s and 1970s.

If you're not familiar with the game of squash, it's like racquet-

WINNING HABIT NO. 14:

ADMIT YOUR MISTAKES AND CORRECT THEM *IMMEDIATELY*

The Master Investor	The Losing Investor
Is aware of his own fallibility. Corrects mistakes the moment they become evident. As a result, rarely suffers more than small losses.	Hangs onto losing investments in the hope that he'll be able to break even. As a result, often suffers huge losses.

ball. You have to chase a small rubber ball (the squash ball is harder than a racquetball and smaller, too—just the right size to fit into your eye socket, so it can be a dangerous sport) around an enclosed court.

The court is small, but the ball is fast. To get to the ball after your opponent has hit it, you have to sprint five to ten yards from a standing start, hit the ball back so it bounces off the front wall, and then get ready to sprint again . . . just a few seconds later. A champion squash player must be ready and able to sprint one short dash after another for four to five solid hours: A championship squash match can last longer than a hotly contested Wimbledon tennis final.

The sport is so physically demanding that people have died on court from heart attacks!

Barrington was determined to win, and win he did by consistently and continually aiming at one simple goal: to make no mistakes.

A mistake in squash, as in tennis, is to miss the ball, or to hit it out of bounds.

So Barrington aimed to *always* hit the ball, and to *always* hit it back to the front wall so that it stayed in play.

Like many simple goals, this one is far from easy to achieve. Barrington had to be incredibly fit and have amazing stamina.

He wore his opponents down. After three or four or five hours, his opponents were tiring. But Barrington was still there, still hitting the ball back, seemingly inexhaustible, while his opponents began to make mistakes, so losing the match.

In a sense, Barrington never *won:* His opponents always *lost.*

The Barrington Fund

If Barrington managed a mutual fund, it would probably be fully invested in Treasury bills at all times. Admittedly, he would never make significant profits, but by just avoiding mistakes he would *never* make a loss.

If you think that sitting on a pile of cash is a bad investment strategy, you should meet a few of the people I've coached over the years. As I mentioned earlier, one of my favorite questions is: "Imagine you'd never made *any* of your investments and just put your money in the bank. Would you be better off today?"

Even I was surprised when Geoff, one of my clients, figured out he'd have *$5 million more* in the bank today. Another client of mine, Jack, had thrown $7 million down the drain!

What these two gentlemen had in common was that they focused purely on profits. (Not that they ever made many.) Neither realized the importance of avoiding mistakes—not until, at my prompting, they added up their losses.

The wide-eyed focus on profits is not an attitude the Master Investor shares. Rather like Barrington, Berkshire vice chairman Charlie Munger "has always emphasized the study of mistakes rather than successes, both in business and other aspects of life," as Buffett wrote in one of his letters to shareholders. "He does so in the spirit of the man who said: 'All I want to know is where I'm going to die so I'll never go there.' "[4]

Similarly, George Soros is constantly on the lookout for errors he may have made. "I've probably made as many mistakes as any investor," he says, "but I have tended to discover them quicker and was usually able to correct them before they caused too much harm."[5]

Since preservation of capital is the Master Investor's first aim, his primary focus is, in fact, on avoiding mistakes and correcting any he makes; and only secondarily on seeking profits.

This doesn't mean he spends most of his day focusing on what mistakes to avoid. By having carefully defined his circle of competence, he has already taken most possible mistakes out of the equation. As Buffett says:

> Charlie and I have *not* learned how to solve difficult business problems. What we have learned is to avoid them . . . . Overall, we've done better by avoiding dragons than by slaying them.[6]

It should be no surprise to learn that Warren Buffett's favorite book on his favorite pastime, other than reading annual reports, is *Why You Lose at Bridge.*

"Unforced Errors"

Most people think of investment mistakes and losses as being equivalent. The Master Investor's definition of a mistake is more rigorous: not following his sytem. Even when an investment that did not fit his criteria ends up being profitable, he still views it as a mistake.

If the Master Investor follows his system religiously, how can he make a mistake of this kind?

Unwittingly.

For example, in 1961 Warren Buffett put $1 million, one-fifth of his partnership's assets, into buying control of Dempster Mill Manufacturing. This company, in a town ninety miles from Omaha, made windmills and farm implements. In those days, Buffett was following Graham's approach of buying "cigar butts," and Dempster fitted perfectly into that category.

As the controlling shareholder, Buffett became chairman. Each month he "would entreat the managers to cut their overhead and trim the inventory, and they would give it lip service and wait for him to go back to Omaha." Realizing he had made a mistake in taking control, "promptly, Buffett put the company up for sale."[7]

But there were no takers.

> ### Experience
>
> "What is the secret of your success?" a bank president was once asked.
>
> "Two words: Right decisions."
> "And how do you make right decisions?"
> "One word: Experience."
> "And how do you get Experience?"
> "Two words."
> "And what are those words?"
> "Wrong decisions."

He hadn't appreciated the difference between being a minority shareholder and having control. Had he owned 10 percent or 20 percent of the stock, he could have easily dumped it. But with 70 percent he was trying to sell control, something nobody wanted.

Turning companies around, Buffett discovered, wasn't his "cup of tea." To correct his mistake, he turned to his friend Charlie Munger who "knew a fellow, name of Harry Bottle, who might be the man for Dempster."[8] Bottle cut costs, slashed inventory, and squeezed cash out of the company—which Buffett reinvested in securities.

Buffett finally sold Dempster, now profitable and with $2 million in securities, in 1963 for $2.3 million. As Buffett later admitted, he can "correct such mistakes far more quickly"[9] when he's just a shareholder than when he owns the business.

"The Secret to My Success"

Buffett readily admits his mistakes, as a glance through his annual letter to shareholders makes abundantly clear. Every other year or so, he'll devote an entire section to his "mistakes du jour."

Likewise, the very foundation of Soros's investment philosophy is his observation that "I am fallible." While Buffett "credits Charlie Munger with helping him understand the value of studying one's mistakes rather than concentrating only on success,"[10] Soros needed no such urging.

His method for handling mistakes is built into his system. "I have a criterion that I can use to identify my mistakes," he writes. "The behavior of the market."[11]

When the market tells him he's made a mistake, he immediately "beats a hasty retreat." If he did otherwise, he would not be following his system.

With his emphasis on his own fallibility, he logically equates recognizing his mistakes with being *the secret to my success.*

Having recognized he's blundered, the Master Investor has no emotional qualms about admitting he was wrong, taking responsibility for his mistake—and correcting it. To preserve his capital, his policy is to sell first, analyze later.

Learn from Your Mistakes

"The chief difference between a fool and a wise man is that the wise man learns from his mistakes, while the fool never does."

—Philip A. Fisher[1]

"One learns the most from mistakes, not successes."

—Paul Tudor Jones[2]

"To make a mistake is natural. To make the same mistake again is character."

—Anon.

IF YOU WANTED TO TEACH someone how to ride a bike, would you give him a book to read? Take him to a lecture where he could hear a long exposition of the physics of bike riding, how to keep your balance, turning and starting and stopping, and so on? Or would you give him a few pointers, sit him on a bike, give him a gentle shove, and let him keep falling off until he figures it out for himself?

WINNING HABIT NO. 15:

TURN MISTAKES INTO LEARNING EXPERIENCES

The Master Investor	The Losing Investor
Always treats mistakes as *learning experiences*.	Never stays with any one approach long enough to learn how to improve it. Always looks for an "instant fix."

You know that to try learning how to ride a bike from a book or a lecture is totally ridiculous. With all the explanation in the world, you still have to learn the same way I and my kids did—by making lots and lots of mistakes, sometimes quite painful ones.

> "Can you really explain to a fish what it's like to walk on land?" Buffett asks. "One day on land is worth a thousand years of talking about it."[3]

In a sense, we're programmed to learn from our mistakes. But what we learn depends on our reaction. If a child puts his hand on a hot stove, he'll learn not to do it again. But his automatic learning might be: Don't put your hand on *any* stove. He must *analyze* his mistake before he can discover that it's okay to put his hand on a cold stove.

Then he goes to school, and what does he learn about mistakes there? In too many schools he is punished for making mistakes. So he learns that making mistakes is *wrong*, that if you make mistakes you're a *failure*.

Having graduated with this carefully ingrained attitude what's his reaction when, as is inevitable in the real world, he makes a mistake? Denial and evasion. He'll blame his investment advisor for recommending the stock or the market for going down. Or he'll justify his action: "I followed the rules—it wasn't *my* fault!" just like the kid who screams "*You* made me do it." The last thing he's going to do with that kind of education is to be dispassionate about his mistake and learn from it. So, just as inevitably, he'll do it again.

When the Master Investor makes a mistake, his reaction is *very* different. First, of course, he accepts his mistake and takes immediate action to neutralize its effect. He can do this because he takes complete responsibility for his actions—and their consequences.

Neither Buffett nor Soros has any emotional hang-up about admitting his mistakes. Indeed, both make it their policy to be frank and open about them. According to Buffett, "The CEO who misleads others in public may eventually mislead himself in private."[4] To Buffett, admitting your mistakes is essential if you are to be honest with yourself.

Soros is equally forthright. "To others," he says, "being wrong is a source of shame; to me, recognizing my mistakes is a source of pride. Once we realize that imperfect understanding is the human condition, there is no shame in being wrong, only in failing to correct our mistakes."[5]

Once the Master Investor has cleared the decks by getting rid of the offending investment, his mind is free to analyze what went wrong. And he always analyzes every mistake. First, he doesn't want to repeat it, so he has to know what went wrong and why. Second, he knows that by making fewer errors he will strengthen his system and improve his performance. Third, he knows that reality is the best teacher, and mistakes are its most rewarding lessons.

And he's curious to learn that lesson.

In 1962, Soros made a mistake that nearly wiped him out. It proved to be possibly his most powerful learning experience.

He had found an arbitrage opportunity in Studebaker stock. The company was issuing "A" shares which would become regular stock a year or so later. They were trading at a substantial discount to the ordinary shares. So Soros bought the "A" shares and shorted the regular Studebaker stock to pocket the spread. He also thought that Studebaker's stock would first decline. When it did, he planned to cover his shorts, and then hold just the "A" shares for the expected recovery. If it didn't, he figured he had locked in the spread.

The Master Investor's Mistakes

A Master Investor's errors usually fall into one or more of six categories:

1. He (unwittingly) didn't follow his system.
2. An oversight: He overlooked something when he made the investment.
3. An emotional blind spot impaired his judgment.
4. He has changed in some way that he hasn't yet recognized.
5. Something in the environment has changed that he hasn't noticed.
6. Sins of omission . . . investments he should have made but didn't.

But Studebaker went through the roof. And to make things worse, the spread widened as the "A" shares lagged behind.

Complicating Soros's predicament, "I had borrowed money from my brother and I was in danger of being entirely wiped out."[6] It was money his brother—who was just starting his own business at the time—could ill afford to lose.

When the trade went against him, Soros didn't beat a hasty retreat, but hung on, even putting up more margin money to keep his short position open. He was overextended; he hadn't prepared an exit strategy to follow automatically if the trade went against him. He wasn't ready for the contingency that he might be wrong.

After a prolonged period during which matters remained touch and go, Soros recouped his money, but the emotional impact of the ordeal was long lasting. "Psychologically it was very important."[7]

This was his first major financial setback, and it caused him to rethink his entire approach to the markets. It's certainly possible to trace many of the components of the investment system that turned Soros into a Master Investor to all the mistakes he made in this particular trade.

Buffett Takes Control

By taking control of Dempster in 1961, Buffett was clearly beginning to move away from the pure Graham system he had been following 'till then. The businessman inside him was seeking an outlet. But in buying a "cigar butt" like Dempster, he was doing it in a Graham-like fashion.

When he went for his next target, Berkshire Hathaway, he had clearly learned from his experience.

By 1963, the Buffett Partnership was the largest shareholder of the company. In May 1965 Buffett took control of the company—though he didn't become chairman until later.

Immediately he told Ken Chace, whom he had previously identified as the man to run Berkshire his way and who was now president, his plans for the company. In a nutshell, he wanted Chace to do to Berkshire what Harry Bottle had done to Dempster: squeeze cash out of Berkshire's dying textile business for Buffett to invest elsewhere. The first company that the new Berkshire bought—two years later—was National Indemnity Co., an insurance company.

In many respects, this is very similar to what Buffett does now, over three decades later. He buys a company with the management in place, and they run the business without his direct involvement—and send him all the spare cash to invest elsewhere. The major difference is that the companies he buys today are no longer cigar butts like Dempster and Berkshire Hathaway.

Buffett's $2 Billion Mistake

Uniquely, Buffett also considers *what could have been* when he analyzes his mistakes.

In 1988 he wanted to buy 30 million (split-adjusted) shares in Federal National Mortgage Association (Fannie Mae), which would have cost around $350 million.

> After we bought about 7 million shares, the price began to climb. In frustration, I stopped buying. . . . In an even sillier move, I surrendered to my distaste for holding small positions and sold the 7 million shares we owned.[8]

In October 1993 he told *Forbes* that "he left $2 billion on the table by selling Fannie Mae too early. He bought too little and sold too early. 'It was easy to analyze. It was within my circle of competence. And for one reason or another, I quit. I wish I could give you a good answer.'"[9]

This was a mistake that, he wrote, "thankfully, I did not repeat when Coca-Cola stock rose similarly during our purchase program"[10] which began later the same year.

"I Am My Most Severe Critic"

George Soros goes far beyond just analyzing his mistakes. As you might expect from someone whose philosophy and approach is based on his own fallibility, Soros views everything with a critical eye—including himself. "I am my most severe critic,"[11] he says.

"Testing your views is essential in operating in the financial markets,"[12] he tells his staff, urging them to be critical of their own ideas and always test them against somebody who holds an opposite view. He follows the same procedure himself, always looking for any flaw in his own thinking.

With this mind-set, Soros is constantly on the lookout for any discrepancy between his investment thesis and how events actually unfold. He says that when he spots such a discrepancy, "I start a critical examination."[13] He may end up dumping the investment, "but I certainly don't stay still and I don't ignore the discrepancy."[14]

Soros's willingness to continually question his own thinking and actions gives him a considerable edge over the investor who is complacent in his thinking and very slow to recognize when something is going wrong.

Like Soros, Buffett can also be hard on himself. Sometimes, too hard.

In 1996, Buffett once again became a shareholder of Disney when it merged with Cap Cities/ABC, of which Berkshire was a major shareholder. Buffett recalled how he had first become interested in Disney thirty years earlier. Then,

> its market valuation was less than $90 million, even though the company had earned around $21 million pre-tax in 1965 and was sitting with more cash than debt. At Disney-land, the $17 million Pirates of the Caribbean ride would soon open. Imagine my excitement—a company selling at only five times rides!
>
> Duly impressed, Buffett Partnership Ltd. bought a significant amount of Disney stock at a split-adjusted price of 31 cents per share. That decision may appear brilliant, given that the stock now sells for $66. But your Chairman was up to the task of nullifying it: In 1967 I sold out at 48 cents per share.[15]

With 20/20 hindsight, it's easy to see that selling at 48 cents per share was a major blunder. But in criticizing himself for doing so, Buffett overlooks the fact that in 1967 he was still largely following Graham's investment model. In that model the rule is to sell a stock once it reaches intrinsic value.

Nevertheless, he has clearly taken to heart Philip Fisher's observation that studying "mistakes can be even more rewarding than reviewing past successes."[16]

As the examples of both Buffett and Soros show, it's better to be overly critical than forgiving of your own mistakes. As Buffett's partner Charlie Munger puts it:

It is really useful to be reminded of your errors. I think we're pretty good at that. We do kind of mentally rub our own noses in our own mistakes. And that is a very good mental habit.[17]

18

Wishing Won't Make It So

"He who would climb the ladder must begin at the bottom."

—ENGLISH PROVERB[1]

"He who wishes to be rich in a day will be hanged in a year."

—LEONARDO DA VINCI[2]

"The only place where success comes before work is in a dictionary."

—VIDAL SASSOON[3]

IN PEOPLE'S MINDS, THE NAMES Warren Buffett and George Soros tend to be linked with their impressive investment track records—24.4 percent and 28.2 percent per year, respectively. It's as though they appeared from nowhere with this genius for investing.

Nothing could be farther from the truth. When Buffett began his Buffett Partnership in 1956, he drew on twenty years of experience of saving, investing, and learning about business and money.

WINNING HABIT NO. **16:**

PAY YOUR DUES

The Master Investor	The Losing Investor
His returns increase with experience; now seems to spend less time to make more money. Has "paid his dues."	Not aware it's necessary to "pay your dues." Rarely learns from experience . . . and tends to repeat the same mistake until he's cleaned out.

Similarly, Soros had already spent seventeen years learning his craft when he established the Double Eagle Fund in 1969.

For both, it was this long apprenticeship that made it possible for them to post such stellar returns from the very first day they entered the fund management arena.

In this respect, Buffett and Soros are no different from, say, Tiger Woods, who started to learn to play golf as soon as he could stand up. It wasn't as though he just burst onto the scene to win his first professional title at the age of twenty-one. He *already had* nineteen years of experience.

Buffett's Head Start

Compared to Tiger Woods, Buffett was a late starter. He didn't buy his first stock until he was eleven years old. And he waited until he was five before starting his first business, a stand in front of his house selling Chiclets to passersby. This was followed by a lemonade stand positioned not in front of his house but in front of a friend's, as he had noticed there was far more traffic there, and so many more customers. At six, he was buying six-packs of Cokes from the general store for 25 cents, and selling them door to door for 5 cents a bottle.

Many kids have a paper route or some other part-time work in order to supplement their pocket money. Not Buffett.

At the age of fourteen, Buffett had *several* paper routes, set up as a business. He was delivering 500 newspapers a day—but he had organized the route so it only took an hour and a quarter. He used his access to customers to sell them magazine subscriptions to maximize his income. He was making $175 a month from this paper route alone, an incredible sum for a teenager in the mid-1940s, money he planned to keep, not spend.

Other business ventures included collecting lost golf balls and selling them—not just a handful, but hundreds at a time. He and a partner owned pinball machines placed in barbershops. That business brought in $50 a week ($365 in today's dollars), and was sold when he was seventeen for $1,200. He even had half ownership of a Rolls-Royce which was rented out at $35 a day.

This experience in starting and running businesses, tiny as they were compared to the smallest of Berkshire Hathaway's acquisitions, gave him an understanding of business that's simply not available from reading a book or taking a course.

Indeed, at Wharton (which he attended before going to Columbia) the nineteen-year-old "disgustedly reported that he knew more than the professors."[4] According to a classmate, "Warren came to the conclusion that there wasn't anything Wharton could teach him. And he was right."[5]

Buffett was also fascinated by stocks and spent a lot of time in his father's brokerage, sometimes chalking up prices on the blackboard. He began to chart prices, "bewitched by the idea of deciphering their patterns."[6] His first stock purchase was Cities Service. He bought three shares at $38—and they soon dropped to $27. Buffett hung on, eventually selling out with a $5 profit. After which the stock kept going up all the way to $200.

While other kids read the sports pages or played ball, the young Buffett pored over the stock tables and read the *Wall Street Journal* after school. His high school teachers even asked him for investment advice.

But although he spent a lot of time studying the stock market, he wasn't really doing all that well. He tried everything—"I collected charts and I read all the technical stuff. I listened to tips,"[7] he later recalled—but nothing worked too well. He had neither a framework nor a system—until he found Benjamin Graham.

When he entered Columbia University in 1950 to attend Benjamin Graham's class on security analysis, he was just twenty years old. But he was already a seasoned investor. He had already made many of the mistakes, and had many of the learning experiences, that most of us don't begin to have until our twenties or even thirties . . .

- he had read every business and investment book he could lay his hands on—over 100 in total;
- he had tried (and discarded) a variety of approaches to investing, including reading charts and listening to hot tips; and
- for a twenty-year-old, he had an unusually wide experience in business, and had already demonstrated his business acumen.

Thanks to the power of compound interest, his unusual head start has added untold billions of dollars to his current net worth.

Buffett's Mentor

For the next six years Buffett absorbed everything he could from Graham, first, as a student where he received the only A+ Graham ever awarded;[8] then, working at Graham-Newman Corp., Graham's fund management company, from 1954 to 1956.

But Buffett was already showing signs that he would excel his teacher.

Buffett was quicker at everything. Graham would amaze the staff with his ability to scan a page with columns of figures and pick out an error. But Buffett was faster at it. Howard

Newman, [Graham-Newman partner] Jerry Newman's son, who also worked there, said, "Warren was brilliant and self-effacing. He was Graham exponential."[9]

And Buffett immediately applied what he had learned.

When he arrived at Columbia in 1950 he had $9,800 accumulated from his teenage business ventures.* When he left New York for Omaha in 1956 to start managing funds on his own, he had turned that sum into $140,000[†]—nearly a million of today's dollars!—an annual compounded return of over 50 percent.

He had acquired his investment philosophy, developed his investment system, and tested it—successfully. He was ready.

The Failed Philosopher

When George Soros graduated from the London School of Economics in the spring of 1953, he was hoping for an academic career. But his grades weren't good enough.

So after graduation he took the first of a series of odd jobs until, as a means of paying the rent, he hit upon the idea that there was money to be made in financial markets.

Soros wrote a personal letter to the managing director of each of the merchant banks in the City of London. One of his few interviews was with the managing director of Lazard Frères, who gave him an appointment for the sole purpose of telling him he was barking up the wrong tree trying to get a job in the City of London. He told Soros:

---

*The equivalent of $9,800 in 1950 dollars is approximately $77,100 today. A remarkable achievement for anyone just turned twenty.
†About $975,000 of today's dollars. An amazing result when you realize the stock market of the early 1950s bears no resemblance to the booms of the 1980s or 1990s.

"Here in the City we practice what we call intelligent nepotism. That means that each managing director has a number of nephews, one of whom is intelligent, and he is going to be the next managing director. If you came from the same college as he did, you would have a chance to get a job in the firm. If you came from the same university, you may still be all right. But you're not even from the same country!"[10]

Eventually, Soros did secure a job in the City with Singer & Friedlander, whose managing director was, like Soros, Hungarian. His time there was hardly illustrious, though what he was learning by doing—for example, to arbitrage gold stocks—began to make him more comfortable with a financial career.

But his time there was hardly an abject failure, either. A relative had given him £1,000 (then $4,800) to invest on his behalf. When he left in 1956 to join F. M. Mayer in New York, he took with him $5,000, which was his share of the profits made on that original £1,000. He clearly had a natural talent for operating in the investment marketplace.

In New York, Soros began arbitraging oil stocks—buying and selling the same securities on different international markets to profit from small price discrepancies.

But he first made his mark on Wall Street as a research analyst covering European stocks, where he had enormous success until John F. Kennedy entered the White House. One of Kennedy's first acts as president in 1961 was to introduce the "interest equalization tax" to "protect" the balance of payments. This 15% tax on foreign investments brought Soros's highflying business in European stocks to a crashing halt.

With little to do, he turned back to philosophy. In 1961 and 1962 he worked weekends and evenings on *The Burden of Consciousness,* a book he had begun writing while studying at the London School of Economics. He did indeed complete it, but it failed to satisfy him.

There came a day when I was rereading what I had written the day before and couldn't make sense of it. . . . I now realize that I was mainly regurgitating Karl Popper's ideas. But I haven't given up the illusion that I have something important and original to say.[11]

It was only then, at the age of thirty-two, that Soros decided to focus his full attention on investing. In 1963 he made his last-but-one move, to Arnhold & S. Bleichroeder, where he began testing his philosophical ideas in the markets. It was here that the Quantum Fund was first conceived and, eventually, born.

In 1967 the First Eagle Fund was launched by Arnhold & S. Bleichroeder with Soros as its manager. A second fund, the Double Eagle Fund, was established in 1969—*seventeen years* after his first job in the City of London. Soros's current net worth in the billions began then with his own investment in the fund of just $250,000. The following year, Jimmy Rogers (author of *The Investment Biker*) became Soros's partner. They set up as independent fund managers—Soros Fund Management—in 1973, taking the Double Eagle Fund with them. It was renamed the Quantum Fund a few years later, and the rest is history.

Easy Money

Everyone would laugh at the idea that you could just pick up a golf club and take on Tiger Woods without any special training. Only a lunatic would bet on a complete novice beating André Agassi at Wimbledon. And who in his right mind would get in the ring with Mike Tyson and expect to last longer than fifteen seconds?

So why do people think they can just open a brokerage account, plonk down $5,000, and hope to make the same kind of returns as Warren Buffett or George Soros?

The myth that investing is an easy way to riches, that no special training or apprenticeship is needed, is implicit in every single one of the Seven Deadly Investment Sins. And it is reinforced by the fortunes that some rank amateurs occasionally make when they're lucky enough to jump on a bandwagon like the Internet boom.

Even Master Investors such as Warren Buffett and Peter Lynch contribute (unwittingly) to this myth when they say that all you need to do is find a few good companies you can buy at the right price and sit on them.

It's true that there are no barriers to entry. You don't need any special physical skills. You don't need to start while you're in kindergarten, as top athletes and concert pianists must. And every investment book, every talking head on CNBC makes it all *sound* so easy.

And investing *is* easy—when you have reached the state of unconscious competence. But to get there, you must first "pay your dues."

Neither Buffett nor Soros actually set out with the intention of paying their dues. But by going through the process of making mistakes with real money, analyzing them, and learning from them, that is exactly what they were doing. By following this process, the losses they incurred were an investment in their long-term success.

Going through the pain of losing real money is an essential component of accumulating experience. How you react to such losses is the crucial element that determines whether you will ultimately succeed or fail as an investor.

Both Buffett and Soros were dedicated to succeeding. They are always willing to "go the extra mile" to reach their goal. A mistake, a loss, does not impact on their confidence in themselves. They don't take it personally. As Buffett puts it: "A stock doesn't know who owns it. You may have all these feelings and emotions as the stock goes up and down, but the stock doesn't give a damn."[12]

By taking responsibility for their actions they feel in control of their own destiny. They never blame the markets or their broker.

They lost money because of something *they* did wrong—and so the remedy was within *their* control.

The investor who doesn't react to his mistakes as Buffett and Soros react to theirs won't stick it out long enough to pay their dues.

Paying the Price

Even investors who are spectacularly successful for a while sometimes fail to pay their dues and inevitably pay the price—just like Long-Term Capital Management.

Long-Term was founded in 1994 by John Meriwether, the former chief of Salomon Brothers' Arbitrage Group, and most of the other traders from the same department. Long-Term started with $1.25 billion, raised mainly with the help of two of its partners, the Nobel Prize–winning economists Robert C. Merton and Myron S. Scholes.

At Salomon, the $500 million a year in profits these traders had averaged trading bond spreads accounted for the bulk of the firm's profits.

For its first few years, Long-Term successfully replicated those profits by following exactly the same strategy. They knew what they were doing, and they did it well.

Too well. By 1997, the partners had a problem: They had too much money, even after they returned a big chunk of it to the investors. And at the same time, the margins on their bread-and-butter business of bond spreads had shrunk as everyone else on Wall Street piled in.

Except for Meriwether, most of the other partners were "quants": people with PhD's in economics or finance who had studied with Merton or Scholes or one of their followers. Underlying their approach was the fundamental belief that "markets are efficient."

At Salomon, they had built computerized models of the bond markets to identify and exploit bond market inefficiencies. Bonds were their circle of competence—and, there, they *had* paid their dues.

But their success had gone to their heads. When faced with the problem of where to put all this new money, they took their bond models and applied them to markets like takeover arbitrage where they had no competitive advantage. Not only were these models unproven and untested outside bonds, the "professors" (as the partners were known) didn't feel that any testing was necessary. They just plunged in with billions of dollars.

Unfortunately for them (as it turned out later), their first forays outside the bond markets were successful. So they expanded to trading currencies, as well as Russian, Brazilian, and other emerging market bonds and spreads on stock options. They even shorted some stocks outright, including Berkshire Hathaway, a trade that eventually cost them $150 million.

Scholes was one of the few partners who was upset about such trades. "He argued that Long-Term should stick to its models; it did not have any 'informational advantage' "[13] in any of these areas. But he was totally ignored.

The other partners acted as if they could walk on water. To them, their previous success proved they were infallible. They had no Plan B to tell them what to do if things fell apart. On the contrary, with mathematical precision they had calculated that a market implosion that would affect all their positions simultaneously was a ten-sigma event, one that might happen once in the life of the universe.

Their first mistake, of course, was going outside their circle of competence. You will not want to make this mistake. You can *expand* your circle of competence by learning and testing a different way of investing. If you're willing to pay your dues *again*. To just dive in with a billion dollars on the line from day one is akin to getting into the ring with Mike Tyson with your eyes closed. A recipe for disaster.

And sure enough, Long-Term imploded in August 1998 when

Russia defaulted on its bonds and the markets went haywire. After having quadrupled their investors' money from $1.25 billion to $5 billion, by October 1998, there was only $400 million left—40 cents on the original dollar.

Of course, their failure to "pay their dues" wasn't the only mistake the "professors" made. Indeed, they violated almost every single one of the 23 Winning Investment Habits. But the way they believed they could jump straight to the end of the learning curve was an integral part of their demise.

If you haven't paid your dues, you'll eventually blow up. It's inevitable.

"It's Frightening Easy"

Like any master of a craft, the Master Investor who has paid his dues develops what some people think of as "a sixth sense where they just know that a stock is going to move. . . . It's visceral. You just sense it."[14]

It could be a backache, as it is for Soros. A mental picture like the one Buffett sees of a company ten or twenty years in the future. Or an internal voice saying, "That's the bottom!" In whatever form it comes, it's the years of accumulated experience stored in the Master Investor's subconscious mind communicating in a kind of mental shorthand.

This is why, for the Master, everything he does seems so effortless.

Before he had achieved the state of unconscious competence, it would have been impossible for Buffett to decide to buy a billion-dollar company in just a few minutes. Nor would Soros have been able to take such a giant position in a currency, as he did when he shorted the pound sterling in 1992. Indeed, until the Plaza Accord in 1985 Soros had lost money on his forays into currencies.

But to some degree, Soros's and Buffett's increasing expertise is disguised by the mountain of money each has to invest. With billions rather than millions of dollars to invest, only an investment "elephant" will make a significant difference to either Master Investor's net worth.

While there are very few "elephant-sized" investments with the prospect of large percentage gains, there are endless investments of this kind for the smaller investor. As Buffett demonstrated in the late 1970s when he and his wife separated and he, personally, was strapped for cash.

Although he was then worth $140 million, it was all tied up in Berkshire stock. He refused to sell a single share of his "work of art." And he would certainly not declare a dividend just to pay his rent.

So he began buying stocks on his personal account.

> "It was almost frightening, how easy it was," a Berkshire employee said. "He analyzed what he was looking for. All of a sudden he had money. . . ." According to the broker Art Rowsell, "Warren made $3 million like bingo."[15]

The investor who believes that all he needs to do is find the holy grail, the right formula, the secret to reading charts, or some guru to tell him what to do and when to do it, can never develop the expertise of a Warren Buffett or a George Soros.

Paying your dues can be a long and arduous process, one that took Buffett and Soros almost twenty years apiece. But they went about the process unsystematically.

Unlike them, you now know that you must begin at the bottom of the learning curve. This gives you an inestimable advantage over the Master Investor who reached Mastery by a process of trial and error.

Keep Your Mouth Shut

TV interviewer: "What are your favorite stocks?"

George Soros: "I'm not going to tell you."[1]

"[Buffett] maintained that he was afraid to talk in bed because his wife might hear."

—ROGER LOWENSTEIN[2]

"My idea of a group decision is to look in the mirror."

—WARREN BUFFETT[3]

WHEN BENJAMIN GRAHAM GAVE HIS course at Columbia University he would use current examples of undervalued stocks to illustrate his methodology. After each class, some of his students would rush out and buy them. More than one of his students paid for his tuition that way.

Warren Buffett aped his mentor in every respect (even his letters to his partners were modeled on Graham's style)—except in this one. In 1953, for example, he taught a class in investment

WINNING HABIT NO. 17:

Never Talk about What You're Doing

The Master Investor	The Losing Investor
Almost never talks to anyone about what he's doing. Not interested or concerned with what others think about his investment decisions.	Is always talking about his current investments, "testing" his decisions against others' opinions rather than against reality.

principles at the University of Omaha but, unlike Graham, he refused to hand out any tips.

When he started his partnership in 1956 he would tell prospective investors: "I'll run it like my own money, and I'll take part of the losses and part of the profits. *And I won't tell you what I'm doing.*"[4]

Then, as now, Buffett simply refused to tell anyone what stocks he was looking at, not even to gain a new investor in his partnership. John Train, who profiled Buffett in *The Money Masters,* was "looking for a good place to park some capital" when he first met Buffett. "When I found that the holdings could not be revealed, I decided not to sign up."[5] Much to his later regret.

When Buffett said he wouldn't tell his investors what he was doing, he meant it.

> One time, a partner barged into the reception area [of Buffett's office] at Kiewit Plaza intent on finding out where the money was invested. Buffett, who was meeting with a banker named Bill Brown—later chairman of the Bank of Boston— told his secretary he was busy. She returned in a moment and said the man *insisted* on seeing him. Buffett disappeared for a minute and then told his secretary, "Price that guy out" [of the partnership]. Turning to Brown, Buffett added, "They know my rules. I'll report to them once a year."[6]

Today, when hundreds of thousands of investors around the world anticipate Buffett's every move, it makes perfect sense for Buffett to keep his mouth shut. But his policy was no different when he had just $100,000 and nobody had ever heard of him.

Until he met Charlie Munger, Buffett refused to talk to *anyone* about any of his investments until after he had sold them. And often, not even then—in case he wanted to buy them back sometime in the future.

And why should he talk to anyone? He knew what he was doing. He had no need to validate his ideas by seeking confirmation from others. "You're neither right nor wrong because other people agree with you," he told shareholders at the 1991 Berkshire Hathaway annual meeting. "You're right because your facts are right and your reasoning is right. That's the only thing that makes you right."[7]

Another reason Buffett keeps his cards close to his chest is that "good investment ideas are rare, valuable, and subject to appropriation just as good product or acquisition ideas are."[8] Investment ideas are his stock in trade. He isn't going to give them away any more than Bill Gates will make Windows source code freely available, or Toyota will reveal to Ford or General Motors its latest engine design or its model lineup for next year.

There is more than self-confidence behind his behavior. Buffett's ideas are *his creations*, his property—and "a tiny bit sacred."[9]

"Keep Quiet and Speculate"

Like Buffett, George Soros keeps his investment ideas to himself. A secretive person by nature, he wanted his fund to have a very low profile. When, in June 1981, he was featured on the cover of *Institutional Investor*, he was depicted "as something of a mystery man, a loner who never telegraphs his moves, who keeps even his associates at a distance."[10]

"George is never very open to me as to what his inner thoughts are," said Gary Gladstein, who has administered the Quantum Fund's operations—and even Soros's personal finances—since

1985. Stanley Druckenmiller concurs: "Although I know about his activities, it's remarkable how little I know. He is of course arrogant but he's also shy. He's definitely shy."[11]

Soros's staff were strictly forbidden to speak to the press. As a result they were known as the secretive Soros Fund. "The last time I went on the record," said one former Quantum Fund manager, James Marquez, "was the day I went to work for George Soros."[12]

Soros didn't want anybody to get wind of what they were up to. "You're dealing with a market. You should be anonymous,"[13] he says. And he went to great lengths to cover his tracks. "Soros keeps the lid so tight it is difficult for any outsider to learn what stocks the group is buying, holding, and shorting."[14]

How, then, could he build billion-dollar positions and keep them quiet? One clue comes from a former London bond trader I know whose firm was a broker for the Quantum Fund. "There was a special phone on the managing director's desk," the ex-bond trader told me. "When it rang, he knew it was Soros. No one spoke to George except the boss. When the orders came to me to execute, I'd be dealing in 1,000 or 10,000 lots instead of the hundred or so that was normal. And I would have to dribble them into the market so as not to leave any tracks."

Soros goes to such lengths for the same reason as Buffett: If others find out what he is doing they'll pile into the market and the price will run away from him.

Unable to find out what he is doing, other traders will try and discern his "footprints" in the market, as happened in October 1995 "when a burst of speculation that Soros was shorting the French franc helped drive that currency sharply down against the German mark."[15]

If a stock market investor like Buffett broadcasts his intentions, the worst thing that can happen is that other investors pile in and drive up the price. For a trader like Soros, who often has large short positions, the downside can be far worse.

In 1978, Soros shorted casino operator Resorts International. So did another trader, Robert Wilson, who having announced his position to all and sundry went off on a round-the-world vacation.

Gambling stocks were hot. While Wilson cruised the fjords in Norway and went shopping in Hong Kong, the public back home poured into Resorts, which soared from $15 to $120. Brokers who knew about Wilson's short position "told their customers that when the stock got high enough Wilson would have to buy all his shorts back, since his resources were not infinite; this, they said, gave a measure of support to the stock."[16]

Eventually, Wilson's brokers tracked him down and told him he had to put up more money or get out. " 'Cover some Resorts,' he ordered. Now he was in the position of squeezing himself."[17]

Quite likely, Resorts stock would have gone up anyway. But by talking about his short position Wilson effectively invited the market to squeeze him. Which it did.

And Soros? He had kept his mouth shut as usual, so nobody knew at the time that he was also short. When he saw what was going on, he quietly covered his shorts and went long to profit from Wilson's folly.

As Wilson's quandary illustrates all too well, Soros is right when he says "Speculators ought to keep quiet and speculate."[18]

But Soros isn't as tight-lipped as Buffett. Certainly since he became famous as "The Man Who Broke the Bank of England" he has kept a high profile, and is inevitably quizzed about his investment outlook.

When he was relatively unknown, while he avoided the press like the plague he did continually talk to other traders and investors. Sometimes, it was to test his ideas. Mostly, though, he wanted to improve his "feel for the market" by finding out what other people were thinking and doing. That usually means giving people at least some inkling of your own thinking.

Not that knowing what Soros is thinking is always of much help. Soros once spent an entire afternoon arguing about the stock market with a trader named Jean-Manuel Rozan. "Soros was vehemently bearish," Rozan recalled, "and he had an elaborate theory to explain why, which turned out to be entirely wrong. The market boomed."

Two years later, Rozan ran into Soros at a tennis tournament. "Do you remember our conversation?" Rozan asked. "I recall it very well,"

Soros replied. "I changed my mind, and made an absolute fortune."[19]

While Buffett loves to talk about business and investing any time of day or night (but won't say a word about anything he's actually doing in the markets), Soros prefers to avoid the subject entirely on social occasions. One of his longtime friends said that for many years he didn't even know what George did for a living.[20]

At one dinner party a guest asked Soros for his investment advice.

The atmosphere changed. George, turning icy, asked his guest, "How much money do you have?" The guest, left uncomfortable by the question, tried to parry by bouncing it back to Soros: "How much money do *you* have?"

And as the other guests looked on, George shot back, "Well, that's my business, but I never asked you what I should do with it." [Bill] Maynes said the man was never asked back.[21]

"Did I Do the Right Thing?"

Like Soros's dinner guest, most investors are continually asking for advice and confirmation about their investments.

Many years ago, a fellow newsletter publisher set up a telephone advice service for his subscribers. One of his staff told me that over half the calls were people asking some variation of the question: "I just bought this stock." Or "I just made a real estate investment." Whatever they'd done, they all asked: *"Did I do the right thing?"*

The rest of the calls were people asking either to be told what to do or seeking confirmation that what they were thinking of doing was the right move.

Needless to say, no one with the self-confidence of a Buffett or a Soros ever phoned in. The Master Investor thinks independently. He simply doesn't need someone to verify the quality of his investment ideas. And that is why he keeps them to himself.

"Phony! Phony! Phony!"

> *"In evaluating people, you look for three qualities: integrity, intelligence, and energy. And if you don't have the first, the other two will kill you."*
>
> —WARREN BUFFETT[1]

> *"I am willing to use different people employing different approaches as long as I can rely on their integrity."*
>
> —GEORGE SOROS[2]

ONE OF MY INVESTMENT COACHING clients was a woman from Singapore. In our initial conversation she told me that she chose her stocks based on the numbers she found in annual reports and elsewhere. "I do it, I'm good at it," she said, "but I don't really enjoy it."

Later in this conversation she mentioned that she considered herself a good judge of character. So I said to her: "Well, why don't you go along to the annual meetings of companies you're looking at so you can meet, or at least observe, the company's managers and

WINNING HABIT NO. 18:

KNOW HOW TO DELEGATE

The Master Investor	The Losing Investor
Has successfully delegated most if not all of his responsibilities to others.	Selects investment advisors and managers the same way he makes investment decisions.

directors. You can see if you'd feel comfortable giving your money to any of these guys to look after."

This is an aspect of Warren Buffett's investment strategy that's usually underemphasized in all examinations of his investment approach: that he loves dealing with people as well as numbers, and he's an incredibly good judge of character.

Walter Schloss is another Graham student who also worked at Graham-Newman Co. He has since averaged around 20 percent a year buying Graham-style investments. Comparing his style to Buffett's, he says:

> I really don't like talking to management. Stocks really are easier to deal with. They don't argue with you. They don't have emotional problems. You don't have to hold their hand. Now Warren is an unusual guy because he's not only a good analyst, he's a good salesman, and he's a very good judge of people. That's an unusual combination. If I were to [acquire] somebody with a business, I'm sure he would quit the very next day. I would misjudge his character or something—or I wouldn't understand that he really didn't like the business and really wanted to sell it and get out. Warren's people knock themselves out after he buys the business, so that's an unusual trait.[3]

As Ken Chace, whom Buffett promoted to run Berkshire, summed it up: "It's hard to describe how much I enjoyed working for him."[4]

"I Knew He Was a Phony"

How has Warren Buffett been able to acquire businesses whose owners end up "working harder for him than they did for themselves"?[5]

He is a superb judge of character. "I think I can tell pretty well what people's motivation is when they walk in," he says.[6]

In 1978, Warren Buffett was one of the few people in Omaha who closed his door to Larry King, a former Franklin Community Credit Union manager-treasurer who served a fifteen-year sentence [and is no relation to the CNN host of *Larry King Live*].

> "I knew that King was a phony," says Buffett, "and I think that he knew I knew. I'm probably the only person in Omaha he never asked for money." How did Buffett know? "It was like he had a big sign on his head that said 'PHONY, PHONY, PHONY.'"[7]

His unusual ability to gauge a person's character accurately is a crucial aspect of Buffett's investment and business success. It's what allows him to buy companies with management in place, confident that the former owners will stay on to run the business indefinitely. He can decide whether a manager is "his kind of people" in moments—an ability Schloss admits he doesn't have.

Whether he's buying a business in whole or in part, Buffett always acts as if he were the owner hiring the management. So when he's buying a stock he is effectively asking himself: "If I owned this company would I hire these guys to run it?" And of course, if the answer is no he won't invest.

For Buffett, every investment is an act of delegation. He is fully aware that he is entrusting the future of his money to other people—and he's only going to do that with people he respects, trusts, and admires.

He has two roles at Berkshire Hathaway. He says his primary role is the allocation of capital, a role he reserves to himself. But a second role, equally important, is to motivate people to work who simply have no need to.

One of his conditions when he purchases control of a company is that the existing owners stay on to manage it. Now independently wealthy, with lots of Berkshire Hathaway stock or cash in the bank, the previous owners continue to work as hard as ever, sometimes for decades—to make money for Buffett instead of themselves!

Part of his success is in choosing to only do business with people who simply love their work the way he does.

And part of it is the loyalty he inspires. Richard Santulli, who invented fractional ownership of private jets—and who sold the company he created, Executive Jets, Inc., to Berkshire Hathaway— put it succinctly when he said: "If Warren asked me to do anything, I would do it."[8]

Such loyalty is rare in today's corporate world. Yet Santulli's sentiment would be echoed word for word by most chief executives of Berkshire's many other subsidiaries. "Buffett's respectful treatment of his managers has instilled in them an ambition to 'make Warren proud,' as one puts it."[9]

Motivating previous owners to work just as hard *after* they've sold their company as they did before is a remarkable feat, one simply not achieved by any other company. By any measure, Buffett is an unsung genius at the art of delegation.

He's so good at delegating that Berkshire has just fifteen people working at company headquarters—the smallest by far of any Fortune 500 company. This allows Buffett to focus on what he does best, allocating capital, which as we've seen is Buffett's genius.

How Soros Learned to Delegate

In contrast to Buffett, delegation doesn't come naturally to George Soros. "I'm a very bad judge of character," he admits. "I'm a good judge of stocks, and I have a reasonably good perspective on history. But I am, really, quite awful in judging character, and so I've made many mistakes."[10]

Nevertheless, he recognized early on that the fund could only continue to grow by expanding the staff—and it was over this issue that Soros and Jimmy Rogers split. Soros wanted to expand the team; Rogers did not.

So they agreed on a three-step plan, Soros said. "The first step was to try and build a team together. If we didn't succeed, the second step was to build one without him; and if that didn't work, the third step was to do it without me. And that is what happened."[11]

In 1980 the partnership broke up. Soros was now in complete charge. But instead of building a team, as he had proposed, he ended up running the fund himself.

> I was the captain of the ship and I was also the stoker who was putting the coal on the fire. When I was on the bridge, I rang the bell and said "Hard left," and then I would run down into the engine room and actually execute the orders. And in-between I would stop and do some analysis as to what stocks to buy and so on.[12]

Not surprisingly, by 1981 Soros was breaking under the strain, and he had his first losing year. The fund lost 22.9 percent. Worse, a third of his investors pulled their money out, fearful that Soros had lost his grip.

So Soros stepped back, turning his fund into a "fund of funds. My plan was that I would give out portions to other fund managers, and I would become the supervisor rather than the active manager."[13]

This turned out to be a mistake, partly because Soros was delegating the task he did best: investing. Soros describes the three years that followed as lackluster ones for the Quantum Fund. But by taking a backseat he was able to recover from a problem he (like all traders) faced, that an investor like Buffett doesn't. It's called "burnout."

Trading is highly stressful. It requires total concentration for extended periods of time. Writing about his experience in 1981, Soros said, "I felt the fund was an organism, a parasite, sucking my blood and draining my energy."[14] He was working like a dog "and what was my reward? More money, more responsibility, more work—and more pain—because I relied on pain as a decision-making tool."[15]

In 1984 Soros took back the helm. Though his experiment in delegation hadn't been fully successful, Soros was rejuvenated and in 1985 the fund was up 122.2 percent.

That was also the year that Gary Gladstein came on board. Now, at last, Soros no longer had to worry about the administrative side of his business.

But Soros kept trying to find a successor to take over his role as chief investor. He finally succeeded when Stanley Druckenmiller joined him in 1988. When Druckenmiller was introduced to Soros's son Robert, he was informed that he was "number nine, my father's ninth successor."[16] As Soros wrote:

> It took me five years and a lot of painful experiences to find the right management team. I am pleased that finally I found it, but I cannot claim to be as successful in picking a team as I have been in actually managing money.[17]

Druckenmiller ran the Quantum Fund for thirteen years. But for the first year it was far from clear how long he would stay. He had been hired to be captain of the ship, but Soros had great difficulty in letting go.

Then, in 1989, the Berlin Wall collapsed and Soros spent most of the next five months setting up his Open Society Foundations in Eastern Europe. "When I finally heard from him, he acknowledged I had done extremely well," Druckenmiller recalled. "He completely let go and we never had a contentious argument since then."[18]

Though delegation never came easily to Soros, eventually, after many trials and tribulations, he in fact delegated more of his responsibilities than Buffett has. When Druckenmiller took full charge, says Soros, "we developed a coach-and-player relationship, which has worked very well ever since."[19] Their relationship was somewhat akin to Buffett's relationship with the managers of Berkshire's operating subsidiaries, though far more intense.

And Soros was happy to let the reins go, to focus on his other activities. While Buffett quips that he plans to hold a séance after his death for his successors. "I will keep working until five years after I die, and I've given the directors a Ouija board so they can keep in touch."[20]

Teamwork

Knowing how to delegate is absolutely essential to investment success—even if you're not Warren Buffett and you don't have to figure out what to do with $31 billion in cash.[21]

We normally think of delegation as something to do when, like Soros, we want to find someone to take over from us. But all successful investing is a result of teamwork. As an investor you must delegate . . .

- when you open a brokerage account, you're delegating the care of your money and the execution of your orders;
- when you invest in a mutual fund, commodity pool, limited partnership, or managed account you're hiring a fund manager, so you're delegating the investment function of decision making and delegating the care of your money;
- whenever you make an investment of any kind, you're delegating significant (and at those times when the market moves dramatically, total) control of your money to Mr. Market (think about that: would you knowingly hire a manic-depressive money manager?); and
- whenever you buy shares of a company, you're delegating the future of your money to the management.

Every act of delegation entails *giving up control*. Merely opening a bank account entails giving up control of your money to a group of people you have never met.

Successful delegation means you know what to expect. You know your brokerage account is segregated from the broker's assets. You know when you give an order to your broker that it will be executed as you specify. You can hang up the phone and focus on other things—without having to keep tabs on him to see that it's done the way you want.

The Master Investor delegates authority, but he never delegates responsibility for delegating a task to someone else. "If you picked the right man, fine, but if you picked the wrong man, the responsibility is yours—not his."[22]

And the Master Investor always takes responsibility for all the consequences of his actions. To be sure, he has more things to delegate than the average investor. But the rationale is the same: to free up his mind so that he can focus on the things he does best.

21

"Whatever You Have, Spend Less"

"Annual Income, £20; annual expenditure, £19 19s 6d. Result: Happiness. Annual Income, £20; annual expenditure, £20 0s 6d. Result: Misery."

—MR. MICAWBER IN CHARLES DICKENS'S
DAVID COPPERFIELD

"Probably the most tangible benefit [of being a billionaire] is that I get very good tennis games."

—GEORGE SOROS[1]

"Money, to some extent, sometimes lets you be in more interesting environments. But it can't change how many people love you or how healthy you are."

—WARREN BUFFETT[2]

BELIEVE IT OR NOT, you can usually tell whether children are going to be wealthy or not by the time they are three or four years old. If

WINNING HABIT NO. 19:

LIVE FAR BELOW YOUR MEANS

The Master Investor	The Losing Investor
Lives far below his means.	Probably lives beyond his means (most people do).

they take their pocket money and immediately blow it on candies—and the next day ask to borrow a dollar you know you're unlikely to ever get back—let's hope this behavior doesn't last them a lifetime. Sadly, too often it does.

But if a child is frugal with his pocket money, always putting aside a chunk of it, you can be confident he has a good chance of achieving financial independence as an adult.

And a frugal kid who invests her pocket money in candies to sell to other kids at a profit might become another Warren Buffett.

Aside from inheriting, marrying, or stealing wealth, there's only one way to accumulate investment capital: Live below your means. This is a behavior that both Warren Buffett and George Soros exhibited from an early age. Their achievement of wealth beyond most people's wildest dreams has not changed those core values. They weren't extravagant as children or teenagers; and they aren't now. The leopard doesn't change his spots.

For most of his life Soros has lived in modest accommodations, often almost indifferent to his surroundings. Once a Swiss art dealer loaned Soros a Paul Klee painting he could easily afford. "He loved it, but sent it back saying he could not separate the painting from the figure on its price tag."[3]

When he married his second wife, Susan Weber, "he sent me out to look for apartments," she said. "Every apartment I show him he turns down. It's too expensive, he says, or it's too big."[4]

Some billionaires insist on traveling around in a chauffeur-driven limousine. Not Soros. He'd grab a taxi, ride a bus, take a tram, or simply walk from one part of town to another. It was

never a matter of saving money, just getting there the most efficient way.

Reflecting on his own wealth, Soros once said: "A benefit of being successful was that I could afford the things I wanted, but I did
not have extravagant tastes. I always lived on a scale that was more
modest than my financial resources."[5]

The Extremist of Omaha

Stories about Buffett's frugality (some call it miserliness) are le-
gion. One day Warren Buffett was riding the elevator up to his office on the fourteenth floor and there was a penny on the floor.
None of the executives from construction conglomerate Peter
Kiewit Sons, riding in the same elevator, took any notice.

> Buffett leaned over, reached down and picked up the penny.
> To the Kiewit executives, stunned that he would bother
> with a penny, the fellow who would one day be the richest
> person in the world quipped, "The beginning of the next
> billion."[6]

Buffett is an extremist on the subject of money. And nowhere is
his extremism more evident than when it comes to spending it.

Or, to be more accurate, *not* spending it.

The basis of his frugality is his future orientation. When he
spends a dollar—or scoops a dime off the street—he's not thinking
of *today's* value of that money. He is thinking about the value that
money could become.

For Buffett thrift isn't just a personal virtue but an integral aspect of his investment method. He admires managers like Tom
Murphy and Dan Burke (of Capital Cities/ABC) who "attack
costs as vigorously when profits are at record levels as when they

are under pressure."[7] He was a fan of Rose Blumkin, whose motto was "Sell cheap and tell the truth,"[8] long before he bought her business, the Nebraska Furniture Mart. She cut costs so ruthlessly that she drove her competitors out of business. Major national furniture chains simply avoid Omaha because they know they cannot compete.

Buffett loves managers who ensure their companies live below their means. While Buffett and Charlie Munger were accumulating stock in Wells Fargo, they found out that Carl Reichardt, the bank's chairman, had told an executive who wanted to buy a Christmas tree for the office to buy it with his own money, not the bank's.

"When we heard that, we bought more stock,"[9] Munger told shareholders at the 1991 Berkshire annual meeting.

Frugality is a natural aspect of both Buffett's and Soros's characters. As their wealth increased, both indulged in minor extravagances. Minor compared to their wealth. Buffett bought an executive jet he named *The Indefensible*. Aside from his apartment in Manhattan, Soros owns a beach house on Long Island, a country home in upstate New York, and a house in London.

But wealth didn't change their natural frugality. It's easy to see how the consequence of living below your means is important when you're starting out. It's the only way you can accumulate capital to invest. What's less obvious is how this mental habit remains crucial to your investment success even after your net worth has soared into the billions.

Very simply, without this attitude to money you won't keep what you have earned. Spending money is simple—anyone can do it. Making money is not. That's why living below your means is the attitude that underlies the *foundation* of the Master Investor's success: preservation of capital.

By keeping what he has, and adding to it by living below his means, the Master Investor lets his money compound indefinitely. And compound interest plus time is the foundation of every great fortune.

Most people want to be rich so they can fly first class, live it up in the Ritz, feast on champagne and caviar, and go shopping at Tiffany's without giving a second thought to their credit card bill.

The problem is that people who have this attitude to money don't wait until they're rich before they start indulging their fantasies, even if only on a small scale. As a result they never accumulate any capital, or even worse go into debt so they can live *beyond* their means . . . and remain poor or middle-class.

Wealth is really a state of mind. In the words of Charlie Munger: "I had a considerable passion to get rich. Not because I wanted Ferraris—I wanted the independence. I desperately wanted it."[10] If you share this attitude, once you have gained that hard-fought independence the last thing you're going to do is jeopardize it by blowing all your money.

The alternative to living below your means is the debt-laden pattern of the middle class: If compound interest isn't working for you, it's working *against* you, bleeding your money away just as a spurting artery drains your life energy.

"We Should Pay to Have This Job"

Asked what he would do if he did retire, Mr. Rupert Murdoch, chairman of News Corp., responded: "Die pretty quickly."[1]

— TIME

"I'll keep [investing] as long as I live."

—WARREN BUFFETT[2]

BOTH WARREN BUFFETT AND GEORGE SOROS have so much money they don't need to get out of bed in the morning if they don't want to. What motivates them to keep making more money when, given their frugal natures, they couldn't possibly ever spend what they have? What drives them?

There are two kinds of motivation: "away from" and "toward."

Someone may be motivated to become wealthy from a fear of being poor. This is an "away from" type of motivation.

So what happens when he has achieved some level of wealth? Having moved away from poverty, the motivation no longer has the power to direct his actions, so he stops.

WINNING HABIT NO. 20:

It's Not About the Money

The Master Investor	The Losing Investor
Invests for stimulation and self-fulfillment—*not* for money.	Is motivated by money; thinks investing is the way to easy riches.

"Away from" motivations can be very, very powerful. If you're walking through the jungle and you're suddenly confronted by a tiger, then fear will cause you to run like hell. But once you have achieved safety, there's no reason to run anymore.

This kind of motivation is like a battery stamped with a "use by" date. After then, it's dead; its power has run out. This kind of motivation won't stir you to pursue a goal over an extended period, like a lifetime.

The exception is when such a motivation is associated with a character-shaping event in one's formative years. This seems to be the case for both Buffett and Soros.

Like most people born in the 1930s, the Great Depression had a lasting impact on the young Warren Buffett, who saw his father lose everything.

The Nazi occupation of Hungary had a far deeper impact on the young George Soros, who even today, with billions of dollars at his disposal, talks about survival as "an ennobled value." In his introduction to *The Alchemy of Finance* he wrote: "If I had to sum up my practical skills, I would use one word: *survival*."[3]

Soros's driving "away from" motivation can explain what he does when he goes to the office, but it isn't enough of a force to keep sending him there every morning when survival is no longer a real issue.

For that, you need a motivation that pulls you *toward* some goal. And if that is a fixed goal, such as becoming a millionaire, or running a four-minute mile, then once achieved it will lose its pulling power.

But if you are inspired by what you do, then any money you make while pursuing your goals is merely a side effect.

Warren Buffett's motivation is easy to understand: He just wants to have fun. "There is no job in the world more fun than running Berkshire and I count myself lucky to be where I am."[4]

Fun to him is "tap dancing" to his office every day, reading piles of annual reports, working with "sensational people," and "making money and watching it grow."[5] As he says:

> "I think if you found an athlete that was doing well—and I'm not comparing myself—but a Ted Williams or an Arnold Palmer or something—after they have enough to eat, they're not doing it for the money. My guess is that if Ted Williams was getting the highest salary in baseball and he was hitting .220, he would be unhappy. And if he was getting the lowest salary in baseball and batting .400, he'd be very happy. That's the way I feel about this job. Money is a byproduct of doing something I like doing extremely well."[6]

Money is just the way Buffett can measure how well he's doing what he loves to do.

"We [Charlie and I] should pay to have this job,"[7] he once told shareholders. Given that his salary is a mere $100,000 per year, in a very real sense he does. If Berkshire were a regular mutual fund that charged a one percent management fee, on $77.6 billion[8] in assets Buffett would be getting $776 million a year. That's quite a haircut.

"There Is More to My Existence Than Money"

Like Buffett, Soros is interested in money "in the same way that a sculptor must be interested in clay or bronze. It was the material in which I worked."[9] Like the sculptor, his focus isn't on the material but on the outcome.

He is indifferent to money itself. Talking about his father's influence he noted that "part of what I learned was the futility of making money for money's sake. Wealth can be a dead weight."[10]

But Soros's primary motivation for investing is very different from Buffett's. He doesn't agree with Buffett that investing is fun. "If you're having fun, you're probably not making any money," he says. "Good investing is boring."[11]

Investing isn't his calling, as it is Buffett's. As a student, Soros imagined himself becoming a famous *intellectual* figure like Keynes, Popper, or even Einstein. It's this ambition that still drives him today.

He describes the first years of his career as a hedge fund manager as "a very stimulating and dynamic period" as he began using his philosophical ideas in the real world. "This is when I started elaborating my concept of boom and bust reflexivity. This is when the philosophy took on a practical application."[12]

As he wrote in *The Alchemy of Finance:*

In the first ten years of my business career . . . selling and trading in securities was a game I played without putting my true self on the line.

All this changed when I became a fund manager. I was putting all my money where my mouth was and I could not afford to dissociate myself from my investment decisions. I had to use all my intellectual resources and I discovered, to my great surprise and gratification, that my abstract ideas came in very handy. It would be an exaggeration to say that they accounted for my success; but there can be no doubt that they gave me an edge.[13]

He discovered that the investment marketplace was the perfect arena to test his ideas. He imagined that by proving his ideas in the real world he would be recognized as a philosopher of note.

This was (and remains) a vain hope—if only for the reason

that the majority of academic philosophers deny that the real world even exists! And as for testing philosophical ideas in the real world, that's just not the way to impress academics.

Of course, some of Soros's writings (such as *The Alchemy of Finance*) are so opaque that few people can really grasp them. So it's no surprise that academics ignore him completely. Not that many investment professionals can understand what he's trying to get at either.

But Buffett has hardly suffered a better fate in academia, even though his writings are crystal clear, his method of investing is far easier to grasp, and his philosophy is derived from the most famous investment academic of all time: Benjamin Graham.

To be fair, we should add that Graham's ideas don't get much more attention in academia these days than Buffett's, despite Graham's superior academic credentials. One possible reason: Like Soros, Graham drew his investment philosophy from—and tested it in—the real world. Successfully.*

At heart Soros is a thinker, not an investor. His primary satisfaction comes from proving his ideas in the marketplace. "It's the adventure of ideas that attracts me,"[14] he says. "I was also inspired by the fact that I was able to combine the two great abiding interests in my life: philosophical speculation and speculation in financial markets. Both seemed to benefit from the combination: Together, they engaged me more than either one on its own."[15]

Like most people who have accumulated wealth, Soros began giving some of it away. But his method is unique. He didn't write a check to a charity or simply endow a foundation. He established his Open Society Foundations as tools for applying his philosophical ideas in the political and social arenas. "Being rich," he once said, "enabled me to do something I really cared about."[16]

Whether he is making money or giving it away, what drives Soros is ideas. As he says himself:

---

*I've always been amused that one meaning of the word "academic" is *not practical or directly useful*. As in the phrase "It's academic," meaning "irrelevant."

The main difference between me and other people who have
amassed this kind of money is that I am primarily interested
in ideas, and I don't have much personal use for money. But I
hate to think what would have happened if I hadn't made
money: My ideas would not have gotten much play.[17]

He also acknowledges that if he hadn't become famous as the Man
Who Broke the Bank of England, it's unlikely there'd be much interest in any of the books, such as *The Crisis of Global Capitalism*,
he has published.

He's still motivated by his childhood dream to be remembered
as an influential thinker like Keynes or Popper. "I wish I could
write a book that will be read for as long as our civilization lasts,"
he writes.[18]

I would value it much more highly than any business success
if I could contribute to an understanding of the world in
which we live or, better yet, if I could help to preserve the
economic and political system that has allowed me to flour-
ish as a participant.[19]

A major reason both Soros and Buffett have accumulated so much
money is that it was never their primary aim. If money was the
motivating factor they would have stopped long before they were
billionaires. Indeed, Buffett himself says he had quite enough
money to retire on in 1956 before he even started his investment
career.

When Soros burned out in 1981, he was already worth $25
million. Even so, he had not achieved what he wanted to do in life.

Both Master Investors were inspired to keep moving by a combination of powerful "away from" *and* "toward" motivations that
still drive and inspire them in their seventies. As a side effect, they
accumulated great wealth. For them, making money is a means to
an end, not an end in itself.

Master of His Craft

"I have enjoyed the process [of making money] far more than the proceeds, though I have learned to live with those, also."

—WARREN BUFFETT[1]

IN 1956 HOMER DODGE, A physics professor in Vermont, drove halfway across the country to Omaha for one reason: to persuade Warren Buffett to invest his money. He had heard about Buffett from his friend Benjamin Graham.

Buffett had just started his first partnership with $105,100 from family and friends. He agreed to start a second one for Dodge, who became his first outside investor with $100,000.

Dodge's son Norton has said, "My father saw immediately that Warren was brilliant at financial analysis. But it was more than that."

The elder Dodge saw a uniquely talented craftsman who loved the process of investing and who had mastered all the tools.[2]

WINNING HABIT NO. 21:

LOVE WHAT YOU DO, *NOT* WHAT YOU OWN

The Master Investor	The Losing Investor
Is emotionally involved with (and gets his satisfaction from) the process of investing; can walk away from any individual investment.	Falls in love with his investments.

The master of any art is, first and foremost, the master of the tools of his trade, of his craft.

The artist has a vision of his painting, of his ultimate goal. But when he paints, his focus is on his craft, on the way he applies his brush to the canvas. He is absorbed by the process of painting. When he is totally involved in what he is doing, the master painter enters a mental state that psychologist Mihaly Csikszentmihalyi calls "flow."[3]

Flow is a state where absorption is so complete that one's entire mental focus is on the task being performed. The painter's visual field will narrow so that all he sees is the painting, the brush—and be aware, in the back of his mind, of his image of the final result. His peripheral vision will be so contracted that he simply won't notice anything going on around him. With his attention directed fully outward, he can even lose his sense of self, becoming instead (so to speak) the process of painting. His sense of time can disappear so completely that hours can go by, meals can be skipped, the sun can set and rise again, and he doesn't even notice.

The master painter loves the process of painting not his tools. And whether he sells his paintings, while not irrelevant, is not the most important thing. Unlike those who paint those landscapes that clutter the walls of hotel rooms, the master painter doesn't paint for money. He paints in order to paint.

The archetypal writer or artist starving in a garret may dream of seeing her book on the best-seller list—or of his paintings hanging in the Guggenheim Museum. But that vision isn't going to motivate anyone to work for years in poverty and obscurity. If it's the *process* of writing or painting—if *that* is where someone finds her satisfaction, then that's where she'll also find her motivation.

The common denominator between people who are masters of their own field is that they are motivated by the *process of doing*. The activity, not the outcome. The result—whether it's money or winning medals for his roses—is an added bonus to entering a state of flow. As John Train put it in *The Midas Touch:*

> The great investor, like the great chess player, is determined to become a master of that particular craft, sometimes without caring whether he only gets rich or immensely rich. It has been rightly said that the reward of the general is not a bigger tent but command. It is, in other words, succeeding in the process itself that fascinates the greatest investors.[4]

Investments for the Master Investor are like paint for the painter, the material he works with. An artist may love painting with oils, but it's the "painting with," not the oils, that he loves.

Keeping Your Eye on the Ball

Whether it be tennis, football, baseball, or hockey, players are always urged to "keep their eye on the ball."

In practice this means: Where is your mental focus? Imagine you're playing your favorite game. I'll use tennis, and you can substitute whatever game you like.

Let's say the score is one set each, and you're down one game to five in the third set. If you lose the next game, you lose the match.

Imagine that you're on the court and your focus is on winning the game. Every time you win a point you think of all the points you're going to have to win in order to win the match. That makes you feel like you're at the bottom of a very deep hole, with a long and difficult climb to get out. Every time your opponent wins a point, the hole gets a bit deeper. If you have ever watched a tennis match (or, indeed, any other sports game) you can tell, from the expression on their faces, which players have this mental focus. They look defeated. Even though the game isn't over, even though other players have come from this far behind and won, it's over for them.

Now imagine that you "keep your eye on the ball." You put all your mental and physical energy into hitting the ball the best you can. *Every* ball. You know what the score is—but in this mental state, that doesn't seem to matter any more. You're no longer winning or losing; you're just playing.

This will not guarantee a win. But I'm sure you can sense that the player who "keeps his eye on the ball" is going to give his opponent a much harder time.

Where you have your mental focus determines your outcome. The average investor makes the mistake of focusing on the profits he hopes to make. In the extreme case, the investor "falls in love" with his investments. Like the gold bug, or the investor caught up in the tech (or other) bubble, he firmly believes, "These investments will make me rich."

The Master Investor focuses on the process. George Soros, for example, is "fascinated by chaos. That's really how I make my money: understanding the revolutionary process in financial markets."[5] In Soros's view, calm and order in the financial world can never be more than a temporary hiatus. So there will be never-ending opportunities for the creation and testing of hypotheses to profit from chaos.

It's worth looking at Soros's most famous investment, shorting the pound sterling, in its proper context as but one of many Quantum Fund investments. In 1992 the fund was up 68.6 percent. If Soros and Druckenmiller had not "taken on" the Bank of England, their fund would still have been up 40 percent, well above their own long-term annual average.

Nineteen ninety-two might have been Soros's most famous

> ### Warren Buffett on Buying a Business
>
> "The first question I always ask myself about [a business's owner] is:
>
> "Do they love the money [the effect] or do they love the business [the process]? . . . because the day after I buy a company, if they love the money they're gone."[8]

year, but it wasn't even his best. In both 1980 and 1985 the value of the Quantum Fund more than doubled. It was Soros's mastery of his craft that made his sterling profit possible.

For many successful investors, the most rewarding and exciting part of the process is the *search*, not the investment he eventually finds. "[Investing] is like a giant treasure hunt,"[6] says stock trader David Ryan. "I love the hunt,"[7] says another.

This makes logical sense. The process of investing includes searching, measuring, buying, monitoring, selling—and reviewing mistakes. Buying and selling, the steps most people focus on, both take but a moment. Searching and monitoring are the most time intensive—and are never-ending processes. Only a person whose source of satisfaction is these activities will devote the time and energy necessary to master them and reach Master Investor status.

When Warren Buffett describes his typical day, it's clear that he, too—when he's not talking to his managers (monitoring)—focuses primarily on *searching*:

> Well, first of all, I tap-dance into work. And then I sit down and I read. Then I talk on the phone for seven or eight hours. And then I take home more to read. Then I talk on the phone in the evening. We read a lot. We have a general sense of what we're after. We're looking for seven-footers. That's about all there is to it.[9]

Does the Master Investor get pleasure from the profits he makes? Of course. But his real pleasure comes from his involvement in the investment process. His priority isn't the investment he makes but the criteria he uses to make it. Any investment that does not meet his criteria is simply unappealing. Or, if he owns it, a mistake—which automatically changes his emotional reaction to it regardless of what he thought of it before.

And once the Master Investor has found an investment that meets his criteria, he's off on the trail looking for another one.

This Is Your Life

"He [Buffett] is thinking about [Berkshire] twenty-four hours a day."

—An employee of a Berkshire subsidiary[1]

"A fanatic worker, [Peter] Lynch lived and breathed stocks, stocks, stocks, morning, noon, and night."

—John Train[2]

ONE EVENING, BUFFETT AND HIS wife Susan had dinner with friends. Their hosts had just come back from Egypt.

After dinner, as their friends were setting up the slide projector to show him and Susan their pictures of the Pyramids, Buffett announced: "I have a better idea. Why don't you show the slides to Susie and I'll go into your bedroom and read an annual report."[3]

Warren Buffett doesn't just enjoy reading annual reports. It's his favorite pastime. "He just had a hobby that made him money," said Ralph Rigby, a Berkshire Hathaway textile salesman. "That was relaxation to him."[4]

Buffett's investment style is relaxation itself. The only time he's likely to come under any pressure at all is when the market is insanely cheap and he has more good investment ideas than money.

WINNING HABIT NO. 22:

LIVE AND BREATHE INVESTING 24 HOURS A DAY

The Master Investor	The Losing Investor
Lives and breathes investing twenty-four hours a day.	Is not fully dedicated to achieving his investment goals (even if he knows what they are).

The last time that happened was in 1974, when he said he felt "like an oversexed guy in a harem."[5]

The lifestyle of the trader could not be more opposite. The extreme is the trader with quote machines all over his house—even one in his bedroom *and* bathroom—so he can check prices anytime of the day or night, regardless of what he is doing. Michael Marcus describes the time when he was trading currencies heavily:

> It was very exhausting because it was a twenty-four-hour market. When I went to sleep, I would have to wake up almost every two hours to check the markets. I would tune in every major center as it opened: Australia, Hong Kong, Zurich, and London. It killed my marriage.[6]

If you want to trade currencies, sleepless nights and ruined weekends go with the territory. You have to be alert all the time—as Soros was one Sunday back in September 1985 when he got wind of the Plaza Accord that would drive the dollar down. So he spent Sunday night at home on the phone to Tokyo, where it was already Monday morning, selling as many dollars as he could.

But Soros's dedication to his chosen profession began much earlier. When his parents arrived in New York in January 1957, having escaped from Hungary the year before, it was Soros's brother, Paul, who met them. "I was busy. I was trading, I couldn't miss a day. I could not miss a day, no."[7]

He had only been in New York three months himself. But already he was working round the clock, buying stocks in Europe and selling them in New York.

What Other Investors and Traders Say

Ed Seykota: I feel my success comes from my love of the markets. I am not a casual trader. It is my life. I have a passion for trading. It is not merely a hobby or even a career choice for me. There is no question that this is what I am supposed to do with my life.[8]

Peter Hull: I don't know a lot about [eighty-one-year-old Australian investor] Jim Millner but I like the idea that he has gone through and kept in the game until he's a very old man. And I would like to do that as well. I want to still be here in forty years if possible. I don't want to retire because retirement is death. I want to stay in the game and investing is one game where you are continually stimulated. This is a career that allows you to keep playing the game for a long time and stay active.[9]

Lou Simpson: I really like what I'm doing. . . . I don't know what I'd do with myself if I retire.[10]

René Rivkin: I love the market, it is my work, my play and my life. I hate weekends because there is no stock market.[11]

Richard Driehaus: Why am I better? I probably stay in it more. A lot of people like to play the piano. But can you really become a virtuoso? It's like the Olympics. Practice, practice, practice. Remember the old saying: The harder I work the luckier I get? Or: Success is 99% perspiration and 1% inspiration? Success requires an addiction to what you are doing and it takes a lot of time.[12]

Michael Marcus: It's too much fun to give up. I don't want to make a lot more money . . . If trading is your life, it is a torturous kind of excitement. But if you are keeping your life in balance, then it's fun.[13]

Paul Tudor Jones: Trading gives you an incredibly intense feeling of what life is all about. Emotionally, you live on the extremes. . . . I wouldn't have it any other way.[14]

Laura J. Sloate: I love what I do, so I do it seven days a week.[15]

Peter Lynch: [While on vacation in Ireland in 1987] I was thinking about Dow Jones and not about Blarney, even at the moment I kissed Blarney's stone.[16]

"I would be wakened at 4:30, which is 9:30 in London, and then maybe every hour. I'd be asleep, pick up the phone, listen to the numbers and decide to make a bid or not. I might cable back a bid and go back to sleep. Sometimes I would then dream that the stock I had just bought went up and there were times when I'd wake up and have a little difficulty figuring out what I had done and what I had dreamed."[17]

Then he would head for the office to find buyers for his overnight purchases. He didn't see his parents for several days after they'd arrived, even though it had been ten years since he had seen them last.

One reason the Master Investor is so successful is that investing is *all* he does. It's not just his profession, it's his life. And so he thinks about investing day and night—even dreaming about it, as Soros did.

No one could become a Wimbledon champion, or equal Pavarotti's status in the world of opera, by practicing tennis or singing in their spare time. But the average investor *can* make handsome profits, even if investing isn't his full-time vocation. But he must emulate the Master Investor's dedication to mastering the craft. To quote Woodrow Wilson:

Nothing in the world can take the place of persistence. Talent will not; nothing is more common than unsuccessful men with talent. Genius will not; unrewarded genius is almost a proverb. Education will not; the world is full of educated derelicts. Persistence and determination alone are omnipotent.[18]

Or as the *I Ching* puts it more succinctly:

Perseverance furthers.

"Eat Your Own Cooking"

*"I manage [the Quantum Fund] as if it were my own money—
which it is to a large extent."*

—George Soros[1]

"Around here, we eat our own cooking," says Warren Buffett about where he puts *his* money. Ninety-nine percent of his net worth is in Berkshire Hathaway stock.

Buffett has the lowest salary of any CEO of any Fortune 500 company, just $100,000 per year. Not much more than a wet-behind-the-ears graduate with a freshly minted MBA from Harvard gets for his first job. As Berkshire pays no dividends, that's the only money he takes home. Unless he were to sell some Berkshire stock, which is the last thing he wants to do.

So if he needs more spending money, what does he do? Applying the same methodology that made him a billionaire, he buys stocks in his personal account—taking advantage of opportunities too small to make a difference to Berkshire's net worth; selling something when he needs a little extra cash.

WINNING HABIT NO. 23:

Put Your Net Worth on the Line

The Master Investor	The Losing Investor
Puts his money where his mouth is. For example, Warren Buffett has 99 percent of his net worth in shares of Berkshire Hathaway; George Soros, similarly, keeps most of his money in his Quantum Fund. For both, the destiny of their personal wealth is identical to that of the people who have entrusted money to their management.	Adds little to his net worth through investments—indeed, his investment activities are often hazardous to his wealth. Funds his investments (and makes up his losses) from somewhere else—business profits, salary, pension funds, company bonus plans, etc.

Similarly, Soros has nearly all his net worth in the Quantum Fund. Soros Management receives a 20 percent share of the fund's profits. If this fee is paid in kind—in shares of Quantum rather than cash—no tax is due until those shares are sold. So, before he started using his wealth to fund his Open Society Foundations, Soros personally owned some 40 percent of his Quantum Fund.

With the bulk of their wealth in Berkshire and Quantum, respectively, Buffett and Soros are no different from any entrepreneur: Bill Gates has most of his net worth in Microsoft stock; Rupert Murdoch's money is in News Corp.; Michael Dell's fortune rests in his shares of Dell Computer. Similarly, millions of businessmen around the world you have never heard of, both big and small, have most of their net worth tied up in their own companies.

There's nothing controversial about that. Indeed, you'd expect to find successful businessmen with most of their net worth in their own business. That's where they know how to make money more easily than anywhere else. That's what they love to do.

In Investment Guru Land

But the moment you walk into Investment Guru Land it's a totally different story. You'll find that the investment guru who eats his own cooking is the exception, not the rule.

And this signals the major difference between the Master Investor and the investment guru. The Master Investor is an investor. The investment guru is a fortune seller. Whether he or she is a fund manager, a newsletter writer, a brokerage house analyst, or a financial advisor—selling *opinions*, not profitable investing, is what it's all about.

And where does the media guru put his or her own money? Good question. One you should ask, especially when you're looking for someone to manage your money.

The investment guru who doesn't eat his own cooking may be entertaining to watch on TV. But if what he's really saying is "Do what I say, not what I do," why on earth would you want to follow his advice or hire him to look after *your* money? (Though it's worth remembering that just because someone *is* following his own advice, it doesn't automatically mean that he's banking any profits.)

Every Master Investor puts his money where his mouth is for the same reason the successful businessman has his net worth tied up in his own business. Investing *his* way is the easiest way he knows to make money. And it's what he loves to do.

How much of your net worth is backing *your* investment strategy? Your answer is the best index of your own confidence in what you are doing.

26

Do You Need to Be a Genius?

"Warren may be as near to a genius at investing as I have observed."

—Paul A. Samuelson[1]*

"It was really to your benefit to talk to him [Soros] about it because he was smart."

—Allan Raphael[2]

"He [Buffett] is the smartest man I have ever met, by a long shot."

—Rich Santulli[3]

---

*The famed economist Samuelson is an ardent proponent of the efficient-market hypothesis. Nevertheless, he made a sizable investment in shares of Berkshire Hathaway. We can only assume that his conscience was salved by the profits he made.

CLEARLY, BOTH SOROS AND BUFFETT exhibit the hallmarks of genius. Both are investment pioneers; both developed their own original investment methods and applied them with outstanding success. Both are inventors and innovators, and could be considered the investment equivalents of Thomas Edison and Alexander Graham Bell.

Does this mean there should be a twenty-fourth Winning Habit: Be a Genius?

Perhaps—if you want to do *everything* that Buffett and Soros did, including inventing or perfecting an entirely new investment method.

But even if you do need to be a Thomas Edison to invent the lightbulb, you don't need to be a Thomas Edison to switch one on. Or to make one—after the genius has blazed the trail for the rest of us to follow. For investors, that trail is laid out in the mental habits and strategies that Buffett, Soros, and other Master Investors all follow religiously.

As Buffett says, "You don't need to be a rocket scientist. Investing is not a game where the guy with the 160 IQ beats the guy with the 130 IQ."[4]

Buffett and Soros share many other characteristics. They both live in the United States, have similar political opinions (for example, both helped fund Hillary Clinton's Senate bid), are male, wear glasses, and are married to women named Susan. None of these is relevant to their investment success.

Intriguingly, they have one other thing in common: Neither has passed any of the many securities industry exams that employees of Wall Street firms are routinely required to take.

When Buffett became CEO of Salomon Brothers in 1991, "there was also a rule that because I was an officer of a securities firm I had to take the Series 7 exam [for stockbrokers]," he recalls. "I kept delaying it until I left because I wasn't sure I could pass it."[5]

Earlier in his career, Soros actually took such an exam—and failed it miserably.

"There came a point when they introduced a certificate for security analysts, a sort of professional qualification. After avoiding it for a while I sat for the exam and I failed in every conceivable topic. At that point I told my assistant that he had to take it and pass it. As I understood it, the importance of the certificate would not start to matter for another six or seven years and by that time I would either be so far ahead that I wouldn't need it, or I would be a failure, in which case, I also wouldn't need it."[6]

When the world's two greatest investors fail or are afraid they'd fail such professional exams, one wonders what the true value of these qualifications is. If neither Buffett nor Soros has them, you certainly don't need them to achieve investment success. What you do need to do is follow the same mental habits and strategies as Warren Buffett and George Soros.

27

Carl Icahn and John Templeton

WARREN BUFFETT AND GEORGE SOROS aren't the *only* well-known investors on the annual *Forbes* magazine list of the world's richest people. Nor are they the only investors on the list who started with nothing.

But until 2003, they were the two *richest*.

In the *Forbes* 2004 list of the world's billionaires, Carl Icahn, with a net worth of $7.6 billion, topped George Soros (at $7.0 billion) for the first time, so becoming the world's *second* richest investor.

So the obvious question is: Does he also practice the 23 Winning Investment Habits?

Carl Icahn: From Options to Takeovers

"If you want a friend on Wall Street, get a dog."

—CARL ICAHN[1]

In late 1977, Carl Icahn began accumulating shares in an Ohio-based manufacturer of stoves, Tappan Company. He kept buying until he owned 20 percent of the company.

What did this New York–born options trader know about stoves—or manufacturing for that matter?

Not much. But he could read a balance sheet. And it was clear—to him—that the breakup value of the company of $20 a share exceeded its market price of $7.50 with a wide margin of safety.

Not everyone agreed that Tappan was a bargain. Litton Industries, for example, had considered taking over the company, but concluded it was in terrible shape, so they backed off.

And Icahn's uncle, who years earlier had lent him $400,000 to buy a seat on the New York Stock Exchange, thought he was crazy. But he changed his mind when his nephew walked away with a profit of $2.7 million on his Tappan stock just one year later.

Tappan had another characteristic that appealed to Icahn: no controlling shareholder. Icahn set about changing that by building his position to 20 percent of the company.

His ultimate aim: to control the financial destiny of the company long enough to make a quick profit by finding another company to take it over at a much higher price. Or to persuade the management to have the company buy his shares back ("greenmail")—he didn't care, as long as he made money.

Shaking Up the Options Business

Icahn went to Wall Street in 1961 as a trainee broker with Dreyfus & Co. making $100 a week. It was boom time. It was easy to sell stocks. And Icahn was a good salesman.

Using a $4,000 grubstake he'd accumulated playing poker while training for the Army Reserve, Icahn was also buying for his own account. Like his clients, almost everything he bought for himself went up.

But when the bubble burst in 1962, Icahn lost everything he had made on the way up—over $50,000. He even had to sell his car, a white convertible, so he could eat.

To say this was a formative experience would be an understatement. But Icahn didn't react as many might have done—by looking for some safer, securer field, like fulfilling his mother's dream by becoming a doctor.

Quite the reverse. He realized that if you could lose so much money so quickly, you could make it just as a fast—if you followed a sound strategy instead of, as he had been doing along with his clients, mimicking the herd.

Icahn quickly bounced back, reinventing himself as an options broker. In the 1960s, there was no such thing as exchange-traded options. Buyers and sellers came together by haggling on the telephone.

It was a tiny investment niche, but rife with exploitable pricing inefficiencies. Which Icahn was quick to capitalize on.

Targeting Market Inefficiencies

He gained a loyal clientele by working the market to get his clients better prices than they could get anywhere else. Other brokers hated him for slashing their fat buy/sell spreads. At one point they even ganged up on him, boycotting him to try to squeeze him out of the business. But the minicartel cracked very quickly: Icahn had too much business to be ignored.

Eventually, in 1967, Icahn went into business for himself with his own seat on the New York Stock Exchange. He published a weekly options bulletin, which became the only publicly available source of options price information.

He expanded into arbitrage. And noticing a similar pricing inefficiency in closed-end mutual funds, which were almost all trading at significant discounts to the value of the assets they owned, he started buying them up.

Like both Buffett and Soros, Icahn clearly believes the efficient-market theory is a load of hooey. His entire Wall Street career has been built on finding and exploiting these kinds of market *in*efficiencies.

Icahn's strategy in buying into closed-end funds was to "shake the tree" to force the management to liquidate the fund at a profit to the shareholders—most important, of course, Icahn himself.

The Lone Ranger and Tonto

Instrumental in Icahn's success was his associate Alfred Kingsley, who joined him in 1968. Icahn delegated the number crunching to Kingsley, who would plow through the data to identify potential investment targets for Icahn to choose from.

One day over lunch, Icahn and Kingsley (who became known on Wall Street as the "Lone Ranger and Tonto") realized they could apply the exact same strategy they'd used to make money in closed-end funds to other listed companies trading significantly below their book value.

And their timing was perfect. After the big bear market of 1973–74, triggered by the first oil shock, stocks rebounded slightly in 1975 but then more or less trended sideways until the biggest bull market in history began in 1982. There were bargains aplenty.

Another factor that appealed to Icahn's distaste for losing money was that in the 1970s inflation was soaring; values for tangible assets like gold and real estate had skyrocketed, but these changes had yet to be reflected in corporate balance sheets. In this environment, plenty of stocks were trading below their book values, but thanks to inflation their discount to liquidation value was *even higher*. This offered Icahn an enormous margin of safety.

Tappan was just the first of many undervalued investments Icahn and Kingsley went after.

Beating the Bushes for a Buyer

But their strategy was always the same. As Icahn himself described it in the offer document for one of his early investment partnerships, their aim was to take

> large positions in "undervalued" stocks and then attempting to control the destinies of the companies in question by (*a*) trying to convince management to liquidate or sell the company to a "white knight"; (*b*) waging a proxy contest; or (*c*) making a tender offer and/or (*d*) selling back our position to the company.[2]

Clearly, Icahn has a well-defined exit strategy that is inherent in his investment system. He doesn't buy anything without having first carefully considered his exit plan. And unlike most investors, Icahn is actively involved in creating his own exit path by "beating the bushes" for the highest bidder.

Kingsley combed through listed companies to find those trading significantly below book or liquidation value, where no one, including the incumbent management, had a significant stake in the company.

After they'd identified a target, Icahn began quietly accumulating stock, buying as much as he possibly could.

When the management noticed, Icahn began playing what was to him like a high-stakes game of poker.

Playing Poker on Wall Street

First was his poker face. He introduced himself and his associate Alfred Kingsley to Tappan's management as friendly investors "who might increase their investment further." And to this end asked a series of näive questions about the company and its products.

Needless to say, Icahn already knew the answers. But he achieved his aim of lulling the Tappan management into a false sense of security, leaving them thinking he and Kingsley were "pleased that we took the time to talk to them about the company."[3]

The great investors rarely talk to anyone about what they are doing in the markets. Icahn was different. In the second step of his strategy, to keep the management off guard, he'd talk and talk and talk. But the net effect was to sow so much confusion that no one had a hope of figuring out what he was really up to.

As he increased his stake in Tappan, the management became more determined to find out what he was really after. Icahn would mumble, ramble, and throw around a bewildering number of possibilities. Including, of course, the prospect of a takeover bid, pointing out that the undervalued price of Tappan's shares was one factor that had attracted him to making the investment.

Or was he just a long-term investor? The management couldn't be sure. They'd have done better if they hadn't listened to Icahn at all.

This process gave Icahn time to continue building his position without unduly forcing up the price of the stock.

His third step was to seek a seat on the board. It was usually around this point that the management realized that whatever Icahn's *real* intent, *their* security might be endangered. Feeling threatened, they took defensive action.

The Prize-Winning Philosopher

Icahn went to Princeton University where—like Soros—he studied philosophy. His thesis, "An Explication of the Empiricist Criterion of Meaning," won first prize. And as it had for Soros, philosophy proved to be a key factor in Icahn's later investment success.

"Empiricism says knowledge is based on observation and experience, not feelings," Icahn said. "In a funny way, studying twentieth-century philosophy trains your mind for takeovers. . . . There's strategy behind everything. Everything fits. Thinking this way taught me to compete in many things, not only takeovers but chess and arbitrage."[4]

Going for the Jugular

The Tappan management proposed an issue of preferred stock. Seeing immediately that this would weaken his position by watering down his equity—and possibly send Tappan's stock down—Icahn initiated the fourth element in his strategy: a proxy battle to win the support of the legions of small shareholders to his agenda. This was a tactic no one on Wall Street had ever used before to deliberately put a company "in play."

Just the threat of Icahn going to the shareholders seeking to reverse a management decision caused the Tappan management to back off.

Sensing weakness, Icahn pounced and launched his proxy campaign anyway, aiming for a seat on the board. He told other shareholders his aim was to see "our company" sold for a price reflecting its true value of $20.18 per share, not the paltry $7.50 the stock had been languishing at on the stock market.

Icahn painted a devastating picture of the current management, pointing out that the company had lost $3.3 million over the past five years, while Tappan's chairman and president had been paid over $1.2 million in salaries and bonuses.

Icahn won his seat, but entrenched board members held their

noses and tried to ignore him. Meanwhile, Icahn set about finding an acquirer for the company. He went to leveraged buyout firms, private equity groups, and major companies in the United States, Europe, and Japan. But none were interested.

Tappan Caves In

At the same time he was pushing management to sell off parts of the company—or all of it—to return money to the shareholders. Eventually management, despairing of seeing Icahn liquidate "their" company, found a buyer in the Swedish home appliance maker Electrolux, which ended up buying Tappan for $18 per share in late 1978.

Icahn ended up with a profit of $2.7 million on his 321,500 shares. Ironically, chairman Dick Tappan became an Icahn convert—and a happy investor alongside Icahn in his many future takeover attempts.

Icahn had found the investment niche that would make him one of the world's greatest—and richest—investors.

His raid on Tappan had worked like a dream. But Icahn didn't even take time out for a glass of champagne, let alone a vacation. He and Kingsley were already hard at work on their next deal. A pattern they continued to follow over the next ten years, during which they used the same strategy to go after fifteen more companies like Tappan.

At any one time they were entirely focused on just one or two investments. Like Buffett and Soros, Icahn always buys as much as he can of the company that is in his sights, sometimes stretching his resources to the limit. He completely ignores the traditional advice about diversification—and reaps enormous rewards as a result.

He and Kingsley targeted companies like Gulf & Western, Goodrich, Marshall Field, and Phillips Petroleum. All traded at large discounts to their book value. None had substantial shareholders, so the management—Icahn's only competitor for control—was vulnerable to Icahn's strategy of a proxy battle. All had readily marketable assets, or were appealing takeover candidates.

As the following table clearly demonstrates, Icahn's system—like those of Buffett and Soros—shares all twelve elements of the complete investment system.

Icahn Measures Discount to liquidation value, vulnerability, and marketability of target company	
1. What to buy	A company with no controlling shareholder that is trading under liquidation value and has the potential of being a takeover target.
2. When to buy it	When it's identified as meeting all his criteria.
3. What price to pay	A price significantly under breakup or liquidation value.
4. How to buy it	Pay cash for stock.
5. How much to buy as a percentage of portfolio	As much as he can.
6. Monitoring progress of investments	A continual process of interaction with the company's management to persuade them to sell, restructure, or liquidate. Seeks and sounds out potential buyers.
7. When to sell	When the company is taken over or when management buys him out ("greenmail"). Will dump his stock when it's clear that his target's defence is too strong or his strategy otherwise isn't working. When he gains control of a company, usually sells assets or otherwise gets his money back—by, for example, using the company's cash flow to fund other raids—without giving up control.

Icahn Measures Discount to liquidation value, vulnerability, and marketability of target company	
8. Portfolio structure and leverage	Portfolio holds only cash, stock in his current targets, and companies he has kept. Will use margin, or loans, to multiply the buying power of his cash.
9. Search strategy	Reads lots of annual reports, SEC filings, and the like.
10. Protection against systemic shocks such as market crashes	Pays less than liquidation value, which he considers his margin of safety.
11. Handling mistakes	Negotiates his way out.
12. What to do when the system doesn't work	Stops. Waits or reconsiders his strategy.

Taking Control

Icahn's second target, after Tappan, was Baird and Warner, a real estate investment trust (REIT) which traded at a discount of at least 57.5 percent to its liquidation value.

As with Tappan, after he'd built his stake, he sought a seat on the board, but was rebuffed with the comment, "What do *you* know about the real estate business?"

Positioning himself as "just another shareholder," he launched a proxy battle—but this time for control, knowing that the REIT's real estate holdings could easily be turned into cash. By highlighting that management had paid itself hundreds of thousands of dollars in fees while skipping a dividend to shareholders—and vowing that, if he won, neither he nor his companies would take penny in fees or salary—he won the vote and moved into the driver's seat.

Very quickly, he sold off the real estate and turned the now cash-rich Baird and Warner into one of his takeover vehicles. The shareholders who stayed on board made piles of money.

ICAHN: FROM MILLIONS TO BILLIONS

Rationale	Tactics	Result

1979: Saxon Industries

Rationale	Tactics	Result
An undervalued company with poor performance—return on assets, when Icahn started buying in July 1979, was just 7 percent, for example. And it had no controlling shareholder.	Icahn began accumulating stock in July 1979, ending up with 766,000 shares at an average price of $7.89. Sought a board seat; complained about the company's poor performance; suggested asset sales; and when he eventually threatened to buy more stock, guaranteeing his control (and putting the management out of a job), they caved in.	The company "greenmailed" him at $10.50 a share. Icahn and his investors walked away with a $2 million profit in three months on an investment of around $8 million.

1982: Dan River

Rationale	Tactics	Result
Book value of $38, more than three times the stock price when Icahn started buying in September 1982. Only 2 percent of the stock closely held.	Icahn accumulated 15 percent of the stock, and threatened the management with a tender offer for 40 percent to 50 percent of the company at $16 to $17 per share, which would give him control. Management went to court to stop him. Icahn won on appeal. Bought $15 million more stock in a smaller tender offer. Management tried—and failed—to find a white knight.	Sold out at $26 per share. Made a profit of $8 million in just over six months.

1982: Dan River

Eventually, management persuaded their employees to cash in their pension fund for an ESOP—which bought Icahn out . . . and entrenched management's control.

1984: ACF

Estimated liquidation value of $60 per share, compared to share price of $32 when Icahn started buying in 1984.

Bought 13.5 percent at $32 to $41 per share. Increased to 18.3 percent, then 27 percent. ACF's management tried to keep control with a leveraged buyout at $50 per share—but Icahn trumped them.

Bought the remaining stock at $54.50 per share, a total of $405 million. Sold two ACF divisions for $325 million and turned ACF into another vehicle for his takeovers.

1984–85: Phillips Petroleum

Selling at about half book value. T. Boone Pickens, who'd made an offer at $60 per share, had been paid to go away. Icahn figured if Pickens, an oil man, was willing to pay $60, it must be a bargain at $46.

Icahn's first mega-deal. Starting in December 1984, accumulated about 5 percent of Phillips at $46 to $47 per share. In February he offered to buy the whole company at $55 through an $8.1 billion leveraged buyout (backed by junk-bond specialist Michael Milken)—or the management could buy *him* out at the same price. Management announced its own recapitalization plan (which included a "poison pill"). Icahn

In March 1985, Phillips bought him out. Icahn walked away with a $50 million profit, *plus* $25 million expenses—just three months after he bought his first share.

1984–85: Phillips Petroleum

launched a proxy battle
to defeat it—and won.

1987–89: Texaco

Texaco snatched Getty Oil away from what Pennzoil thought was a done deal. Pennzoil sued and won a judgment totaling $11.1 *billion*. Texaco filed for Chapter 11 bankruptcy in April 1987. Icahn realized the stock would bounce high if Texaco management could be persuaded to settle with Pennzoil.

Icahn started buying just before the crash of 1987. By mid-November he'd accumulated 5,885,000 Texaco shares at an average price of $33.95. Then acquired another 10 percent of Texaco at $29 from the Australian corporate raider Robert Holmes à Court, who was squeezed by the crash and needed cash. With 12.5 percent, Icahn was now the biggest shareholder.
In righteous indignation, management pinned its hopes on beating Pennzoil in court, even though its chances were slim. In December 1987, the bankruptcy court judge ruled that the shareholder and creditor committees could negotiate directly with Pennzoil. Icahn joined the other shareholders in pushing for a settlement. Pennzoil eventually agreed to $3 billion— over the objections of the Texaco management.

Icahn then proposed to buy the whole company for $60, financed in part by the sale of some Texaco assets. Management blocked Icahn from making his offer to the shareholders, and responded with its own plan . . . involving the sale of some assets and a special dividend. Icahn lost that battle— but won the war when he sold his Texaco stock for $2.07 billion at $49 a share on June 1, 1989. In a year and a half he'd made a profit of over $500 million.

Icahn's Margin of Safety

Baird and Warner investment is a good illustration of how Icahn protects himself from the risk of loss. When he began buying it at $8.50 a share, it was trading at a nice discount to its book value of $14. But Icahn and Kingsley figured that its liquidation value was, conservatively, at least $20, which gave him a huge, built-in margin of safety.

And in the worst case, as he was buying real estate at over 50 percent off, he was getting double the average rental yield at the time.

But not every one of his investments worked out so well. USX—formerly United States Steel—was his fifteenth (and last) investment in the takeover era of the 1980s. And in this instance, the management had his measure and was immune to his tactics. Indeed, after he'd built a 13.5 percent stake and took his case for restructuring the company to the shareholders in a proxy battle, he lost to management!

In 1991, after five years of sparring with the USX management, Icahn finally agreed to a standstill agreement that basically tied his hands. So he quickly dumped his stock for a mediocre profit. In this case, he probably would have been better off putting his money in T-bills.

From this experience Icahn realized that the takeover era of the 1980s had come to an end. Company managements had woken up to the dangers they faced from takeovers and leveraged buyouts by people like Icahn, T. Boone Pickens, Michael Milken, and Kravis Kohlberg Roberts. So they'd erected powerful barriers, such as staggered boards and poison pills, to deter the raiders.

What's more, the investment firm Drexel Burnham Lambert had gone belly up, so the source of much of the capital that fueled these corporate raids disappeared. And the rising stock market made bargains harder and harder to find.

Icahn realized it was time for him to step back and wait for the market to swing back in his favor.

Which it did. Indeed, the ten years from 1994 to 2004 were Icahn's best. During the period he compounded his wealth at the staggering rate of 50.5 percent[5] per year!

In one of his forays, he took a 5.6 percent stake in RJR-Nabisco with the aim of creating value by splitting the company into its tobacco and food components. In 2000 Icahn swooped on the Sands Casino in Atlantic City, which had been in bankruptcy for two years and could be bought for a song. Learning from his experience with TWA, he invested wisely in upgrading the casino, turning it into a money spinner.

Icahn's Biggest Mistake

Like Buffett, Icahn avoids major mistakes by sticking to his criteria. But when he does make a mistake, it can sometimes take him a while to realize it, admit it, and take action to correct it.

The best example is his investment in TWA, which he bought into in 1985. TWA met most of his criteria—it was undervalued, and there was no controlling shareholder. But it did not meet his criteria as a potential takeover candidate: The only companies likely to be interested in buying TWA were other airlines, and most of them were in the same cash-poor boat.

Eventually another bidder did appear: Frank Lorenzo of Texas Air. His initial offer of $22 a share—which Icahn managed to push up to $26—did offer a nice premium to Icahn's entry price of $18 per share. But by then—in a departure from his system—Icahn had already decided to take over the entire company and run it himself.

Ownership of an airline, or newspapers, TV stations, and sports teams, can be an ego-boosting experience. And Icahn had "fallen in love" with the idea of running an airline—violating the habit of being emotionally involved in the *process* of investing, not the investment itself.

By taking control, he had also violated his investment system and sailed into uncharted waters.

TWA may have been undervalued, but it was not like an undervalued REIT, which can easily be liquidated at a profit. For example, you could sell one plane at a good price, but if you tried to unload 50, there'd only be buyers at a massive discount.

Worse, TWA was a poorly managed company in a lousy industry. To remain competitive it needed a massive investment in new planes and equipment. But Icahn's style was typically to take money out of the company, not put money in.

And Icahn did eventually succeed in getting his money out. First by using TWA's cash flow to help finance his bids for Texaco and USX. And then, in 1988, by arranging a leveraged buyout, financed with junk bonds, which gave him his all initial investment back *and* ownership of 90 percent of the restructured TWA.

Clearly Icahn's negotiating skills served him well once again.

However, aspects of this deal came back to haunt him. The airline needed massive investments in new planes and equipment to keep flying. Instead, Icahn had milked the company of its cash and left it saddled with enormous debts.

He'd got his money back, but there was an important factor he had overlooked. By owning more than 80 percent of TWA, Icahn could be held liable for the company's future pension obligations—potentially $1.2 billion.

When TWA subsequently sought Chapter 11 protection in 1992, the federal Pension Benefit Guaranty Corporation sought to hang Icahn with this liability.

Once again he negotiated his way out. Without an injection of money—$200 or $300 million—TWA would have had to shut down totally and stop flying. The unions would have been left with the satisfaction of stiffing Icahn, but without jobs.

Political pressure to save TWA's thousands of jobs was a factor Icahn used to great advantage in persuading the Pension Benefit Guaranty Corporation to give way.

But he did have to lend TWA $200 million to keep it flying.

This was a powerful lesson for Icahn: When you take control of the business, if you're not going to liquidate it, you have to be prepared to run it and invest money in it.

It's a lesson he has used to expand his investment system, using his proven takeover strategy to occasionally target a company—like the Sands Casino or XO Communications—that he would like to own and knew he could run successfully.

Cleaning Up After the Dot.Com Boom

The collapse of the Internet boom also produced a swath of situations tailor-made for Icahn. His skill in identifying undervalued bargains led him to make a bid for Global Crossing and grab up companies like XO Communications, which still had valuable assets but had been dragged under in the collapse and could now be had for pennies on the dollar.

Throughout his career Icahn has single-mindedly focused on his investment endeavors. For example, his wife has complained more than once that she never sees enough of him. One reason: After she goes to bed he goes to his office at home and starts a *second* working day!

Contemptuous of slothful managers running underperforming businesses at half throttle, Icahn's overriding motivation has always been to "shake up the establishment." As with Buffett and Soros, the money he makes is secondary for him. He enjoys the thrill of the chase.

And, indeed, Icahn shows no sign of slowing down. In 2004, at the tender age of sixty-eight, when most ordinary people are polishing their golf clubs, and with $7.6 billion already in his pocket, Icahn announced he was setting up a $3 billion hedge fund. Seeded with $300 million of his own money, he invited investors who'd like to put up $25 million or more to join him.

John Templeton:
The Global Bargain Hunter

"If you are really a long-term investor, you will view a bear market as an opportunity to make money."

—JOHN TEMPLETON[6]

Sir John Templeton, now ninety-two years old, became a legendary investor by loading up on cheap stocks in emerging markets like Japan and Argentina for his Templeton Growth Fund back in the 1950s and 1960s—*long* before the concept became a commonplace.

But his first major investment was in the United States. In 1939, figuring war would bring the ten-year-old Great Depression to an end, Templeton bought around $100 worth of every stock on the major American stock exchanges trading under $1. He bought 104 stocks in all—including, he insisted to his broker, those in bankruptcy.

Four years later, some of the companies Templeton had invested in had gone out of business. But many others had gone up, some by as much as 12,500 percent! Overall, he'd turned his original investment of $10,000 into $40,000 (over a million in today's dollars), an increase of 41.4 percent per year.

Applying Graham's Principles

If this strategy sounds familiar, that's because it is. It was based on Benjamin Graham's principles. Indeed, in the 1930s, Templeton attended a course in securities analysis given by Graham. Just like Buffett, Templeton developed his own unique variant of Graham's basic system.

Templeton's first major investment was typical of the investments he would make throughout his lengthy investment career:

Only Buy Bargains. Ignore the popular stocks, the ones that are owned by institutions and followed by Wall Street analysts. Do your own digging to find stocks that few people are interested in.

But Templeton also cast his net far wider than Graham had, or Buffett ever would, searching all over the world for companies he could buy for a fraction of their real worth. He wasn't just looking for bargain stocks; he wanted the *best* bargains *in the world*.

Buy in Bear Markets. The best time to buy is when the market is down and most investors—including the professionals—are too scared to invest.

Like Buffett, and Graham before him, Templeton would only invest when he could be sure of having a large "margin of safety." The time you're most likely to be able to get that is when the market is on its knees.

In this respect he is like Buffett, who will go on a spending spree when stock markets collapse—and at other times has to wait patiently for months or more to find an investment that meets his criteria.

By taking a global view, Templeton knew that he could almost always find a bear market *somewhere* in the world.

Invest Actuarially. Focus on a narrow segment of the market and within that class of investments, following Graham, buy a range of stocks that fit your criteria. Some of these may end up losing money, but the winners will more than offset the losses.

Invest with a "Trigger." Templeton looks for an event—such as the advent of the Second World War, which ended the Great Depression and signaled the beginning a new boom—which will change the fortunes of his investments.

Rarely are such triggers as clear-cut. Most of Templeton's success results from following his belief that markets move in cycles, that inevitably a bear market will follow a bull market, and vice versa. The trigger, then, is the inevitable change in the market's direction.

These are the basic elements of the investment strategy that he followed—with much refinement—over the next fifty-three years.

With one exception: For his first major investment back in 1939 Templeton used 100 percent leverage. He didn't have $10,000, so he borrowed the entire amount!

"The World's Markets Are Interconnected"

John Templeton was born in a small town in Tennessee in 1912. His family was comfortable but not exceptionally well off. In his second year studying economics at Yale, the Great Depression set in and his father told him he could no longer finance his education.

So Templeton was forced to work his way through his final years at university. As a result, he learned to appreciate the value of a dollar, being forced by necessity to shop around for the best bargain for every purchase he made—including food, clothing, furniture, and accommodation. He managed to stretch his budget, making every dollar do the work of two. This became a lifetime habit.

And it didn't affect his studies. He graduated with flying colors, even winning a Rhodes scholarship to Oxford.

He became interested in stocks while at Yale, observing, like Graham, that stock prices fluctuated wildly while the underlying value of the businesses was far more stable.

At Oxford, though he was studying law, he "was really preparing myself to be an investment counselor, particularly by studying foreign nations."[7] So he took the opportunity to travel widely around Europe and Japan, visiting thirty-five different countries altogether.

His viewpoint—commonplace now, but highly unusual in the 1930s—was that the world's investment markets were interconnected. To be a successful investor it wasn't enough to understand a company's market and competitors on its home turf: You needed an appreciation of how foreign companies and economies might affect that company's destiny.

When Templeton returned to the United States, he joined Merrill Lynch's new investment counseling division in New York. And in 1940 he established his own counseling firm.

The initial period was tough going. By the end of the Second World War he still had only a handful of clients, but his results were evidently excellent. Word of Templeton's abilities spread, money started pouring in, and in 1954 he set up the first global investment fund.

Getting Time to Think—Tax-Free

Eventually his firm grew to be managing $300 million. Templeton found himself so busy with the day-to-day running of the business that he felt he didn't have enough time to think. Like Soros, he believes that to be a successful investor you need to have the time to stop and contemplate what's going on.

But rather than delegate more of his responsibilities, in 1968 he decided to make a clean break. He sold out to Piedmont Management and at the age of fifty-six basically started all over again with only the Templeton Growth Fund, which Piedmont didn't want.

He left the United States, moving from Wall Street to the far more relaxed lifestyle of the Bahamas. What's more, after giving up his U.S. citizenship and becoming a British subject, he could live there tax-free. This move would later save him around $100 million in taxes, when he sold his family of mutual funds to Franklin Group in 1992.

From November 1954, when he started the Templeton Growth Fund, until Franklin bought him out, he achieved an annual compound return of 15.5 percent. During the same period the Dow Jones Industrials rose by only 5.8 percent a year.

Even more impressive than its performance when making

money was his fund's record in bear markets. According to one study, in the twenty years to 1978, the Templeton Growth Fund was consistently ranked in the top twenty of four hundred funds in rising markets. But its performance leapt to the *top five* in declining markets, demonstrating how Templeton had managed to achieve the number one objective of every successful investor: preserving your capital before worrying about how you're going to increase it.

Loading Up on Cheap Japanese Stocks

Instrumental in Templeton's success was his prescient move in the late 1960s to begin investing heavily in Japan. He noticed that there were bargains galore on the Tokyo stock exchange.

At that time, Japan was known worldwide for its cheap and shoddy products. But Japanese stocks were even cheaper, with great companies that investors hadn't even noticed selling, on average, for just three times earnings. While American stocks were then trading at fifteen times earnings.

The Spiritual Investor

Templeton views his money as a "sacred trust" that he can use to help other people.

In 1987 he established the John Templeton Foundation with the aim of spurring "spiritual progress." He established an annual $1 million award for achievements in religion. Recipients have included Mother Teresa and Billy Graham.

He has always felt that the spiritual side of life was crucial to everyone's well-being. As an investment counselor, his view of what he was doing wasn't that he was making piles of money, but that he was helping people be in a position to achieve their goals—both material and spiritual.

But Templeton didn't just want bargains. He wanted *quality* bargains. So he scoured the Japanese market for soundly managed companies with promising products and projected growth rates of at least 15 percent a year. As soon as he found one, he'd immediately start buying. He bought stocks like Hitachi, Nissan, Matsushita, and Sumitomo.[8] Companies that today are household names but back then were hardly known outside of Japan.

He poured so much money into the Tokyo market that by the time he'd finished buying, he'd put over 50 percent of his fund's assets into these "made-in-Japan" bargains.

Clearly, Templeton knew a bargain when he spotted one and wasn't shy about buying as much as he could.

Tokyo stocks peaked on New Year's Eve, 1989, with stocks selling for as high as 75 times earnings. The bear market that followed has still not come to an end.

But Templeton was out long before. As he admits himself, he sells too soon. He was completely out of the Japanese market by 1986, when stocks were going at "just" 30 times earnings.

His exit rule is to sell a stock when he finds a new bargain to buy. For example, in 1979 Nissan's stock price had risen so far it was selling at 15 times earnings, while in the United States, Ford was going for just 3 times earnings. So to Templeton, Ford at that point was the far better buy.

He is constantly monitoring his portfolio, measuring the valuation of the stocks he owns against those of others he is researching. When he finds a new bargain, he'll take profits and redeploy his capital.

Templeton's Criteria

Templeton has a hundred-odd different factors he examines for investing in a company—though not all of them will be relevant in each case.

But four factors, he says, are always crucial to measuring the profit expectancy of an investment:

1. The P/E ratio
2. Operating profit margins
3. Liquidating value
4. The growth rate, *particularly* the consistency of earnings growth[9]

One way he used to investigate these criteria was to visit the companies. But when he moved to the Bahamas, determined not to slip back into a situation where he didn't have time to think, he began grooming managers who could follow his investment principles and take over the investment decision making.

As part of their training, he sent *them* out to visit managements with a standardized questionnaire in hand. He had developed and honed the questions over his first three decades as an investment manager.

Today the various Templeton Funds continue to be managed by his protégés, including Mark Mobius and Mark Holowesko. Both have become famous in the fund management industry in their own right, continuing to use the same tools and techniques that Templeton pioneered. Mobius, for instance, will not invest in a company that hasn't been visited by him personally or by a member of his investment team.

Templeton's Greatest Coup

Though Templeton sold his fund company in 1992 to devote more time to his charitable and spiritual pursuits, he still kept his eye on the markets.

In 2000, at the tender age of eighty-seven, Templeton made a brilliant and enormously profitable foray back into the stock market—and proved that even if you can't teach an old dog new tricks, that old dog can certainly use his old tricks in new ways.

Like most other value investors, Templeton was flabbergasted as dot-com stocks zoomed to absurdly high levels. Many investors, realizing these stocks were wildly overvalued, shorted them all the way up—selling shares they didn't own expecting to be able to buy them back cheaper.

But the market was like a speeding train: Nothing could stop it from going higher. So some lost their shirts. Others, like Julian Robertson, eventually couldn't bear the pain anymore; he quit in disgust, shutting down his fund entirely.

Not Templeton. He bided his time until January 2000—three months *before* NASDAQ peaked—when he discovered a trigger that allowed him to initiate one of the most creative short-sale strategies ever.

The venture capitalists and insiders who floated these Internet companies were typically restricted from selling their stock until six months or a year after the company had gone public.

Templeton's insight was to use the end of this lockup period as his trigger. He systematically initiated short positions in eighty-four different dot-com companies eleven days before the lockup period for each stock expired. He projected that the increased supply of stock from insiders rushing to cash in their "lottery tickets" would drive prices for these stocks down.

Did it ever. Many he bought back when they reached just 5 percent of the price he'd sold them at. And following his normal rule of "getting out early," some he bought back when they'd dropped to thirty times earnings.

Eighteen months later, he'd added $86 million to his net worth.[10] Not bad for an old codger.

Bernhard Mast: "Minting Gold" in Hong Kong

"First of all, you have to protect yourself from yourself"

—BERNHARD MAST*

I first met Bernhard in Hong Kong when I was testing my Investor Personality Profile,† which pinpoints your weaknesses and strengths as an investor. From his answers to the questionnaire I could clearly see that he was following all the Winning Investment Habits—except one. Which puzzled me. He didn't appear to be following Habit No. 11—which is to act instantly once you have made up your mind to buy or sell something.

So I queried him about this, wondering if there was some flaw in the format of my questions.

He told me that he reviews his portfolio and makes his investment decisions in the morning but he places all his orders through a bank in Switzerland. Due to the time difference, Bernhard can't phone his orders in until afternoon in Hong Kong, when Zurich opens for business.

As I got to know him and understand his strategy, it became clear that he was, indeed, following *all* 23 Habits.

Bernhard is living proof that you don't need to be a high-profile investor with hundreds of millions of dollars, or even an investment professional, to successfully apply the Winning Habits.

What's more, he has no ambition to have his name up in lights like Buffett or Soros. He doesn't want to manage other people's money and prefers to remain anonymous. His goal is very simple: "When I'm seventy-five, I *don't* want to be stacking shelves at a supermarket to earn money to put food on my table. I've seen it happen to others, and it's *not* going to happen to me,"[11] he told me.

---

*"Bernhard Mast" prefers to remain completely anonymous, so this is not his real name.
†See www.marktier.com/ipp.htm.

What he sees as the greatest threat to his future financial security is the loss, over time, in the purchasing power of paper currencies. As he points out, a dollar today buys less than 5 percent of what a dollar bought a hundred years ago. In contrast, the purchasing power of an ounce of gold has remained relatively constant.

This is a topic Bernhard has studied in detail. He even wrote his PhD thesis at the University of St. Gallen on central banks and their gold reserves (though as he got an exciting job offer in Asia he never actually handed in his thesis). He's fascinated by the history and theory of money. And today his knowledge in this field forms the basis of his investment philosophy.

His first investment was in silver in 1985. He recalls going on holiday and not even reading a newspaper for ten days. In a taxi on the way to the airport to catch his flight home, he noticed in the newspaper that silver had gone up 20 percent. He took his profits right away.

The Investment "Genius" Gets Wiped Out

Bernhard was, at that time, just dabbling in the markets. His main focus was on building his business. He told me he didn't make another significant investment until 1992. A friend of his worked on the trading desk of one of the big Swiss banks. Together, they went heavily into silver call options, buying $60,000 worth. Soon after they'd gone into the market, the price of silver soared. They made ten times their money!

"We felt like geniuses," Bernhard recalled.

So what happened next, I wanted to know. They tried to repeat their success by shorting the S&P index. But American stocks didn't fall; they began to creep up. Being "geniuses," Bernhard and his friend added to their short position, only to see the market go through the roof. "I was wiped out," Bernhard told me. "I gave

back all my profits on the silver options, plus my original investment—and then some."

It was then Bernhard realized that, to invest successfully, the
first thing he had to do was "protect myself from myself."

Devising the Rules

Bernhard sat down and did something very few people ever do. He
spent several months building a detailed investment strategy, and
more time testing it, so he could achieve his primary aim: ensuring he
would have financial security and independence for the rest of his life.

He defined his overriding investment objective as preserving the
purchasing power of his capital. He believes the safest way to achieve
this goal is with investments in precious metals, chiefly gold.

Bernhard divided his assets into four parts: life insurance, real
estate, fully owned gold bullion, and a trading portfolio consisting
of mining stocks and forward positions in precious metals.

He keeps them all separate, even to the extent of using different banks for the mortgage on his property and for storing his gold
bullion.

The first three asset classes are the bedrock of his financial security. His aim in his trading portfolio is to make profits he can use
to increase his ownership of gold.

Bernhard thinks that commodities, including gold, are currently undervalued. And this is the basic premise of the investment
system he has devised.

Getting Leverage on Gold

Bernhard owns gold, but as gold pays no interest, his holdings
don't increase over time. To achieve that objective, he seeks to use

the leverage of gold mining stocks, which he says "typically rise by a factor some two or three times the corresponding rise in the gold price."

He has developed a complete investment system with detailed criteria for selecting mining stocks to buy.

His first screen is location. He refuses to invest in any company operating in Russia or China. Or places like Zimbabwe, Mongolia, and Indonesia. Why? "I simply don't trust these markets," he says. "Property rights in these countries just plain aren't secure. They're riddled with corruption; and governments do whatever they feel like."

Bernhard is justifiably afraid that he could wake up one morning and learn that the mines of a company he owns have been shut down or confiscated, leaving his shares worthless. For him, investing in any of these countries is simply not worth the potential risk of loss.

Next, Bernhard looks at currencies. When I interviewed him in June 2004, he owned no mining stocks in Australia or South Africa—two of the world's major gold producers. The reason: Both the Australian dollar and South African rand had risen dramatically against the US dollar.

"I had some South African gold shares until about a year ago," Bernhard told me, "but I got out when I realized they can't make any money. Even though they're sitting on tons of gold, since the rand has skyrocketed against the dollar, they can't take it out of the ground at a profit."

His next filter is management. Like Buffett, he wants to be sure that management treats the shareholders well. He wants to invest with managers who've successfully found and developed deposits in the past. He also reviews the company's current projects to evaluate their prospects.

Bernhard gathers all this information using the Internet. "You couldn't have done this five years ago," he says. "But now, there's an enormous amount of information readily available." Company websites provide annual reports, financial data, press releases, and the like. Stock price data is readily available, as are charts of past prices, which to him are useful tools.

The Importance of Position Sizing

Forty-seven stocks from a universe of some 350 that he has screened meet all his criteria. Following the typical actuarial approach, he owns them all, but he doesn't have an equal investment in each. His capital allocation hinges on his assessment of where the company is in the development cycle.

To him, mining stocks fall into three categories:

- producing companies that typically pay dividends;
- companies which have proven discoveries they're still in the process of developing, often in partnership with one of the majors like Newmont Mining; and,
- pure exploration companies, which are just as likely to burn up all their cash as they are to strike it rich with a big discovery.

Bernhard feels that companies in the second category—those nearing production—offer the best risk-reward trade-off. They're about to turn from consumers of cash to significant cash generators. So his portfolio is weighted heavily toward this category.

And—at the moment—he gives the smallest weighting to the

"The Best Financial Decision I Ever Made"

"Moving to Hong Kong was the best financial decision I ever made," Bernhard told me. "The tax rates are so low I can compound my money faster here than just about any other place in the world."

When he first moved there it was to accept an attractive job offer. Tax rates were the last thing on his mind.

He also admits that having no children has saved him a small fortune, giving him far more capital to invest—and compound.

And in a city with more Rolls-Royces per capita than anywhere else in the world, Bernhard doesn't even own a car. "Why have a car in a place where the buses are great and taxis are cheap and plentiful."

existing producers, as he feels they offer the least leverage on the price of gold.

He also has detailed rules about timing his purchases and sales of these stocks.

He will only buy stocks that meet his criteria when gold is under $350 per ounce. "Following this rule," he told me, "I've bought hardly anything over the past six months." Only if gold dips below $350 would he add to his stock holdings.

When one of his stocks doubles, he sells half, getting his initial investment back. As a result, he says, "about a third of my stocks I own for free."

Another exit rule is to begin banking his profits if gold goes over $450 an ounce. If gold rises as he expects, sometime over the next few years he will have sold all his mining stocks and will be looking for some other investment field.

He spends three hours a day looking at political and economic developments that could affect his assets; searching for new candidates to add to his list of qualified stocks; and monitoring the stocks he already owns to ensure they continue to meet his investment criteria. If they don't, he dumps them.

Bernhard pays cash for his stocks, and then uses them as collateral to finance forward purchases of gold bullion, which is the second element of his trading strategy.

If gold rises above $450 per ounce, he will begin cashing in his stock profits. He will take that money and use it to take delivery of the gold he has purchased with forward contracts. This bullion he adds to his nest egg of precious metals.

To protect himself against a catastrophic drop in the price of gold and avoid being wiped out, he has stops set to liquidate his entire trading portfolio. Moreover, he has a large cushion of protection. "I have my gold position at an average price of around $310 an ounce," compared to the current price of $408, "so gold has to drop a long, long way before I have to worry."

His overall approach is exceptionally conservative. Unlike the average homebuyer, who'll increase his mortgage to gain spending money when the price of his house goes up, Bernard doesn't even count unrealized gains when he values his holdings.

The only profits he counts as part of his net worth are the ones he has actually cashed in. And while he doesn't include paper profits, he *does* subtract paper losses. In other words, he values his portfolio at his cost, or the market price—whichever is *lower*.

"Investing Is Like Playing Chess"

Bernhard's underlying premise is that commodities are undervalued. Eventually they'll be fully valued. So he recognizes his current system will stop working someday.

Indeed, he fully expects that some time in the next five to ten years he will have sold all his mining stocks, taken delivery of his gold forward contracts, and possibly even sold some of his bullion nest egg.

"Investing is like playing chess. You have to contemplate the present, but you also have to look ahead to the forth, fifth, sixth, or seventh move." So he's already looking at expanding his universe into energy stocks, a field where he's beginning to test a variation of his system.

Like the well-known investors we've already talked about, Bernhard has devised a system which has all twelve necessary elements. And like their approach to investing, his is highly personalized and specialized, clearly drawing on his own unique background, his studies, his experience, and interests.

"Some of my friends think I'm crazy," Bernhard says. "But I'm very happy with my current strategy, and I sleep very well every night.

"I follow it," he told me, "because it's the safest way I know of, right now, to preserve the purchasing power of my capital. If I knew a better way, I'd do it. I'd switch today."

While his method is certainly unusual, it works for him. And he follows it religiously. To ensure he doesn't deviate from it, he keeps a written set of guidelines—his rules—and continually refers to them.

He admits that he does occasionally make a mistake. "And if you do," he said, "*don't panic!* If you panic, you freeze up, you become your own worst enemy. I just say to myself, 'Oops,' review what I did dispassionately, and take the necessary action."

He told me he reviews his list in detail every six months, evaluates his actions to ensure he's been following his rules, and sees if he's learned or discovered something that could improve them.

Such rigor and dedication is unusual in any field. But it is what has made Bernhard—like Buffett, Soros, Icahn, and Templeton—a highly successful investor.

PART TWO

Making the Habits Your Own

Laying Foundations

ONE DAY I WAS HAVING a tennis lesson when my coach pointed to the next court and asked me: "How long do you think they've been playing tennis?"

On the next court were two couples in their late fifties or early sixties playing doubles. For a few moments I watched them play. I could see that none of the players was doing any of the things I'd just been taught to do. In fact, they were hitting the ball the way I did before I'd had any lessons.

So I said: "A few years, I suppose."

"More like fifteen to twenty years," my coach replied. "They've never had a lesson. They've never improved their performance, and they never will. Even though you're still a beginner, using what you've just learned you could go up against players like them and win."

Even if you know you're never going to get to Wimbledon, or don't stand a chance of playing against Tiger Woods in the Masters, you know that you can improve your game immensely by learning the techniques the pros have mastered.

In the same way, even if you don't expect to become the next

Warren Buffett or George Soros, learning the habits of the world's greatest investors will inevitably improve your investment results.

Take an Inventory

Before you can get wherever you want to be, you have to know where you are. That's why the first thing a tennis or golf coach will do is ask you to hit a few shots. He can then assess what you're doing right and what you're doing wrong and figure out where he can begin to help you improve.

That's exactly what I'd do if you were to ask me to be your investment coach. I'd ask you a series of questions about your past investments, about the profits and losses you have made, and draw out your investment behaviors so that I can identify your good and bad investment habits.

You can easily do this yourself. Just rate your own performance for each of the 23 Winning Investment Habits.

I'm sure you'll find you're already practicing some of those habits. Which ones?

And you're probably already aware of times you have behaved more like a losing investor than a winner.

For other habits your behavior may oscillate from one day to the next, depending on your emotional state, or change with the kind of investment you're looking at.

This was Geoff's pattern. You may recall meeting him in chapter 16: a client of mine who'd have been about $5 million better off if he had kept his money in the bank and never invested at all.

When Geoff analyzed his past investments, he found that he had made money on the investment properties he bought when he acted solely on his own judgment. "I could see they were screaming bargains," he told me. "They were practically being given away."

Everything else he touched turned gold into lead. Even in real estate—when he invested with a partner.

Why the difference? He only bought stocks on the advice of others. Having lost money this way, he then invested several million dollars in a real estate development deal with one of his stock market advisors! (Now, ten years later, if he's lucky he'll get his money back.)

So why didn't he make more real estate investments on his own? He was blinded by the excitement of the riches *other* people were making in stocks, and it never occurred to him to analyze his own strengths and weaknesses. Like too many would-be investors, the only thing he brought to the party was his fat checkbook.

Winners and Losers

What I'd asked Geoff to do was to categorize his past investments into winners and losers. This is a powerful exercise that will immediately help you pinpoint what you have been doing right and what you have been doing wrong.

Simply take all the investments you have ever made and put them into two piles: the ones that made you money and the ones that cost you money.

Then examine the investments in each pile to find what they have in common with each other—and how they differ from the investments in the other pile.

Think about each investment and ask yourself what actions you took: Why did you buy it? How did you go about buying it? Did you do your own research or follow someone else's opinion? Did you act decisively or procrastinate? Were you confident you knew what you were doing, or were you still plagued by doubts as you called the broker? (If you felt confident, was it really overconfidence?) When you bought, did you know what developments would cause you to sell? Did you buy as much as you could—or just put a token amount of money on the line?

By analyzing each of your past investments in the context of

"I'm a Loser"

Geoff's investment problems were deeper than just his behaviors. His fundamental belief about himself as an investor was "I'm a loser."

When I pointed out that he had in fact made money successfully in one investment area he simply shrugged and reminded me that he was a loser. "And even losers get lucky sometimes."

Before Geoff could adopt *any* successful investment habit, I had to work with him to change his negative belief about himself.

We tend to think of our beliefs as fixed. In fact, they change over time. To take a trivial example, you probably once believed in Santa Claus, the Easter Bunny, and the Tooth Fairy. And if you think back, you're bound to realize that many of your more complex beliefs have also changed over time.

Unlike Geoff, Warren Buffett and George Soros both believe that they deserve to succeed and make money and that they are in control of their own destiny. These beliefs are essential for investment success.

Beliefs are often formed from experience. If you're like Geoff, you may need some help to change your beliefs. For most people, though, simply changing your experiences by practicing the 23 Winning Investment Habits can be enough to transform negative beliefs into positive ones.

the 23 Winning Investment Habits you'll build up a detailed picture of your own investment strengths and weaknesses.

And you may even find, as Geoff did, that there's one particular class of investments where you are a consistent winner. That could well be your circle of competence.

When Geoff made money, it was because he knew what he was doing. I worked with him to pinpoint the behaviors and mental processes he had applied to his successful real estate investments and transfer those same behaviors to other investment areas.

For clients who are already doing most things right, I only need to focus on the few things they are doing wrong.

Occasionally, I've had the pleasurable experience of meeting someone who practices all 23 Winning Investment Habits and merely wanted to check where he stood. I can't know where you fall on this spectrum of possibilities. That's something you can easily judge for yourself. What I can provide here is a road map for adopting the habits in a logical sequence. Even if you are already practicing every one of the 23 Winning Investment Habits, it will still pay you to run through the checklist. I'll bet you'll find things that you're doing that you didn't even know you were doing.

Clarify Your Investment Goals

THE MASTER INVESTOR KNOWS WHY he's investing: He finds intellectual stimulation and self-fulfillment (Habit No. 20). He
knows his purpose. To be successful, you must first clarify yours.

You could be investing for your retirement, so perhaps your underlying goal is security. Perhaps you're like Charlie Munger and
seek independence. Or your primary goal could be the welfare of
your children.

As you think about your reasons for investing you'll put your financial goals in their proper context, and realize they are secondary: a means for supporting some "higher" purpose.

Then ask yourself whether you're dedicated to achieving those
goals—or whether they are just dreams.

The difference is *motivation*. A dream is something you'd like
to have but are not really motivated to achieve. A goal is something
you're willing and often happy to work toward. For the Master Investor there is no doubt: He lives and breathes investing twenty-
four hours a day. It is his life (Habit No. 22).

Unless you see yourself following in Buffett's and Soros's footsteps, you're unlikely to go to quite this extreme. And you don't

need to. What you do need to do is commit the time and energy it takes to achieve *your* investment objectives, whatever they may be. Only through dedication will you achieve them.

It should be immediately obvious that *losing* money will only make it harder for you to achieve your underlying goal. How can losing money possibly help you achieve security? Will you be *more* secure or *more* independent with *less* money? Clearly not.

That's why, like the Master Investor, your first financial goal must be preservation of capital. Keeping what you have—however much or little it is (Habit No. 1).

By the same token, spending more than you earn will eat into your capital (or send you farther into debt). Only by living below your means can you build capital in the first place, keep what you have—and then add to it (Habit No. 19). Preserving capital and living below your means are the mental attitudes to money that set the wealthy apart from the poor and middle-class. They are the foundation of wealth. Adopting them is the only certain road to wealth.

What's Your Investment Niche?

One of the little-known and usually overlooked secrets of the successful investor is that he *specializes*. Even investment elephants like Buffett and Soros occupy a small fragment of the multitrillion-dollar investment marketplace. Not having billions of dollars to invest, your niche can be even smaller and more focused than the Master Investor's.

What defines your investment niche is your circle of competence. Like the Master Investor, you should only act when you know what you are doing. That means keeping within the limits of what you know—and never straying into the unknown (Habit No. 7).

So it's essential you define your own circle of competence. To do so, simply ask yourself:

- What am I interested in? What class of investments and what aspects of investing fascinate me?
- What do I know now?
- What would I like to know about, and be willing to learn?

The more detailed and specific you can be, the better. And don't be put off if everyone laughs at the area you have chosen.

For example, how would you like to specialize in investing in *rent-controlled* real estate in New York? Sounds insane, doesn't it.

But a friend of mine has made millions doing just that and little else. How? He knows the New York rent control laws backward, forward, inside, and out. He knows how to make minimal improvements to a property so that rents can be increased—which naturally hikes the resale value of the properties he buys. In fact, most New Yorkers aren't even aware that it's possible to increase the rent on a rent-controlled apartment. So my friend has the last laugh—and has that profitable little niche pretty much all to himself.

A doctor I know leverages his medical knowledge by investing exclusively in health-related stocks. A friend of mine now uses the skills he learned as a floor trader to support himself by day-trading stock index futures—usually from a beach somewhere in the world via the Internet.

There's bound to be something that you do or know that you can build into your own personal investment niche. Just as important is to be aware of what you *don't* know and *don't* understand. As Warren Buffett says: "What counts for most people in investing is not how much they know, but rather how realistically they define what they don't know."[1]

Defining your circle of competence is an essential step—but it's not enough. The hallmark of the true Master Investor is that he is never tempted to step outside the boundaries of his investment niche (Habit No. 8).

Saying no to that temptation can be one of the more difficult disciplines for the novice investor.

But if you're truly fascinated by the class of investments you have selected, like the Master Investor you'll be focusing on the process of investing rather than the investments themselves (Habit No. 21). This is one shield against straying into the unknown.

Another powerful antidote to temptation is success. As one of my clients put it: "Now that I know how to make money, those 'greener' fields look decidedly brown."

Of course, for the beginning investor success is something to look forward to, not to rely on today. What you can do today is create, as the Master Investor has done, an investment philosophy that will anchor you within your circle of competence (Habit No. 3).

What Moves the Market?

You probably have some beliefs about the nature of the market. But have you ever made those beliefs explicit? Have you ever examined them to see if they're valid and noncontradictory? Do they, in fact, guide the way you have invested?

Just as goals drive our actions, so beliefs govern them. If you are a devotee of the efficient-market hypothesis and believe that markets are rational and the price is always "right," then you believe that it's impossible to beat the market. The only strategy that is consonant with that belief is to invest in an index fund.

As we saw in chapter 5, the Master Investor believes that the market is sometimes or always wrong. He has developed a theory about why that is the case and a method of profiting from it.

A successful investment system needs to be built on the foundation of an investment philosophy that's consonant with reality. An investment philosophy is a set of beliefs about:

- the nature of investment reality: how markets work, why prices move;
- a theory of value, including how value can be identified and what causes profits and losses; and
- the nature of a good investment.

Buffett's Shortcut

When Warren Buffett first read *The Intelligent Investor* he was
hooked. Benjamin Graham gave him everything Buffett had been
looking for in a complete package: an investment *philosophy,* a
proven investment *method,* and a complete and well-tested *system.*
"All" he had to do was learn how to apply it.

Graham became his mentor. Buffett studied with Graham,
worked for him, and became a Graham "clone."

Buffett, of course, was not Graham. So eventually he departed
from Graham's system. Nevertheless, by modeling himself on
Graham, Buffett took a huge leap along the learning curve
towards becoming a Master Investor. "A few hours spent at the
feet of the master," Buffett recalls, "proved far more valuable to
me than had ten years of supposedly original thinking."[2]

George Soros also chose a mentor: Karl Popper. But Popper's
theories weren't directly applicable to investing. It took Soros
years to build a successful system based on Popper's philosophical
foundation. Years that Buffett didn't have to spend. "The best
thing I did was to choose the right heroes,"[3] Buffett said.

Think about what you believe moves markets. Do prices reflect
fundamentals? If so, in the short-term or the long term? Or both?

"Fundamentals" is a broad term. Do you focus on general economic conditions? Changes in the money supply and interest
rates? Levels of supply and demand in a commodity market? Or
would you prefer to look at the characteristics of an individual
company? Or, perhaps, a specific industry?

Or maybe you believe that prices have little or nothing to do
with fundamentals at all, that what moves prices is investor psychology. Or the balance between the number of shares of a particular stock being offered for sale and how many buyers are
interested in it at any particular moment.

If you're a technical analyst, you might believe that all of this is
irrelevant and everything is "in the chart."

The best way to clarify your beliefs is to write them down. This
may seem like a daunting prospect—but you don't need to devise a

---

Soros's Protégé

George Soros was to Stanley Druckenmiller what Benjamin Graham was to Warren Buffett.

After reading *The Alchemy of Finance* Druckenmiller sought Soros out. "George Soros had become my idol," he said. When Soros offered him the job of managing the Quantum Fund, Druckenmiller needed little convincing. "I thought [working for Soros] was a no-lose situation. The worst thing that could happen was that I would join Soros and he would fire me in a year—in which case I would have received the last chapter of my education."[4]

---

theory as complex as Soros's. Your belief about the nature of the markets can be as simple and straightforward as Graham's and Buffett's belief that market prices eventually reflect the underlying fundamentals but often deviate wildly from them in the shorter term.

Once you have clarified your beliefs about why prices move the next step in establishing your investment philosophy is to define what you mean by "value." You may agree with Graham and Buffett that an investment has a measurable, "intrinsic" worth. Or you may take Soros's view that value is a continually moving target determined by the changing perceptions and actions of actors in the marketplace. Or you may think that value, while measurable, is also contextual in the way that a glass of water to a man in the desert dying of thirst has a far greater "intrinsic" (or life-supporting) value than the same glass of water to you or me.

The Good Investment

By pinpointing what you think represents value, you can now create your definition of a good investment. You should be able to summarize it in one sentence. Consider these examples:

Choose Your Mentor

The fastest way to master anything is to study with a master of the art.

If someone has already perfected the method of investing that appeals to you, why reinvent the wheel? Seek him out. If necessary, offer to work for him for nothing (as Buffett offered to Graham).

If that's not possible, you can still adopt your mentor by long distance. Read and study everything you can about him and his methods. When you're thinking about making an investment, always ask yourself: "What would *he* do?"

Putting yourself in somebody else's shoes helps your subconscious mind take on some of that person's natural behaviors and characteristics that you wouldn't necessarily notice by simply reading about and consciously copying his actions. Before filming started on *Rain Man,* Dustin Hoffman spent three weeks literally shadowing the person the story was based on. At one point in the filming he was crossing the street when the lights changed. Though not in the script, Hoffman stopped in the middle of the road. They later discovered that that's exactly what the original character would have done in the same situation.

Even if you later modify the method you have adopted from your mentor, modeling yourself on him you will make it easier for you to acquire most of the 23 Winning Investment Habits of Warren Buffett and George Soros.

As Warren Buffett observes: "The key in life is to figure out who to be the batboy for."[5]

Warren Buffett: a good business that can be purchased for less than the discounted value of its future earnings.
George Soros: an investment that can be purchased (or sold) prior to a reflexive shift in market psychology/fundamentals that will change its perceived value substantially.
Carl Icahn: a company with no controlling shareholder trading below its breakup value that's a potentially appealing candidate for a takeover.

Benjamin Graham: a company that can be purchased for substantially less than its intrinsic value.

There are hundreds of other possibilities. A few more examples:

The Corporate Raider: companies whose parts are worth more than the whole.

The Technical Analyst: an investment where technical indicators have identified a change in the price trend.

The Real Estate Fixer-Upper: run-down properties that can be sold for much more than the investment required to purchase and renovate them.

The Arbitrageur: an asset that can be bought low in one market and sold simultaneously in another at a higher price.

The Crisis Investor: assets that can be bought at fire-sale prices after some panic has hammered a market down.

Coming to your definition of a good investment is easy—*if* you're clear about the kinds of investments that interest you and have clarified your beliefs about prices and values.

What's Your Investment Personality?

Perhaps you share Buffett's definition of a good investment. Does that mean you should model yourself on him?

Not necessarily. For example, you could follow Buffett's rules for buying investments but use trailing stops, as some traders do, as your exit strategy.

A handful of successful investors invert Benjamin Graham's investment strategy. They pinpoint companies selling far *above* their intrinsic value—and sell them short.

In addition to deciding what kind of investments to focus on, you also need to select your investment strategy. One way to select the method that suits you best is to decide whether you're primarily an Analyst, Trader, or Actuary (the three investor archetypes introduced in chapter 15). By now you have probably already realized which investment personality fits you best. If not, you need to think about whether your investment horizon is long, short, or medium term. Are you planning to buy and hold; go short as well as long; trade in and out; or take a purely actuarial approach like the professional gambler?

A related consideration is your talents, skills, and abilities. Are you mathematically inclined? If you are, it doesn't mean you'll necessarily follow in Buffett's footsteps. You might prefer to develop a mathematically based, computerized trading system to select a

---

"Arbitrageurs Die Young"

When George Soros was offered a job by F. M. Mayer in New York, his application for a United States visa was knocked back on the grounds that no twenty-five-year-old could be an expert in anything.

Mayer consulted the legendary Franz Pick, who monitored free (i.e., "black") gold and currency markets around the world and published the annual *Black Market Yearbook*.

"Pick submitted an affidavit in support of Soros, saying that the position of arbitragist was very taxing and that the risks that such people constantly assumed took a dreadful toll on their health and nerves and consequently they tended to die young."[6] Pick's letter got Soros the visa he needed.

Though he didn't die young, Soros eventually burned out, as Pick had forecast in his admittedly overdramatic letter. Twelve years later his protégé, Stanley Druckenmiller, suffered the same fate.

By comparison, it's easy to imagine Buffett running Berkshire until he reaches his preferred retirement age—somewhere north of Methuselah.

Stress is a factor you should consider when choosing your method and building your investment system. Successful traders deal with stress with a variety of tools, including keeping fit, meditation, taking complete breaks—or by altering their system to reduce or eliminate the level of stress.

class of investments that, on average, has a positive profit expectancy—a purely actuarial approach.

Or maybe you're a "people person" and would find it easiest to dig up investment ideas by talking to managers, competitors, retailers, suppliers, and others in the business. Or perhaps your element might be reading the emotions of traders on the floor of the exchange.

The key is to adopt the method and strategy that best suits your personality and best uses your skills and abilities. One shortcut is to study different investors and traders until you find the approach that resonates most with you. Once you have done this, you'll be ready to start building your investment system.

What Are *You* Going to Measure?

"If you can't measure it, you can't control it."

—MEG WHITMAN, CEO eBay[1]

THE LINK BETWEEN YOUR INVESTMENT philosophy, your investment method, and your investment system is your investment criteria.

From all possible good investments in your investment niche, how do you know when you have found one to buy? What makes a home run stand out from the others? It will be one that meets all your investment criteria—a detailed checklist of the characteristics of what you have defined as a good investment, against which you can measure the quality of any particular investment.

As you'll recall, Buffett is measuring the characteristics of a good business, including the quality of the management, the nature of its franchise, the strength of its competitive position, its pricing power, its return on equity—and, of course, its price. While Soros is measuring the quality of his investment hypothesis against events as they unfold.

Your investment criteria are the features of an investment in your chosen niche that you can measure *today* which you know will consistently make you profits over time.

Your investment criteria give you six crucial elements of your investment system: what to buy, when to buy it, when to sell it, how much to pay, how to gauge whether everything is on track once you have invested—and what to focus on when you're searching for investments. So you need to specify them in as much detail as you can.

Your Margin of Safety

As we saw in chapter 6, "You Are What You Measure," a complete investment system has twelve elements. They are all bound together by the Master Investor's highest priority: preserving capital. His method of preserving capital is to avoid risk (Habit No. 2). He accomplishes this aim by embedding his preferred method of risk control into all aspects of his system.

Buffett's primary risk-control method is to always have what he calls a "margin of safety." Although this term has become associated with Benjamin Graham and Warren Buffett, in fact *every* successful investor has his own version of the margin of safety: It's the way he minimizes risk.

You may decide to be like Soros and discipline yourself to get the hell out the minute you find yourself in uncharted waters—sell first and ask questions later. Or you may use an actuarial approach to risk control.

Whatever margin of safety you choose, for it to work it must be one of the foundations upon which your system is built—and be woven into your system's rules.

Applying Your Criteria

The Master Investor treats investing like a business. He doesn't focus on any single investment but on the overall outcome of the continual application of the same investment system over and over and over again. He establishes procedures and systems so that he can compound his returns on a long-term basis. And that's where his mental focus is: on his investment process (Habit No. 21).

Once you're clear what kind of investments you'll be buying, what your specific criteria are, and how you'll minimize risk, you need to establish the rules and procedures you'll follow to gain the Master Investor's long-term focus.

The first step is to plan the structure of your portfolio. Will you be buying stocks? Stocks and options? Futures? Writing puts or calls, or using spreads or straddles? Investing in real estate? Is your focus on commodities, currencies, or bonds? Or would you prefer to delegate investment decision making to carefully selected money managers? These are just a few of the many possibilities you can choose from.

Having made those decisions (which, of course, might be blindingly obvious from identifying your investment niche) you need to define other elements of your system before you leap into the market.

Will you use leverage? If you're going to invest in futures, you may think you'll automatically be using leverage.

Not so. The use of leverage must always be a conscious and preplanned decision. If you keep the full face value of a futures contract in the account, your margin is 100 percent, the same as paying cash for a stock.

Although both Soros and Buffett use leverage, they are both cash-rich. I advise you to follow their example, focusing on the "cash-rich" part, at least until (like them) you have reached the stage of unconscious competence in your investing.

Even then, if you use leverage, follow the Master Investors' example and use it sparingly. (And *never* meet a margin call.)

How are you going to minimize the impact of taxes and transaction costs? Master Investors focus on the long-term rate of compounding. One way they improve that rate is (as we've seen—Habit No. 6) to construct their system in a way that minimizes the taxes which need to be paid and keeps transaction costs as low as possible.

There are many different ways to achieve this. Some depend on the kinds of investments you make or on the period you plan to hold them. Where you live and where your investments are kept is another factor. If, like me, you're an extremist on this subject, you might consider arranging your affairs so you're liable for hardly any taxes at all.

Whatever your situation, you should use all available means to defer or reduce taxes so that your money can compound tax-free for as long as possible. By doing so, you'll harness the power of compound interest to add several percentage points to your annual rate of return—without having to make a single investment decision.

What do you need to delegate? Unless you have a banking license and a seat on the stock (or commodity) exchange, you're going to need to delegate some of your investment functions.

Few people think of opening a brokerage or bank account as an act of delegation. But it is: You're hiring someone (do you know who they are?) to look after your money. Will it be there when you want it? (Banks and brokerage companies do go bust. Okay, you're insured . . . but how long will it take you to get your money back?) Will you get the service and execution capabilities you require?

The wealthier you are and the more complex your affairs, the more delegation you'll have to do (Habit No. 18). You may need to choose lawyers, accountants, tax advisors, trust companies, and other advisors.

When you buy, how much are you going to buy? When the Master Investor finds an investment that meets his criteria he buys as much as he can. His only limit is the money he has available. As a result, his portfolio is concentrated, not diversified.

By specializing in your investment niche, all your investments will come from the same category. You have already thrown the mainstream version of diversification out the window (Habit No. 5).

Nevertheless, regardless of your investment approach you will need to establish rules for what's called "position sizing." In other words, how much of your portfolio are you going to put into each individual investment? If the amount varies between different investments, why?

In a sense, position sizing boils down to gaining confidence in what you are doing. Once you reach the point of knowing your kind of bargain the moment you see one, you'll be both happy and comfortable to go for the jugular.

How will you protect your portfolio against systemic shocks such as market panics? When the founders of Long-Term Capital Management developed their system, they dismissed what they called ten-sigma events as so statistically improbable that they weren't worth worrying about.

When the Asian financial crisis of 1997 was quickly followed by the Russian debt default of 1998, LTCM was hit by two ten-sigma events in a row—and blew up.

Ten-sigma events may be improbable, but that doesn't mean they're impossible. The Master Investor has structured his portfolio and investment strategy so that he will survive even the most extreme market conditions.

If the market collapses overnight, will you live to invest another day? You have to structure your system so that the answer to this question is yes!

The first thing to do is to acknowledge that anything can and will happen in the markets. Generate several worst case scenarios in your mind. Then ask yourself: If any of these things happened, how would you be affected—and what would you *do?*

As we've seen, one of Soros's protections against such systemic risk is his ability to act instantly, as he did in the crash of 1987 when even most investment professionals simply froze up.

The Master Investor's primary protection—and this is true for both Buffett and Soros—is their judicious use of leverage. Every

Hire a Master Investor?

"The average trader should find a superior trader to do his trading for him, and then go find something he really loves to do."
—ED SEYKOTA[2]

To judge by the amount of money in mutual funds and with professional investment managers, the majority of people delegate the entire investment process to others.

This is a perfectly legitimate option. Investing takes time and energy, and for many of us that time and energy can be better invested somewhere else.

If this is your choice, you can still achieve superior investment returns by taking Ed Seykota's advice and finding a successful investor to do your investing for you.

But how to judge whether a money manager is likely to be successful or not? Find a person who follows the 23 Winning Investment Habits.

It's also important to find someone whose investment style is compatible with your personality. For example, Warren Buffett is obviously extremely comfortable having Lou Simpson manage GEICO's investments. That's because they share the same investment philosophy and method. By the same token, you could imagine that Buffett wouldn't sleep very well at night if he gave money to a commodity trader—or even to George Soros himself.

To successfully delegate the task of investing means you must be clear about your own investment philosophy and preferred style. Only then can you find someone who will manage your money in the same way you would like to do it yourself.

At the very least, you need to be able to identify whether the manager has a clear investment philosophy; a complete investment system; whether the system follows logically from the philosophy; whether he's good at "pulling the trigger"—and whether he "eats his own cooking."

Most investors choose their money managers or mutual funds by looking at their track record or by following their broker's or friends' recommendations, or they are seduced by a good marketing story. None of these methods has any relationship to a manager's long-term performance. Evaluating managers by determining how closely they follow Buffett's and Soros's mental habits and strategies is virtually guaranteed to improve your investment returns.

time the market crashes we hear stories of people who lose their shirt because they were overleveraged. The Master Investor simply doesn't get himself into this position. You should follow his example—even if this means flouting yet another standard Wall Street maxim: Be fully invested at all times.

How are you going to handle mistakes? The Master Investor makes a mistake when he doesn't follow his system, or when he has overlooked some factor that, once taken into account, means he shouldn't have made that investment.

Like the Master Investor, you need to recognize when you may have strayed from your system and be awake to factors you might have overlooked. When you realize you have made a mistake, admit it and simply get out of your position (Habit No. 14).

Then review what led you to commit that error—and learn from it (Habit No. 15). Focus on what is under your control—your own actions.

If you're like most people, the hardest aspects of learning from your mistakes are being willing to admit them, and then to be self-critical and to analyze your mistakes objectively.

If you overlooked something, how did that happen? Was some information "too hard" to dig up? Was it a factor you'd not appreciated the importance of before? Did you act too quickly? Were you too trusting of the management? There are a host of such errors that can be made, and the only thing you can be sure about is that you're going to make them. Don't take it personally; like the Master Investor, just be sure you won't make the same mistake again.

If there was some system rule you didn't follow, then you weren't following your system religiously (Habit No. 13). Again, analyze why. Did you follow your heart, not your head? Did you break this rule knowingly? Did you hesitate too long?

This kind of problem should only crop up when you first set out to apply your system. It may just be that you're at the beginning of the learning curve—or it could be that the system you have devised, or parts of it, aren't truly compatible with your personality.

What's crucial is that you have the mental attitude of accepting your mistakes and treating them as something to learn from.

Keep Your Powder Dry

Cash is a drag on your portfolio, says the conventional wisdom. Its returns are low and often negative after inflation and taxes.

But cash has a hidden embedded option value. When markets crash, cash is king. All of a sudden assets that were being traded at five and ten times the money spent to build them can be had for a fraction of their replacement cost.

Highly leveraged competitors go bankrupt, leaving the field free for the cash-rich company.

Banks won't lend money except to people who don't need it—such as companies with AAA credit ratings and people with piles of money in the bank.

In times like these the marketplace is dominated by forced sellers who must turn assets into cash regardless of price. This is when the investor who has protected his portfolio by being cash-rich is rewarded in spades: people will literally be beating a path to his door to all but give away what they have in return for just a little bit of that scarce commodity called cash.

What are you going to do when your system doesn't seem to be working? There may be times when you lose money—even though you have followed your system religiously and you're as certain as you can be that you have overlooked nothing.

It's important to realize that some investment systems can and do stop working. If this appears to be the case, the first thing to do is to exit the market completely.

Sell everything. Step right back and review every aspect of what you have been doing—including your investment philosophy and investment criteria.

Maybe something has changed. Perhaps it's you. Have you become less dedicated? Is your motivation still high? Have your interests changed? Are you distracted by some other problem such as divorce or a death in the family? Or are you simply stressed out?

More often, the cause of the change is external. Maybe your tiny niche has been invaded by Wall Street institutions loaded with

---

The Complete System

A complete investment system has detailed rules covering these twelve elements:

1. What to buy
2. When to buy it
3. What price to pay
4. How to buy it
5. How much to buy as a percentage of your portfolio
6. Monitoring the progress of your investments
7. When to sell
8. Portfolio structure and the use of leverage
9. Search strategy
10. Protection against systemic shocks such as market crashes
11. Handling mistakes
12. What to do when the system doesn't work

An exercise that will help you build your system is to photocopy the table on pages 85–86—which shows Buffett's and Soros's rules for each of these twelve elements—and add an extra column: *Me.*

You may be able to fill out some of the fields already. You'll know you system is complete when you can fill out all twelve.

---

capital and the margins that were once profitable have become too thin to sustain you.

Markets can become more efficient. Is the inefficiency you were exploiting no longer there?

Have you changed your environment? Floor traders who move to screen-based trading are often surprised to discover that the system that made them money on the floor of the exchange depended upon cues such as the noise level on the trading floor or the body language of other traders. Missing those cues, they are forced to develop a different approach to regain their feel for the market.

Have you been so successful you have just got too much money to handle? That is a factor that affected both Buffett and Soros. It's a "problem" we can all hope to have.

By considering all of these issues you'll create an investment system that is unique to you. By taking the time to cover every one of the twelve elements in detail, you will ensure that your system is *complete*.

The Master Investor's Benchmarks

Before beginning to test your system you must establish a measure that will tell you whether or not it is working. The first test, obviously, is whether or not it makes you money. But is that enough?

If your system is profitable, you'll be getting a return on your capital. But will you also be getting an adequate return on all the time and energy you have to devote to implementing your investment strategy?

The only way to tell is to compare your performance to a benchmark.

Buffett and Soros measure their performance against three benchmarks:

1. Have they preserved their capital?

2. Did they make a profit for the year?

3. Did they outperform the stock market as a whole?

The importance of the first two is obvious. The third benchmark tells you if you're being paid for your time; whether your system is paying you more than, say, just investing in an index fund—or leaving your money in the bank.

The benchmarks you choose will depend on your financial goals, and how you value your time. There is no "one-size-fits-all." But only when you have established your benchmark can you measure whether your system is working or not.

Intelligent Diversification

Master Investors spurn diversification (Habit No. 5) for the simple reason that diversification can never result in above-average profits (as we saw in chapter 7).

But if all you want to do is preserve your capital, *intelligent* diversification is a perfectly valid option. "When 'dumb' money acknowledges its limitations," says Buffett, "it ceases to be dumb."[3]

Diversification may seem like a simple and obvious strategy. But it is no more than a method to achieve certain goals. So those goals must first be defined. Only then can you build a system that will meet them.

The Wall Street wisdom is to put X percent of your portfolio into bonds, Y percent into stocks, and Z percent into cash—with stock market investments further diversified into a variety of categories from so-called conservative "widow and orphan" stocks to high-risk "flavor of the month"–type stocks.

But the aim of this strategy isn't to preserve capital (which it may) but to reduce the risk of loss. These are two quite different objectives.

I've only seen one well-thought-out investment strategy that successfully applies diversification to the aim of not just preserving capital, but increasing that capital's real purchasing power over time. It was developed by Harry Browne, who named it the Permanent Portfolio. Its purpose, he says, "is to assure that you're financially safe no matter what the future brings."[4]

Browne started from the premise that it's impossible to predict the future price of any investment. But it is possible to foresee the impact of different economic conditions on different classes of assets. For example, when inflation is high the price of gold usually rises, while the higher interest rates that usually accompany rising inflation push down the prices of long-term bonds. During a recession, however, interest rates usually fall, so bonds rise, sometimes skyrocketing, while gold and stocks tend to fall in value.

Browne identified four different classes of investments, each "a cornerstone of a Permanent Portfolio because each has a clear and reliable link to a specific economic environment."[5]

Stocks, which profit in times of prosperity;
Gold, which profits when inflation is rising;

Bonds, which rise in value when interest rates fall; and,
Cash, which provides stability to the portfolio and gains in
purchasing power during deflation.

With 25 percent of the portfolio in each category, at almost
any time the value of one of those categories will be rising. There
will, of course, be occasional periods when everything is stagnant.
But those times are rare.

The key to making the Permanent Portfolio work is volatility.
By choosing the most volatile investments in each category, the
profit on just one quarter of the portfolio's assets can more than
compensate for any declines in the other categories. So Browne
recommends investing in highly volatile stocks, mutual funds that
invest in such stocks, or long-term warrants for the stock market
portion of the portfolio. By the same reasoning, he advises
holding thirty-year bonds or even zero-coupons for the bond
portion, as they are far more sensitive to interest rate changes
than bonds that mature in just a few years time.

The portfolio can also be diversified geographically to protect
against political risk by holding a portion of the gold or cash
holdings offshore—in, say, a Swiss bank.

The portfolio only needs to be rebalanced once a year to bring
each category back to 25 percent of the portfolio. For the rest of
the year you can literally forget about your money.

The "turnover" of the portfolio is minimal, rarely more than 10
percent a year. So both transaction costs and taxes are kept very
low. And in the years that you are earning income, the chances
are that you'll be adding to your portfolio every year. With the
Permanent Portfolio approach, that would usually mean buying
more of the investments that have fallen in price. So most years
you'd only be liable for taxes on interest and dividend income
from your bonds, T-bills, and stocks. You would rarely pay any
capital gains taxes on your investments until you retire.

The return on this approach is a quite remarkable 9.24 percent
per annum (from 1970 to 2002), compared to 10.07 percent per
annum for the S&P 500 index. And, as this chart shows, the
Permanent Portfolio appears to rise inexorably in value while
stocks provide many sleepless nights.

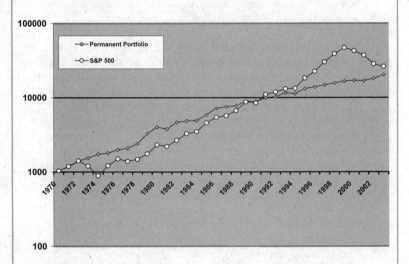

Harry Browne's Permanent Portfolio is a well-thought-out investment system that applies intelligent diversification to the objective of preserving capital and, indeed, increasing that capital's purchasing power over time.

Its returns pale by comparison to those achieved by Buffett and Soros. The difference is the amount of time and energy that you must devote to your investments: as little as a few hours per year to successfully manage a Permanent Portfolio, compared to the intensity of time and effort that most other investment systems require.

If you have decided that there are other things you'd rather do in life than worry about your money, intelligent diversification is an option worth considering. You might like to adopt Browne's Permanent Portfolio approach, or you might prefer to create your own method of intelligent diversification. The important thing is, like Browne's Permanent Portfolio, the method you use should still meet all the Master Investor's standards for a complete investment system.

31

Gaining Unconscious Competence

"Instinct—the subconscious—is much more reliable than statistics."

—PHILIP CARRET[1]

"Nothing is stronger than habit."

—OVID[2]

HAVING GOT THIS FAR, IT's now time to test your system in the real world with real money—and pay your dues (Habit No. 16).

If you have applied all the steps so far, you should be in the state of conscious competence in your chosen investment niche. *Successfully* "paying your dues" means graduating into the state of unconscious competence where applying all your rules has become second nature.

The crucial test is how you will react under pressure and stress. It's at these times your old habits are most likely to emerge from wherever they were hiding in your subconscious—and get in your way. Replacing habits you don't want and mastering new ones requires constant repetition.

One way to achieve unconscious competence is to test your system in a methodical way, keeping records of everything you do—and why you did it.

Testing Your System

The first step is to decide how you are going to find investments that meet your criteria. You can find investment ideas just about anywhere. What you need to determine is what hunting ground is most fruitful for you. By establishing your investment niche you have effectively put yourself in the position where, like the Master Investor, you have to do your own research.

It's important to realize that this is a continual process. Most investors are reactive: They wait till something comes to their attention. To succeed, be proactive like the Master Investor, and make sure you are always searching for investments that fit your criteria (Habit No. 9).

There will inevitably be times when you may feel discouraged because you cannot find anything to buy. Be like the Master Investor and just keep looking (Habit No. 10).

Even when you get an investment idea from somewhere else—be it a newsletter, a magazine, or a friend—you need to make sure it's in your circle of competence; and personally check it against your investment criteria. This will inevitably involve you in doing some of your own digging.

You may be tempted to "test" your rationale with somebody whose judgment you respect. If this person is like your investment mentor, this can be useful. But beware.

Maurice was a budding trader who followed a technical system he had devised. He once came up with an investment idea that he thought was compelling, but he was unsure about it. So he checked it out with an experienced technical trader he looked up to as an expert—who pooh-poohed the idea. So Maurice did nothing—much to his regret when he watched from the sidelines as the investment soared exactly the way he had anticipated. Had Maurice kept his mouth shut (Habit No. 17) and followed his own judgment instead of being swayed by the guru's opinion, he would have made a bundle of money.

If you have done your research properly, it's unlikely that even the expert will know as much about this investment as you do. Besides, any judgment he makes will be based on *his* method, goals, and personality—not yours.

And you can't always be completely certain whether the expert is giving you a considered opinion or just doesn't want to look like a fool. Back in the days when I was a guru myself, somebody came up to me at a seminar and asked me what I thought about coffee. I didn't know the first thing about the coffee market. But I was a guru, and how could a guru not have an opinion? So I invented something on the spot.

When you keep your own counsel, you make your own mistakes. When you depend on someone else's advice, there's always the temptation to blame him when something goes wrong. Worse, you may take credit for successes that weren't your own. To pay your dues you must make your own mistakes, own up to them, take responsibility for them—and learn from them.

Before You Call Your Broker . . .

Once you have found an investment that meets all your criteria and is trading at a price you're willing to pay, there are still some other steps I advise you to take *before* you call your broker:

1. *Write down* **why you are buying it and why you are willing to
   pay the price you have in mind.**

Think of an investment you made two years ago. Do you remember why you bought it? Why you were happy (at that time) to
pay that price? Unless you have almost total recall, like Warren
Buffett, the chances are your memory is hazy at best.

By writing everything down you can easily refresh your memory and monitor the progress of your investment. And more important, when the investment doesn't work out, you can go back
and see what, if anything, you did wrong.

2. *Write down* **what would cause you to sell it.**

The Master Investor knows why he would sell an investment
before he buys it (Habit No. 12). It's an integral part of his system.

The average investor usually focuses on what to buy. Selling is
too often an afterthought. When it may be time to sell, he often
can't remember why he bought it or what he expected to happen.
So the selling decision becomes an agonizing reappraisal of his
original buying decision—or simply an emotional reaction.

If you don't know when you're going to sell, don't buy.

Writing down your predetermined exit criteria for every investment you make will give you a discipline that most investors don't
have. Adopting this habit alone could transform your investment
results.

Doing this also helps you to monitor the progress of the investment. And the right time to sell it will become glaringly obvious.

3. *Write down* **what you expect to happen to your investment.**

This should be simple. You might expect a company to continue increasing its market share. Perhaps you anticipate institutions piling into the stock and driving up the price. You could be
expecting a takeover. Whatever you expect to happen if everything goes well, write it down in as much detail as possible.
Then . . .

4. *Write down* all the other things that could happen.

You'll need a lot more space to do this. I won't even begin to list the possibilities. Suffice to say what trips up most investors is the unexpected. And in markets the unexpected is to be expected. You must train yourself to be prepared for the worst scenarios you could imagine.

5. *Write down* what you are going to do if any of these other things happen instead of what you expect.

You have absolutely no control over what the market is going to do. What you *can* control is how you react. As the trader William Eckhardt recalled:

> An old trader once told me: "Don't think about what the market's going to do; you have absolutely no control over that. Think about what you're going to do if it gets there."[3]

For each of your scenarios, write down how you want to react if that scenario comes to pass. If the market does "get there," you'll already know what you want to do. Buffett calls this the "Noah rule: Predicting rain doesn't count; building arks does."[4]

This won't guarantee, however, that you will be able to "pull the trigger" instantly. A powerful technique that will help you realize that goal is called "mental rehearsal." Visualize each scenario. Then put yourself in that context and see yourself acting as you want to act; then play the scene again through your own eyes. Pay attention to what feelings come up, and repeat the visualization process as many times as necessary until you can see yourself coolly practicing Habit No. 11 and acting instantly.

It's also a good idea to visualize your investment reaching or exceeding your expectations and similarly rehearse seeing yourself taking a profit.

Whenever you make a mistake, use this same technique to replay what you did in your mind—and rehearse doing what you would rather have done.

By focusing on what you can control, being prepared for what can go wrong as well as what can go right, and practicing the actions you will at some point have to take, you will be able to emulate the Master Investor's dispassionate ability to act instantly.

6. Monitor your investments—and your own performance.

Though you clearly can't monitor an investment until after you've bought it, it's essential to have established procedures to do so *before* you call your broker.

The process of monitoring is an extension of your search strategy. It involves continuing to measure exactly the same criteria that led you to make the investment in the first place.

Exactly *how* are you going to do this? How often? What information will you need to gather—and where will you find it?

By having written records, you'll find this process relatively straightforward. You'll always be able to tell whether or not an investment is meeting your criteria and easily refresh your memory about what you may need to do.

And just as important, you'll be able to judge your own performance and reactions against your intentions.

Putting Your Money
Where Your Mouth Is

When you begin testing your system for the first time, while you may be confident it will work, you can't be certain. So at this stage it's best to commit only money you can afford to lose.

As you pay your dues, acquire the habits of the Master Investor, and prove (and if necessary refine) your system, you will eventually achieve the state of unconscious competence.

You will know when you have reached this point when you happily invest your entire net worth in your system without giving it a second thought (Habit No. 23).

32

It's Easier Than You Think

"What we do is not beyond anybody else's competence. It is just not necessary to do extraordinary things to get extraordinary results."

—WARREN BUFFETT[1]

WHEN I MENTIONED TO ONE woman that I was writing this book, she asked me how many Winning Investment Habits there were. When I told her, she exclaimed, "Twenty-three! Why so many? Can't you make it three?"

I'm afraid not, which may make adopting all the habits seem like a daunting proposition. The good news is that just by adopting a few of them you will immediately see an improvement in your investment results.

That's what I did. I adopted a kind of cross between Benjamin Graham's and Warren Buffett's systems, buying Hong Kong–listed stocks in well-managed companies with low P/Es and high yields. One of these companies turned out to be more poorly managed than I could have ever imagined. It was eventually delisted and I suffered a total loss. But I didn't take it personally. I learned from the error and moved on.

When everyone else was getting rich in dot-com stocks, I wasn't tempted. I stuck to my system. Nevertheless, I had one bonus from the Internet boom. I bought shares in a company that rented the exhibition booths at trade shows and the like. One day I noticed that the stock had doubled since I'd last checked the price a week or so before. Unfortunately, I also noticed that a couple of days before it had been even higher.

I did some digging and quickly discovered the stock had soared because the company was having discussions—just talking!—with an American outfit about somehow putting its business onto the Internet. So I immediately called my broker and told her to dump the stock. It was obvious to me this was like winning the lottery, a windfall gain. Sure enough, a few months later the stock had fallen to less than I'd originally paid for it.

But I can't claim that I have always acted instantly as I did then. Far from it.

I'd owned a stock for a while because it had a 25 percent dividend yield (that is *not* a typographical error). But the company's business fell off as the economy soured and it cut its dividend. This happened while my mental focus was on finishing this book, so I procrastinated for quite some time before selling the stock for far less than I'd have gotten if I'd acted immediately.

Despite my far-from-perfect record in practicing the 23 Winning Investment Habits, I still banked an average 24.4 percent annual return on my Hong Kong stock portfolio for the six years from 1998 to 2003.

But improving your performance isn't the only benefit you can expect from adopting the Winning Investment Habits. You'll also be far more relaxed when making investment decisions. You may even find the process of investing now contributes to your peace of mind rather than being a source of anxiety. You'll no longer view the successes of others with a sense of envy, bewilderment, or self-doubt. Rather, you'll probably react by thinking something like, "Well, that's an interesting way of investing—but it's not for me."

You'll no longer be on an emotional roller coaster governed by the manic-depressive changes in Mr. Market's mood.

Indeed, having purged from your mind any belief you may have once had in the Seven Deadly Investment Sins, you'll suddenly realize that 90 percent of what you read in the financial press and hear from talking heads on financial TV programs is totally irrelevant.

The financial media is dominated by the belief that the only way to make money is to predict the market's next move—the First Deadly Investment Sin. Having purged those beliefs from your mind, you may find yourself wondering whether you really need to continue reading the *Wall Street Journal* every day. Or maybe you'll find it a regular source of amusement, as I do—and wonder why you ever wasted your time watching those financial TV channels.

By adopting these habits you'll develop your own way of looking at the markets, and of doing things, that will separate you once and for all from the investment herd.

Where to Get Help

IF YOU WANT TO LEARN more about *The Winning Investment Habits of Warren Buffett and George Soros,* I publish an e-mail newsletter that will help you get started and keep going.

Like this book, the newsletter aims to help you practice the Winning Investment Habits yourself. It's available only by e-mail to keep "transactions costs" down—both yours and mine.

To browse some past issues, go to www.marktier.com. You'll find:

- My market commentary—something quite different from what you might expect. For example, don't expect me to make any predictions about the market or give you any advice about what to buy or sell.
- Problems and obstacles other people have had adopting the Winning Investment Habits—and how they solved them. Learning from *other* people's mistakes is a great shortcut to success.
- You'll also have the opportunity to raise your own questions and concerns and get my suggestions on what to do.

Again, to learn more, and browse some past issues, just go to my Web site: www.marktier.com.

I'll also post information there on when and where I'll be giving courses, seminars, and other talks. I'll be offering these all over

---

Attention: Money Managers, Financial Advisors, Institutional Investors, and Other Investment Professionals

Readers of this book will turn into very demanding customers. And they'll put you on the spot by asking you all kinds of difficult questions as they decide whether you're really the right people to look after their hard-earned money.

Get a head start—and a jump on your competitors—by getting Mark Tier to help you install a culture of investment excellence in your organization.

Find out more at www.marktier.com/4managers.htm

---

the world, so there's bound to be something happening somewhere near you soon.

And you can also . . .

Discover *Your* Investment Personality

Compare *your* investment habits to the Master Investors' by taking my unique *Investor Personality Profile* questionnaire. Find out just what you've been doing wrong—and, just as importantly, what you've been doing right.

You'll get a detailed inventory of your investment strengths and weaknesses and personalized advice on what steps you need to take to adopt the Winning Investment Habits—to quickly start to improve your investment performance.

Discover *your* investment personality at www.marktier.com/ipp.htm.

Investment Books Worth Reading

There are thousands of investment books available—with dozens more being issued every month. Some of them are worth reading.

Here are the books that I've found very helpful. They also expand on some aspects of the material in this book.

The Seven Deadly Investment Sins

If you're afflicted by a belief in any of the Seven Deadly Investment Sins, I implore you to read *The Fortune Sellers* by William A. Sherden. Sherden does more than just survey the whole gamut of fortune sellers, from weather forecasters to economists to market gurus. He *measures* their predictions against what he calls the "naïve forecast."

The naïve forecast is simply: Tomorrow's weather will be the same as today's; inflation next year will be the same as it was this year; next year's earnings will be up (or down) X percent, just like they were this year. And so on.

Through rigorous analysis, Sherden shows that only one class of forecasters beats the naïve forecast with any regularity: weather forecasters. But only for forecasts for up to four days in the future. And even then, by only a small margin.

So next time you're tempted to listen to some guru's market prediction, remember that you can beat *any* guru—*on average*—by simply "predicting" that the market will do tomorrow what it did today. Sherden *proves* this in his book.

And in his *Why the Best-Laid Investment Plans Usually Go Wrong*, Harry Browne has a wonderful collection of market and economic forecasts whose authors I'm sure wish they'd never written them.

The Seven Deadly Investment Sins need "powerful magic" to be exorcised—exactly what you'll find in these two books.

Warren Buffett

Books about Warren Buffett are about as scarce as wheat fields in Nebraska. Unless you're a Buffett junkie, the problem is what to read and what *not* to read?

By starting with Roger Lowenstein's biography *Buffett: The Making of an American Capitalist* and then reading *The Warren Buffett Way* by Robert Hagstrom you'll be introduced to both the man and his method.

To hear it straight from the horse's mouth pick up a copy of *The Essays of Warren Buffett,* edited by Lawrence A. Cunningham. These are actually extracts from Buffett's annual letters to his partners and shareholders, organized by topic.

Even better, read Buffett's letters in full. You'll find them, from 1977 to the present, at the Berkshire Hathaway Web site, www.berkshirehathaway.com.

Berkshire Hathaway has also reprinted Buffett's letters to shareholders (1977 to 1995) in two volumes, available for $30 direct from Berkshire Hathaway, Inc., 1440 Kiewit Plaza, Omaha, Nebraska 68131.

If you want to delve deeper into Buffett's method, I can highly recommend *The Real Warren Buffett* by James O'Loughlin.

Andrew Kilpatrick's *Of Permanent Value* is a wonderful compilation of stories and anecdotes about Buffett's experience, his investments, his hobbies, and his outlook on life (plus hundreds of pithy Buffett quips and quotes).

Reading *Buffettology* (by Mary Buffett and David Clark) will help you get a handle on Buffett's investment system. But be warned: The authors oversimplify and attempt to provide a formula that encapsulates Buffett's stock-picking ability. Oversimplification is a helpful way to *start* learning something. So if you read this book, remember to graduate beyond its formulaic approach before putting your money on the line.

One book you'll do just fine *without* reading is Richard Simmons's *Warren Buffett Step-by-Step: An Investor's Workbook*. Like the authors of *Buffettology*, Simmons attempts to reduce Buffett's system to a formula (and even produces an equation which he doesn't adequately explain). Unlike *Buffettology*, it does not have the redeeming virtue of adding significantly to your understanding of Buffett's methodology.

There are many other books on Warren Buffett—and I think I've read all of them. Here I've recommended the ones I think will allow you to cover the most ground most quickly.

George Soros

Far less, sad to say, has been written about George Soros, no doubt because both the man and his methods are far more complex and less accessible than is the case with Buffett.

The best introduction is Robert Slater's (unauthorized) biography, *Soros: The Life and Times of the World's Greatest Investor*. Slater emphasizes Soros's investment methods and achievements, and it's a great way to gain familiarity with his approach.

A more recent biography, *Soros: The Life and Times of a Messianic Billionaire* by Michael T. Kaufman, was written with full access to Soros and his papers. So it is a far deeper portrait of Soros, the man. And, as you'd expect, there's a lot in Kaufman's book that you won't find in Slater's. Kaufman also had greater access to Soros's Open Society Foundations, so there's more information on his charitable activities.

To really understand Soros's investment methods, it's essential to read his own writings. I suggest you start with *Soros on Soros*, which, given its interview format, is easier to digest than his book *The Alchemy of Finance*, which can be rough going at times—though definitely worth the effort.

Robert Slater also published a brief volume of what he perceived to be Soros's twenty-four trading secrets, *Invest First, Investigate Later.* Though an excellent summary, much of the material is simply drawn from his biography of Soros.

Other Master Investors

It's worth studying the methods of as many other Master Investors as you can find, especially if you discover that neither Buffett's nor Soros's approach fits you. Here are some suggestions:

Only one book has been written about Carl Icahn: *King Icahn* by Mark Stevens. It's a fascinating journey into his mind and his methods.

Peter Lynch has written about his way of investing in several books, including *One Up on Wall Street* and *Beating the Street.*

Philip Fisher deserves a far higher profile than he has. I urge you to read his book *Common Stocks and Uncommon Profits.*

Benjamin Graham, of course, needs no introduction. His *Intelligent Investor* should be required reading for anyone planning to buy stocks. And if you're really serious, pick up a copy of his classic *Security Analysis* as well.

Bernard Baruch is another legendary investor. James Grant wrote an excellent biography, *Bernard Baruch: The Adventures of a Wall Street Legend.*

A more obscure book that I can highly recommend is *You Can Be a Stock Market Genius* by Joel Greenblatt. The title still turns me off—but the book is well worth reading. It's a wonderful reinforcement of the importance of specializing in your own investment niche.

John Train has several books profiling the methods of successful investors: *The Midas Touch, The Money Masters, The New Money Masters,* and *Money Masters of Our Time.* This is a great way of being introduced to a variety of different approaches, one or more of which you may want to study further.

Sir John Templeton is one of the investors whose methods he analyzed in *The Money Masters* (which is also included in *Money Masters of Our Time*). Templeton's approach is also examined by Nikki Ross in her book *Lessons from the Legends of Wall Street*.

Investment Gurus by Peter J. Tanous is another useful book surveying a number of different investors.

In *Market Wizards* and *New Market Wizards*, Jack Schwager has done a sterling service by finding and interviewing some of the greatest traders of our generation. Traders talk far more about their systems, methodology, and thought processes than most investors do. As a result, even if the last thing you want to do is buy a futures contract, you'll find these two books of interviews a valuable source of proven ideas for building and testing your own investment system.

Risk and Uncertainty

An understanding of risk and uncertainty is essential for investment success. Simply the best book on this topic I've ever seen is *Fooled by Randomness* by Nassim Nicholas Taleb.

Peter Bernstein has also written a classic on this topic: *Against the Gods: The Remarkable Story of Risk*. Though you'll find this book has more of a historical emphasis, it will also (like *Fooled by Randomness*) open your eyes to the importance of understanding the laws of probability.

Probability

You simply can't be a Master Investor if you don't understand probability. Since a lot of probability theory is counterintuitive, this causes many people problems.

One way to overcome this obstacle is with a book called *Conned Again, Watson* by Colin Bruce. In a series of tales, Sherlock Holmes and his sidekick Dr. Watson solve a variety of crimes and other misdemeanors through Holmes's understanding of the laws of chance. If your reaction to probability is like a kid's reaction to castor oil (you know it's good for you but you can't stand it), here's a sugar-coated solution.

Why Smart People Make Big Money Mistakes (and How to Correct Them) by Gary Belsky and Thomas Gilovich explains how our thought processes are often flawed when it comes to money and investing. A superficial understanding of probability is often a big part of the problem.

Possibly the best introduction to probability theory—best because it's clearly presented—is *Probability Without Tears* by Derek Rowntree. Unfortunately, it's out of print—but you can probably find a used copy on eBay or Amazon.com.

Trading

If trading, rather than investing, is your calling, Van Tharp's *Trade Your Way to Financial Freedom* is essential reading. Even nontraders can benefit enormously from this book. Tharp is a psychologist who specializes in helping traders overcome their mental blocks. Though designed for commodity traders, most of what Tharp has to say is equally applicable to investors. There's excellent guidance on how to build a system, and an analysis of the importance and significance of position sizing I've not seen anywhere else.

Living Within Your Means

The Richest Man in Babylon by George Clason is the classic on this subject. Give it to your kids (after you have read it yourself).

In *Rich Dad, Poor Dad* Robert Kiyosaki shows how the amount of money you have in the bank is a direct consequence of your beliefs and behaviors. The rich *are* different—because the way they think about money is different.

Kiyosaki does much more than just show you the differences. You'll also learn how you can start thinking about money the same way the rich do—and change your own fortunes as a result.

The Millionaire Next Door by Thomas Stanley and William Danko shows that the one thing millionaires who've *kept* their millions have in common is that they spend less than they earn.

Taxes

I'm no expert on taxes—and I neither need to be nor want to be. All I can say is that you should follow in Buffett's and Soros's footsteps and keep your taxes (and other transaction costs) as low as possible. So it's essential to gain familiarity with the tax laws that affect you. The approach that I would follow if I were in your shoes is outlined by Terry Coxon in his book *Keep What You Earn*. You can also check www.passporttrust.com and www.yoot.info for details and information.

Transaction Costs

In *Trading Is Hazardous to Your Wealth: The Common Stock Invest-*
ment Performance of Individual Investors, a paper published in *The*
Journal of Finance (Vol. 4, No. 2, April 2000), the authors Brad M.
Barber and Terrance Odean showed that investors who traded
stocks actively had, on average, a far lower return than investors
who followed a buy-and-hold strategy.

They came to this conclusion by analyzing the performance of
66,465 accounts from a discount brokerage for the period 1991 to
1996. Though somewhat technical, it's well worth reading. It's
available in PDF format from http://faculty.haas.berkeley.edu/
odean/papers/returns/Individual Investor Performance Final.pdf

Other Investment Books
Worth Reading

For other views on investing from people not directly involved in
the industry (including academics) some of the better choices include *A Random Walk Down Wall Street* by Burton Malkiel, *Stocks*
for the Long Run by Jeremy Siegel, and *Irrational Exuberance* by
Robert Shiller.

Charles Mackay's *Extraordinary Popular Delusions and the Mad-*
ness of Crowds is the classic study of how crowd psychology can
grab hold of the market.

And I recommend Roger Lowenstein's *Why Genius Failed: The*
Rise and Fall of Long-Term Capital Management. Read this so you
can avoid making the same mistakes!

The Permanent Portfolio Approach

If you'd like to follow up on Harry Browne's Permanent Portfolio approach to investing, you'll find it outlined in detail in his *Why the Best-Laid Investment Plans Usually Go Wrong* (mentioned above). Or check out *Fail-Safe Investing*, available from his Web site, www.harrybrowne.org. (You'll also find what I believe is some of the sanest and best-written commentary on current issues you can read anywhere.)

Another option is a mutual fund based on Harry Browne's investment philosophy. It's called the Permanent Portfolio Fund. Call 1-800-531-5142 if you'd like to see a prospectus. (Note: Until 2004 I was an independent director of this fund.)

A Computer Game

Railroad Tycoon is a wonderful computer game that should be issued with a warning: BEWARE: THIS GAME CAN BE ADDICTIVE. I speak with considerable authority on the topic!

You're the CEO of a railroad. Depending on which of the dozens of different scenarios you choose to play, you'll have up to thirty-one computer-generated competitors. You can also play with real competitors over the Internet. It's your job to build your company into the richest, the biggest, or the most profitable of all; carry the most freight; or become the richest player in the game (and, in some scenarios, all of these and more).

Built into the game are economic cycles that go from boom to depression and back (though not always predictably) and the normal constraints that every manager must face between issuing equity, debt, where best to invest (build more track, buy more trains, invest in the industries you serve, take over a competitor), and so on. In your stock market account, you can buy shares in your company—or the competition's. With or without margin.

It's a great teaching tool for teenagers, who can learn about building a business, the economy, and investing without knowing it while they have a lot of fun.

One of the most powerful lessons you can learn from *Railroad Tycoon* is about leverage. It's frightening to see your entire wealth disappear in just *minutes* because you were overleveraged and you face a margin call you can't meet—while your company goes bankrupt. But it's a lot cheaper to learn this lesson on a computer than with the help of your friendly stockbroker.

Appendix I

The 23 Winning Investment Habits

The Master Investor	The Losing Investor
1. Preservation of Capital Is *Always* Priority No. 1	
Believes his first priority is *always* **preservation of capital,** which is the cornerstone of his investment strategy.	Has only one investment aim— "to make a lot of money." As a result, often fails to keep it.
2. *Passionately* Avoid Risk	
As a result (of Habit No. 1), is **risk-averse.**	Thinks that big profits can only be made by taking big risks.
3. Develop Your Own Unique Investment Philosophy	
Has developed his own investment philosophy, which is an expression of his personality, abilities, knowledge, tastes, and objectives. As a result, no two highly successful investors have the same investment philosophy.	Has no investment philosophy—or uses someone else's.

The Master Investor	The Losing Investor

4. Develop Your Own, *Personal* System
for Selecting, Buying, and *Selling* Investments

Has developed—and *tested*—his own **personal system** for selecting, buying, *and selling* investments.	Has no system. Or has adopted someone else's without testing and adapting it to his own personality. (When such a system doesn't work for him, he adopts another one— which doesn't work for him either).

5. Buy As Much As You Can

Does not believe in diversification; always buys as much as he can of an investment that meets his criteria.	Lacks the confidence to take a huge position on any one investment.

6. Focus on *After*-tax Return

Hates to pay taxes (and other transaction costs) and arranges his affairs to legally minimize his tax bill.	Overlooks or neglects the burden that taxes and transaction costs place on long-term investment performance.

7. Only Invest in What You Understand

Only invests in what he understands.	Doesn't realize that a deep understanding of what he is doing is an essential prerequisite to success. Rarely realizes that profitable opportunities exist (and quite probably abound) within his own area of expertise.

8. Refuse to Make Investments That *Do Not* Meet Your Criteria

Refuses to make investments that do *not* meet his criteria. Can effortlessly say "No!" to everything else.	Has no criteria; or adopts someone else's. Can't say "No!" to his own greed.

The Master Investor	The Losing Investor

9. Do Your Own Research

Is continually searching for new investment opportunities that meet his criteria and actively engages in his own research. Likely to listen only to other investors or analysts whom he has profound reasons to respect.	Is looking for the thousand-to-one shot that will put him on easy street. As a result, often follows the "hot tip of the month." Always listening to anyone styled as an "expert." Rarely makes a deep study of any investment before buying. His research consists of getting the latest "hot" tip from a broker, an advisor—or yesterday's newspaper.

10. Have Infinite Patience

Has the patience when he can't find an investment that meets his criteria to wait indefinitely until he finds one that does.	Feels that he has to be doing something in the market at all times.

11. Act *Instantly*

Acts instantly when he has made a decision.	Procrastinates.

12. Hold a Winning Investment
Until There's a *Predetermined* Reason to Sell

Holds a winning investment until a predetermined reason to exit arises.	Rarely has a predetermined rule for taking profits. Often scared a small profit will turn into a loss, so he cashes it in—and regularly misses giant gains.

13. Follow Your System *Religiously*

Follows his own system *religiously*.	Continually "second-guesses" his system—if he has one. Shifts criteria and "goalposts" to justify his actions.

The Master Investor	The Losing Investor

14. Admit Your Mistakes and Correct Them *Immediately*

Is aware of his own fallibility. Corrects mistakes the moment they become evident. As a result, rarely suffers more than small losses.	Hangs on to losing investments in the hope he'll be able to break even. As a result, often suffers huge losses.

15. Turn Mistakes into Learning Experiences

Always treats mistakes as *learning experiences.*	Never stays with any one approach long enough to learn how to improve it. Always looks for an "instant fix."

16. Pay Your Dues

His returns increase with experience; now seems to spend less time to make more money. Has "paid his dues."	Not aware it's necessary to "pay your dues." Rarely learns from experience . . . and tends to repeat the same mistake until he's cleaned out.

17. Never Talk About What You're Doing

Almost never talks to anyone about what he's doing. Not interested or concerned with what others think about his . investment decisions.	Is always talking about his current investments, "testing" his decisions against others' opinions rather than against reality.

18. Know How to Delegate

Has successfully delegated most if not all of his responsibilities to others.	Selects investment advisors and managers the same way he makes investment decisions.

19. Live Far Below Your Means

Lives far below his means.	Probably lives beyond his means (most people do).

20. It's Not About the Money

Invests for stimulation and self-fulfillment— *not* for money.	Is motivated by money; thinks investing is the way to easy riches.

The Master Investor	The Losing Investor

21. Love What You Do, *Not* What You Own

Is emotionally involved with (and gets his satisfaction from) the process of investing; can walk away from any individual investment.	Falls in love with his investments.

22. Live and Breathe Investing 24 Hours a Day

Lives and breathes investing twenty-four hours a day.	Is not fully dedicated to achieving his investment goals (even if he knows what they are).

23. Put Your Net Worth on the Line

Puts his money where his mouth is. For example, Warren Buffett has 99 percent of his net worth in shares of Berkshire Hathaway; George Soros, similarly, keeps most of his money in his Quantum Fund. For both, the destiny of their personal wealth is identical to that of the people who have entrusted money to their management.	Adds little to his net worth through investments—indeed, his investment activities are often hazardous to his wealth. Funds his investments (and makes up his losses) from somewhere else— business profits, salary, pension funds, company bonus plans, etc.

Appendix II

Records of the Two Master Investors

WARREN BUFFETT'S RECORD: 1956–2002

Year	Net Value of Buffett Partnership/Per Share Book Value of Berkshire[2]	Dow Jones 30 Index/ S&P 500 (dividends included)[3]	Buffett Relative to Index[4]	Dow Jones 30/S&P 500 Index[3]	Buffett Partnership/ Berkshire Hathaway (book value)[2]
	Annual Percentage Change[1] in . . .			$1,000 invested in 1956 now worth[1]:	
1957[5]	9.3%	−8.4%	17.7%	$916.00	$1,093
1958	32.2%	38.5%	−6.3%	$1,268.66	$1,445
1959	20.9%	20.0%	0.9%	$1,522.39	$1,747
1960	18.6%	−6.3%	24.9%	$1,426.48	$2,072
1961	35.9%	22.4%	13.5%	$1,746.01	$2,816
1962	11.9%	−7.6%	19.5%	$1,613.32	$3,151
1963	30.5%	20.6%	9.9%	$1,945.66	$4,112

	Annual Percentage Change[1] in . . .			$1,000 invested in 1956 now worth[1]:	
Year	Net Value of Buffett Partnership/Per Share Book Value of Berkshire[2]	Dow Jones 30 Index/ S&P 500 (dividends included)[3]	Buffett Relative to Index[4]	Dow Jones 30/S&P 500 Index[3]	Buffett Partnership/ Berkshire Hathaway (book value)[2]
1964	22.3%	18.7%	3.6%	$2,309.50	$5,029
1965	36.9%	14.2%	22.7%	$2,637.45	$6,884
1966	16.8%	−15.6%	32.4%	$2,226.00	$8,041
1967	28.4%	19.0%	9.4%	$2,648.95	$10,324
1968	45.6%	7.7%	37.9%	$2,852.91	$15,032
1969[6]	16.2%	−8.4%	24.6%	$2,613.27	$17,467
1970	12.0%	3.9%	8.1%	$2,715.19	$19,563
1971	16.4%	14.6%	1.8%	$3,111.60	$22,772
1972	21.7%	18.9%	2.8%	$3,699.70	$27,713
1973	4.7%	−14.8%	19.5%	$3,152.14	$29,016
1974	5.5%	−26.4%	31.9%	$2,319.98	$30,612
1975	21.9%	37.2%	−15.3%	$3,183.01	$37,316
1976	59.3%	23.6%	35.7%	$3,934.20	$59,444
1977	31.9%	−7.4%	39.3%	$3,643.07	$78,407
1978	24.0%	6.4%	17.6%	$3,876.22	$97,224
1979	35.7%	18.2%	17.5%	$4,581.70	$131,933
1980	19.3%	32.3%	−13.0%	$6,061.58	$157,396
1981	31.4%	−5.0%	36.4%	$5,758.50	$206,819
1982	40.0%	21.4%	18.6%	$6,990.82	$289,546
1983	32.3%	22.4%	9.9%	$8,556.77	$383,070
1984	13.6%	6.1%	7.5%	$9,078.73	$435,168
1985	48.2%	31.6%	16.6%	$11,947.61	$644,918
1986	26.1%	18.6%	7.5%	$14,169.87	$813,242
1987	19.5%	5.1%	14.4%	$14,892.53	$971,824
1988	20.1%	16.6%	3.5%	$17,364.69	$1,167,161
1989	44.4%	31.7%	12.7%	$22,869.30	$1,685,380
1990	7.4%	−3.1%	10.5%	$22,160.35	$1,810,098
1991	39.6%	30.5%	9.1%	$28,919.26	$2,526,897
1992	20.3%	7.6%	12.7%	$31,117.12	$3,039,857
1993	14.3%	10.1%	4.2%	$34,259.95	$3,474,557

1994	13.9%	1.3%	12.6%	$34,705.33 $3,957,520
1995	43.1%	37.6%	5.5%	$47,754.53 $5,663,212
1996	31.8%	23.0%	8.8%	$58,738.08 $7,464,113
1997	34.1%	33.4%	0.7%	$78,356.59 $10,009,376
1998	48.3%	28.6%	19.7%	$100,766.58 $14,843,904
1999	0.5%	21.0%	−20.5%	$121,927.56 $14,918,124
2000	6.5%	−9.1%	15.6%	$110,832.15 $15,887,802
2001	−6.2%	−13.0%	6.8%	$96,379.64 $14,902,758
2002	10%	−22.1%	32.1%	$75,079.74 $16,393,034
2003	21.0%	28.7%	−7.7%	$97,894.36 $19,835,571
47-year compounded annual return		**9.7%**	**23.4%***	

Notes to the Table:

1. Percentage changes for each full calendar year.

2. Percentages for the Buffett Partnership, net of all fees, 1957 to 1968. From 1969, book value of Berkshire Hathaway. Assumes full value at liquidation of Buffett Partnership reinvested in Berkshire Hathaway.

3. When he formed the Buffett Partnership, his target was to exceed the Dow Jones 30 Index by 10% per year. He has used the S&P500 Index as his benchmark for Berkshire Hathaway.

4. Buffett's performance minus the Dow or S&P Index.

5. Buffett Partnership to 1968.

6. Berkshire Hathaway book value, 1969 to present, which is Buffett's *own* measure of his performance.

Sources: For Buffett Partnership, *Buffett: The Making of an American Capitalist* by Roger Lowenstein, pages 69 & 93; for Berkshire Hathaway Inc.'s book value, Berkshire Hathaway annual reports.

---

*NOTE: The figure of 23.4% for Buffett's 46-year compounded average annual return is based on Buffett's *own* measure of his performance: the *book value* of Berkshire Hathaway. The average of 24.4% used in the text is calculated on the value of *shares* in Berkshire Hathaway.

APPENDIX II

GEORGE SOROS'S RECORD: 1969–2002

Year	in Net Asset Value of Quantum Fund [2]	in S&P 500 with Dividends included[2]	Soros Relative to Index[3]	S&P 500 Index	Quantum Fund (net asset value)[2]
	Annual Percentage Change[1] in . . .			**$1,000 invested in 1969 now worth[1]:**	
1969	29.38%	−8.4%	37.78%	$916.00	$1,293.82
1970	17.50%	3.9%	13.60%	$951.72	$1,520.24
1971	20.32%	14.6%	5.72%	$1,090.68	$1,829.09
1972	42.16%	18.9%	23.26%	$1,296.81	$2,600.24
1973	8.35%	−14.8%	23.15%	$1,104.89	$2,817.45
1974	17.51%	−26.4%	43.91%	$813.20	$3,310.79
1975	27.58%	37.2%	−9.62%	$1,115.70	$4,223.76
1976	61.90%	23.6%	38.30%	$1,379.01	$6,838.06
1977	31.17%	−7.4%	38.57%	$1,276.96	$8,969.45
1978	55.12%	6.4%	48.72%	$1,358.69	$13,913.70
1979	59.06%	18.2%	40.86%	$1,605.97	$22,130.91
1980	102.56%	32.3%	70.26%	$2,124.70	$44,828.36
1981	−22.88%	−5.0%	−17.88%	$2,018.46	$34,571.15
1982	56.86%	21.4%	35.46%	$2,450.42	$54,229.58
1983	24.95%	22.4%	2.55%	$2,999.31	$67,758.79
1984	9.40%	6.1%	3.30%	$3,182.27	$74,128.24
1985	122.19%	31.6%	90.59%	$4,187.86	$164,708.61
1986	42.12%	18.6%	23.52%	$4,966.80	$234,079.03
1987	14.13%	5.1%	9.03%	$5,220.11	$267,150.79
1988	10.14%	16.6%	−6.46%	$6,086.65	$294,229.58
1989[4]	31.64%	31.7%	−0.06%	$8,016.12	$387,323.81
1990	29.57%	−3.1%	32.67%	$7,767.62	$501,855.47
1991	53.30%	30.5%	22.80%	$10,136.74	$769,344.43
1992	68.11%	7.6%	60.51%	$10,907.14	$1,293,344.92
1993	63.25%	10.1%	53.15%	$12,008.76	$2,111,385.58
1994	3.95%	1.3%	2.65%	$12,164.87	$2,194,785.31
1995	39.04%	37.6%	1.44%	$16,738.86	$3,051,629.49
1996	−1.48%	23.0%	−24.48%	$20,588.80	$3,006,465.38
1997	17.13%	33.4%	−16.27%	$27,465.46	$3,521,472.90

1998	12.17%	28.6%	−16.43%	$35,320.58	$3,950,036.15
1999	34.65%	21.0%	13.65%	$42,737.90	$5,318,723.67
2000	−15.00%	−9.1%	−5.9%	$38,848.75	$4,520,915.12
2001	13.80%	−11.90%	25.70%	$34,225.75	$5,144,801.41
2002	−0.05%	−22.10%	22.05%	$26,661.86	$5,142,229.01
2003	15.00%	28.70%	−13.70%	$34,313.81	$5,913,563.36
1969–2003 **compounded** **annual return**		**10.0%**	**28.6%**		
1969–1988 **compounded** **annual return** **(Soros's management)**		**9.5%**	**32.9%**		
1989–31 March 2000[5] **compounded** **annual return** **(Druckenmiller's management)**	**18.6%**	**26.6%**			

Notes to the Table:

1. Percentage changes for each full calendar year (except 1969, from January 31st).

2. Percentages for the net asset value of the Quantum Fund (from May 2000, Quantum Endowment Fund), net of all fees, assuming dividends reinvested.

3. Soros's performance minus the S&P Index.

4. Stanley Druckenmiller took over active management of the Quantum Fund in 1989. George Soros became "coach."

5. Druckenmiller retired in April 2000. Soros changed the name to the Quantum Endowment Fund.

Sources: For Quantum Fund: 1969 to 1984, *The Alchemy of Finance* by George Soros, page 146; 1985 to present, Soros Fund Management.

Acknowledgments

Both money and psychology have always fascinated me. It was the first interest that led me into the investment industry. In this book I've been able to put both my fascinations together.

As part of my interest in psychology, I studied Neuro Linguistic Programming [NLP], most simply described as applied psychology, eventually becoming a Master Practitioner.

A core concept of NLP is that if someone can do something well, anyone can learn to do it well. An NLP process called "modeling" is the application of that concept—and the origin of the idea of finding out what Warren Buffett, George Soros, and other great investors have in common.

So I must first thank George Zee, who brought many prominent NLP teachers to Hong Kong—and Leo Angart, who continued to organize NLP seminars when George Zee retired.

From Judith DeLozier, Robert Dilts, and David Gordon I learned the process of modeling, which forms the basis of this book.

Robert H. Meier kindly allowed me to access his treasure trove of articles and research material on investments that he'd collected over some twenty-five years of studying the markets. This aided my research immensely.

Writing a book, it turns out, is a team effort. Maurice Cruz's counsel was invaluable in helping me form many of the concepts in this work. And it's safe to say that if Tim Staermose hadn't spent several months working with me, this book would still be unfinished. Many's the time he pointed out where I was getting off-track, and much of the clarity in the writing is due to his invaluable assistance.

Terry Coxon found several ways (and places) to further improve the quality of the manuscript.

Michelle Celi cheerfully typed the manuscript several times, including tens of thousands of words that never made it into the final draft. And Raquel Narca was supportive throughout the slow process of getting this book into shape, and made countless valuable suggestions as it was being written.

Several people read the book in manuscript at different stages and made valuable comments that improved it no end. For their help I thank Larry Abrams, Gloria Altus, David Bergland, Bruno Bissinger, Norman de Brackinghe, Bay Butler, Hugh Butler, Peter Chen, Robert W. Czeschin, Robyn Flemming, Laurent Gounelle, John Greenwood, Loray Greiner, Don Hauptman, Bernhard Mast, Dan Rosenthal, Bruce Tier, Don Tier, Whitney Tilson, Kris Wadia, and Al Zuckerman.

References

Allen, Frederick, *Secret Formula: How Brilliant Marketing and Relentless Salesmanship Made Coca-Cola the Best-Known Product in the World.* New York: HarperBusiness, 1994.

Baruch, Bernard. *My Own Story.* New York: Holt, Rinehart & Winston, 1957.

Berkshire Hathaway Annual Reports. Omaha: Berkshire Hathaway, various dates.

Berkshire Hathaway Inc. Letters to Shareholders, 1977–1986. Omaha: Berkshire Hathaway, n.d.

Berkshire Hathaway Inc. Letters to Shareholders, 1987–1995. Omaha: Berkshire Hathaway, nd.

Bianco, Anthony. "The Warren Buffett You Don't Know." *Business Week.* July 5, 1999.

Browne, Harry. *Why the Best-Laid Investment Plans Usually Go Wrong.* New York: Morrow, 1987.

Buffett, Mary, and David Clark. *Buffettology: The Previously Unexplained Techniques That Have Made Warren Buffett the World's Most Famous Investor.* New York: Rawson Associates, 1997.

Carret, Philip L. *The Art of Speculation.* New York: Wiley, 1997.

Chatman, Seymour, ed. *Benjamin Graham: The Memoirs of the Dean of Wall Street.* New York: McGraw-Hill, 1996.

Coxon, Terry. *Keep What You Earn.* New York: Times Business, 1996.

Csikszentmihalyi, Mihaly. *Flow: The Psychology of Optimal Experience.* New York: Harper Perennial, 1990.

Edwards, Robert D., and John Magee. *Technical Analysis of Stock Trends.* Boston: John Magee Inc., 1966.

Fisher, Philip A. *Common Stocks and Uncommon Profits and Other Writings.* New York: Wiley, 1996.

Graham, Benjamin. *The Intelligent Investor*. 4th revised edition. New York: Harper & Row, 1973.

———, and David Dodd. *Security Analysis*. New York: McGraw-Hill, 1934.

Hagstrom, Robert G., Jr. *The Warren Buffett Portfolio*. New York: Wiley, 1999.

———. *The Warren Buffett Way: Investment Strategies of the World's Greatest Investor*. New York: Wiley, 1994.

Hughes, Anthony, Geoff Wilson, and Matthew Kidman, *Masters of the Market: Secrets of Australia's Leading Sharemarket Investors*. Milton, Queensland: Wrightbooks, 2003.

Kaufman, Michael T. *Soros: The Life and Times of a Messianic Billionaire*. New York: Knopf, 2002.

Kent, Robert W., ed. *Money Talks*. New York: Facts on File Publications, 1985.

Kilpatrick, Andrew. *Of Permanent Value: The Story of Warren Buffett*. Birmingham Ala.: AKPE, 1996.

———. *Warren Buffett: The Good Guy of Wall Street*. New York: Primus, 1992.

Kroll, Stanley. *The Professional Commodity Trader*. New York: Harper & Row, 1974.

LeBaron, Dean, Romesh Vaitilingam, and Marilyn Pitchford. *Dean LeBaron's Book of Investment Quotations*. New York: Wiley, 2001.

Lefèvre, Edwin. *Reminiscences of a Stock Operator*. Burlington Vt.: Fraser Publishing Co., 1980.

Littlewood, Nigel. *Rivkin's Rules*. Melbourne, Victoria: Information Australia, 2000.

Lowe, Janet. *Warren Buffett Speaks: Wit and Wisdom from the World's Greatest Investor*. New York: Wiley, 1997.

———. *Value Investing Made Easy: Benjamin Graham's Classic Investment Strategy Explained for Everyone*. New York: McGraw-Hill, 1996.

Lowenstein, Roger. *Buffett: The Making of an American Capitalist*. London: Weidenfeld & Nicolson, 1996.

——. *When Genius Failed: The Rise and Fall of Long-Term Capital Management.* New York: Random House, 2000.

Lynch, Peter. *Beating the Street.* New York: Simon & Schuster, 1994.

——. *One Up on Wall Street.* New York: Penguin, 1989.

Mackay, Charles. *Extraordinary Popular Delusions and the Madness of Crowds.* New York: Noonday Press, 1974.

Malkiel, Burton G. *A Random Walk Down Wall Street.* New York: Norton, 1996.

Miles, Robert P. *The Warren Buffett CEO: Secrets from the Berkshire Hathaway Managers.* New York: Wiley, 2002.

Neuberger, Roy R. *So Far, So Good—The First 94 Years.* New York: Wiley, 1997.

Niederhoffer, Victor. *The Education of a Speculator.* New York: Wiley, 1997.

O'Loughlin, James. *The Real Warren Buffett.* London: Nicholas Brealey Publishing, 2002.

Outstanding Investor Digest, various issues.

Palmer, Jay. "Market Mover." *Barron's.* November 6, 1995.

Porter, Michael E. *Competitive Advantage, Creating and Sustaining Superior Performance.* New York: Free Press, 1985.

——. *Competitive Strategy: Techniques for Analyzing Industries and Competitors.* New York: Free Press, 1980.

——. *On Competition.* Boston: Harvard Business Press, 1998.

——. *The Competitive Advantage of Nations.* New York: Free Press, 1990.

Reynolds, Siimon. *Thoughts of Chairman Buffett: Thirty Years of Unconventional Wisdom from the Sage of Omaha.* New York: HarperBusiness, 1998.

Ross, Nikki. *Lessons from Legends of Wall Street.* Chicago: Dearborn, 2000.

Schlender, Brent. "The Bill and Warren Show." *Fortune,* July 20, 1998.

Schwager, Jack D. *Market Wizards: Interviews with Top Traders.* New York: New York Institute of Finance, 1989.

——. *The New Market Wizards: Conversations with America's Top Traders.* New York: HarperBusiness, 1992.

Sherden, William A. *The Fortune Sellers.* New York: Wiley, 1998.

Slater, Robert. *Invest First, Investigate Later & 23 Other Trading Secrets of George Soros.* Chicago: Irwin, 1996.

———. *Soros: The Life, Times and Trading Secrets of the World's Greatest Investor.* New York: Irwin, 1996.

Serwer, Andy. "Tech Is King: Now Meet the Prince." *Fortune,* December 6, 1999.

Smith, Adam. "12 Minds That Made the Market." *Bloomberg Personal Finance,* December 1999.

Soros, George. *The Alchemy of Finance: Reading the Mind of the Market.* New York: Wiley, 1994.

———. *Soros on Soros: Staying Ahead of the Curve.* New York: Wiley, 1995.

Soros, Tivadar. *Masquerade: Dancing Around Death in Nazi-Occupied Hungary.* New York: Arcade Publishing, 2001.

Spurgeon, Devon. "Envelope Please: Warren Buffett Hints at Successor." *Asian Wall Street Journal.* October 19, 2000.

Stanley, Thomas J., and William D. Danko. *The Millionaire Next Door.* Atlanta: Longstreet Press, 1996.

Steinhardt, Michael. *No Bull: My Life In and Out of Markets.* New York: Wiley, 2001.

Stevens, Mark. *King Icahn.* New York: Dutton, 1993.

Taleb, Nassim Nicholas. *Fooled by Randomness.* New York: Texere, 2001.

Tanous, Peter J. *Investment Gurus.* New York: New York Institute of Finance, 1997.

Tharp, Van. *Trade Your Way to Financial Freedom.* New York: McGraw-Hill, 1999.

Train, John. *The Midas Touch.* New York: Harper & Row, 1988.

———. *The Money Masters.* New York: Harper & Row, 1980.

———. *The New Money Masters.* New York: HarperBusiness, 1989.

———. *Money Masters of Our Time.* New York: HarperBusiness, 2000.

Notes

A NOTE ON FOOTNOTES: I'm always annoyed when I have to keep turning to the back of the book to find a footnote in which the author expands upon whatever point he was making. So in this book those discursive footnotes that add to or expand on the text have been marked with an asterisk (*) and placed at the bottom of the page.

The footnotes that provide sources are numbered and are all here, at the *end* of the book. They'll tell you in which book or article I found the quote. If that doesn't interest you, simply ignore them. You won't miss a thing.

Chapter 2

[1]"Are Stocks Too High?" *Fortune,* September 18, 1987, pages 28–40.

[2]George Soros, *The Alchemy of Finance* (Wiley, New York, 1994), page 301.

[3]Warren Buffett, "1981 Letter to Shareholders," *Letters to Shareholders, 1977–1986* (Berkshire Hathaway, Omaha, n.d), page 33.

[4]"Penelope Wang, "Garzarelli Is Back," *Money,* May 2000.

[5]John Train, *The Midas Touch* (Harper & Row, New York, 1988), page 83.

[6]Roger Lowenstein, *Buffett: The Making of an American Capitalist* (Weidenfeld & Nicolson, London, 1996), page 111.

[7]Warren Buffett, Berkshire Hathaway Annual General Meeting, April 29, 2000.

[8]"While Stocks Slide, Wall Street Binges on Pay and Perks," *Asian Wall Street Journal,* September 19, 2000, page 8.

Chapter 3

[1]George Soros, *Soros on Soros* (Wiley, New York, 1995), page 61.

[2]Jack Schwager, *Market Wizards* (New York Institute of Finance, New York, 1989) page 189.

[3]Soros, *Alchemy of Finance,* pages 12–13.

[4]Soros, *Soros on Soros,* page 26.

[5]Tivadar Soros, *Masquerade: Dancing Around Death in Nazi-Occupied*

Hungary (Arcade Publishing, New York, 2001), page 71.

[6] *Ibid.*, page 69.

[7] *Ibid.*, page 74.

[8] Soros, *Soros on Soros*, pages 28–29.

[9] *Ibid.*, page 29.

[10] Michael T. Kaufman, *Soros: The Life and Times of a Messianic Billionaire* (Knopf, New York, 2002), page 127.

[11] *Ibid.*, page 5.

[12] Lowenstein, *Buffett*, page 20.

[13] *Ibid.*, page 87.

[14] Andrew Kilpatrick, *Of Permanent Value: The Story of Warren Buffett* (AKPE, Birmingham, Ala., 1996), page 59.

Chapter 4

[1] Dean LeBaron, Romesh Vaitilingam, and Marilyn Pitchford, *Dean LeBaron's Book of Investment Quotations* (Wiley, New York, 2001).

[2] Janet Lowe, *Warren Buffett Speaks* (Wiley, New York, 1997), page 105.

[3] Robert G. Hagstrom, Jr., *The Warren Buffett Way* (Wiley, New York, 1994), pages 94–95.

[4] Jack Schwager, *Market Wizards*, page 186.

[5] Slater, *Soros: The Life, Times, and Trading Secrets of the World's Greatest Investor* (Irwin, Chicago, 1996), page 60.

[6] *Ibid.*, page 175.

[7] Lowe, *Warren Buffett Speaks*, page 106.

[8] Kaufman, *Soros*, page 143.

[9] Information from Slater, *Soros*, page 147.

[10] Kaufman, *Soros*, page 143.

[11] Michael Steinhardt, *No Bull: My Life In and Out of Markets* (Wiley, New York, 2001), page 176.

[12] Nassim Nicholas Taleb, *Fooled by Randomness* (Texere, New York, 2001), page 189.

[13] Warren Buffett, "1982 Letter to Shareholders," *Letters to Shareholders, 1977–1986*, page 61.

[14] Benjamin Graham, *The Intelligent Investor*, 4th ed. (Harper & Row, New York, 1993), page 284.

Chapter 5

[1] Robert W. Kent, ed., *Money Talks* (Facts on File Publications, New York, 1985), page 42.

[2] Warren Buffett, "1990 Letter to Shareholders," *Letters to Shareholders, 1987–1995* (Berkshire Hathaway, Omaha, nd), page 79.

[3] Van Tharp, *Trade Your Way to Financial Freedom* (McGraw-Hill, New York, 1999), page 64.

[4] Lowe, *Warren Buffett Speaks*, page 93.

[5] Kilpatrick, *Of Permanent Value*, page 56.

[6] Warren Buffett, "1987 Letter to Shareholders," *Letters to Shareholders, 1987–1995*, page 12.

[7] Benjamin Graham and David Dodd, *Security Analysis*, 1934 edition (McGraw-Hill, New York, 1984), page 493.

[8] Lowenstein, *Buffett*, pages 67–68.

[9] *Ibid.*, page 80.

[10] Philip A. Fisher, "Developing an Investment Philosophy," in *Common*

Stocks and Uncommon Profits (Wiley, New York, 1996), page 209.

[11]*Ibid.,* page 211.

[12]*Ibid.,* page 210.

[13]*Ibid.,* pages 208–209.

[14]*Ibid.,* page 209.

[15]Adam Smith, "12 Minds That Made the Market," *Bloomberg Personal Finance,* December 1999, page 71.

[16]Fisher, *Common Stocks,* page 85.

[17]*Ibid.,* page 231.

[18]Hagstrom, *Warren Buffet Way,* page 47.

[19]Soros, *Soros on Soros,* page 33.

[20]Adam Smith television program, April 15, 1993.

[21]Soros, *Soros on Soros,* page 48.

[22]"The Man Who Moves Markets," *Business Week,* August 23, 1993, pages 50–60.

[23]As quoted in Slater, *Soros,* page 48.

[24]Soros, *Alchemy,* page 1.

[25]*Ibid.,* page 8.

[26]Soros, *Soros on Soros,* page 71.

[27]Soros, "The Case for Mortgage Trusts," *Alchemy,* page 62.

[28]Soros, *Alchemy,* page 62.

[29]*Ibid.,* page 63.

[30]Kaufman, *Soros,* page 132.

[31]Warren Buffett, "1993 Letter to Shareholders," *Letters to Shareholders, 1987–1995,* page 126.

Chapter 6

[1]Jack Schwager, *The New Market Wizards: Conversations with America's Top Traders* (HarperBusiness, New York, 1992), page 248.

[2]Schwager, *New Market Wizards,* page 159.

[3]Schwager, *New Market Wizards,* page 99.

[4]Berkshire Hathaway Annual General Meeting 2000.

[5]Slater, *Soros,* pages 67–68.

[6]Soros, *Soros on Soros,* page 79.

[7]*Ibid.,* pages 79–80.

[8]*Ibid.,* page 81.

[9]*Ibid.,* page 81.

[10]Kaufman, *Soros,* page 239.

[11]Schwager, *New Market Wizards,* page 208.

[12]Warren Buffett, "1993 Letter to Shareholders," *Letters to Shareholders, 1987–1995,* page 136.

[13]Warren Buffett, "Chairman's Letter to Shareholders," *2000 Berkshire Hathaway Annual Report,* page 3.

[14]Frederick Allen, *Secret Formula: How Brilliant Marketing and Relentless Salesmanship Made Coca-Cola the Best-Known Product in the World* (HarperBusiness, New York, 1994), page 390.

[15]*Ibid.,* page 390.

[16]Berkshire Hathaway Annual Meeting, 2000.

[17]Hagstrom, *Common Stocks,* page 80.

[18]Berkshire Hathaway Annual Meeting, 2000.

[19]Warren Buffett, "1990 Letter to Shareholders," *Letters to Shareholders, 1987–1995,* page 81.

[20]Lowenstein, *Buffett,* page 330.

[21]*Ibid.,* page 132.

[22]*Wall Street Journal,* July 7, 1987.

[23]Slater, *Soros,* page 68.

[24]Lowenstein, *Buffet,* page 135.

[25]Berkshire Hathaway Annual Report, 2003.

Chapter 7

[1]Schwager, *New Market Wizards,* pages 207.

[2]Lowe, *Warren Buffett Speaks,* page 160.

[3]Slater, *Soros,* page 159.

[4]Schwager, *New Market Wizards,* pages 207–208.

[5]Andy Serwer, "Tech Is King: Now Meet the Prince," *Fortune,* December 6, 1999, page 45.

[6]Bernard Baruch, *My Own Story* (Holt, Rinehart & Winston, New York, 1957), page 256.

[7]Slater, *Soros,* page 103–104.

[8]Schwager, *New Market Wizards,* page 207.

[9]Warren Buffett, "1990 Letter to Shareholders," *Letters to Shareholders, 1987–1995,* page 79.

[10]Anthony Hughes, Geoff Wilson, and Matthew Kidman, *Masters of the Market* (Milton, Queensland: Wright books, 2003) page 213.

Chapter 8

[1]Siimon Reynolds, *Thoughts of Chairman Buffett: Thirty Years of Unconventional Wisdom from the Sage of Omaha* (HarperBusiness, New York, 1998).

[2]Kilpatrick, *Of Permanent Value,* page 408.

[3]Warren Buffett, "1989 Letter to Shareholders," *Letters to Shareholders, 1987–1995,* page 46.

[4]Soros, *Soros on Soros,* page 62.

[5]*Ibid.,* page 244.

[6]www.cs.rpi.edu/-thaps/quotes.html

Chapter 9

[1]Graham, *Intelligent Investor,* page 286.

[2]Warren Buffett, "1982 Letter to Shareholders," *Letters to Shareholders, 1977–1986,* page 53.

[3]Schwager, *Market Wizards,* page 315.

[4]Lowenstein, *Buffett,* page 234.

[5]www.nyse.com as of July 31, 2004.

[6]Lowe, *Warren Buffett Speaks,* page 120.

Chapter 10

[1]Kilpatrick, *Of Permanent Value,* page 673.

[2]Schwager, *Market Wizards,* page 181.

[3]Kilpatrick, *Of Permanent Value,* page 673.

[4]Lowenstein, *Buffett,* page 114.

Chapter 11

[1]Kilpatrick, *Of Permanent Value,* page 472.

[2]*Kent, Money Talks,* page 139.

[3]Reynolds, *Thoughts.*

[4]Kilpatrick, *op. cit.,* page 670.

[5]*Ibid.,* page 27.

[6]*Ibid.,* page 417.

[7]Reynolds, *Thoughts.*

[8]Soros, *Soros on Soros,* pages 40–41.

[9]*Ibid.,* page 41.

[10]*Ibid.,* pages 51–52.

[11]Hughes, *Masters of the Market,* page 28.

Chapter 12

[1]Kilpatrick, *Of Permanent Value,* pages 672–673.

[2]"The World's Greatest Money Manager," *Institutional Investor,* June 1981, pages 39–45.

[3]Slater, *Soros,* page 79.

[4]Warren Buffett, "1990 Letter to Shareholders," *Letters to Shareholders, 1987–1995,* page 77.

[5]*Outstanding Investor Digest* (Berkshire Hathaway reprint, Vol. XIII, Nos. 3 & 4, September 24, 1998), page 47.

[6]Soros, *Soros on Soros,* page 17.

[7]Reynolds, *Thoughts.*

[8]Slater, *Soros,* page 65.

[9]Reynolds, *Thoughts.*

[10]Schwager, *Market Wizards,* page 286.

Chapter 13

[1]*Outstanding Investor Digest,* (Berkshire Hathaway reprint, Vol. XIII, Nos. 3 & 4, September 24, 1998) page 47.

[2]*Ibid.,* page 48.

[3]Kilpatrick, *Of Permanent Value,* page 324.

[4]Lowenstein, *Buffett,* page 250.

Chapter 14

[1]Schwager, *Market Wizards,* page 65.

[2]Nikki Ross, *Lessons from the Legends of Wall Street* (Dearborn, Chicago, 2000), page 129.

[3]Berkshire Hathaway Annual Meeting, 2002.

[4]Hughes, *Masters of the Market,* page 303.

Chapter 15

[1]Schwager, *Market Wizards,* page 160.

[2]Schwager, *The New Market Wizards,* page 245.

[3]*Ibid.,* page 291.

[4]*Ibid.,* page 119.

Chapter 16

[1]"The Man Who Moves Markets," *Business Week,* August 23, 1993, pages 50–60.

[2]Warren Buffett, "1992 Letter to Shareholders," *Letters to Shareholders, 1987–1995,* page 117.

[3]Berkshire Hathaway Annual Meeting, 2000.

[4]Warren Buffett, "1985 Letter to Shareholders," *Letters to Shareholders, 1977–1986,* page 106.

[5]Kaufman, *Soros,* page 98.

[6]Warren Buffett, "1989 Letter to Shareholders," *Letters to Shareholders, 1987–1995,* page 62.

[7]Lowenstein, *Buffett,* page 67.

[8]*Ibid.,* page 76.

[9]Warren Buffett, "1981 Letter to Shareholders," *Letters to Shareholders, 1977–1986,* page 42.

[10]Hagstrom, *Warren Buffett Way,* page 84.

[11]Soros, *Alchemy,* page 305.

Chapter 17

[1] www.capitalideasonline.com/quotes/oct2002.htm

[2] Schwager, *Market Wizards,* page 123.

[3] Hagstrom, *Warren Buffett Way,* page 220.

[4] Warren Buffett, *An Owner's Manual* (Berkshire Hathaway, Inc., Omaha, Nebraska, 1996), page 8.

[5] Soros, *Soros on Soros,* page 11.

[6] Kaufman, *Soros,* page 100.

[7] *Ibid.,* page 100.

[8] Warren Buffett, "1991 Letter to Shareholders," *Letters to Shareholders, 1987–1995,* page 102.

[9] Kilpatrick, *Of Permanent Value,* page 418.

[10] Warren Buffett, "1991 Letter to Shareholders," *Letters to Shareholders, 1987–1995,* page 102.

[11] Soros, *Soros on Soros,* page 249.

[12] *Ibid.,* page 45.

[13] *Ibid.,* page 12.

[14] *Ibid.,* page 12.

[15] Warren Buffett, "1995 Letter to Shareholders," *Letters to Shareholders, 1987–1995,* page 172.

[16] Fisher, *Common Stocks,* page 68.

[17] *Outstanding Investor Digest,* (B.H. reprint, Vol. XIII, Nos. 3 & 4, September 24, 1998) page 44.

Chapter 18

[1] Kent, *Money Talks,* page 195.

[2] *Ibid.,* page 174.

[3] *Ibid.,* page 323.

[4] Lowenstein, *Buffett,* page 28.

[5] *Ibid.,* page 32.

[6] *Ibid.,* page 12.

[7] Lowe, *Warren Buffett Speaks,* page 88.

[8] Lowenstein, *Buffett,* page 46.

[9] *Ibid.,* page 54.

[10] Soros, *Soros on Soros,* pages 36–37.

[11] *Ibid.,* page 44.

[12] Kilpatrick, *Of Permanent Value,* page 682.

[13] Roger Lowenstein, *When Genius Failed: The Rise and Fall of Long-Term Capital Management* (Random House, New York, 2000), page 128.

[14] Peter Tanous, *Investment Gurus* (New York Institute of Finance, New York, 1997), page 163.

[15] Lowenstein, *Buffett,* page 234.

Chapter 19

[1] Slater, *Soros,* page 144.

[2] Lowenstein, *Buffett,* page 64.

[3] Train, *Midas Touch,* page 70.

[4] Kilpatrick, *Of Permanent Value,* pages 66–67.

[5] Train, *The Money Masters,* (Harper & Row, New York, 1980), page 10.

[6] Lowenstein, *Buffett,* pages 84–85.

[7] Kilpatrick, *op. cit.,* page 400.

[8] Warren Buffett, "1983 Letter to Shareholders," *Letters to Shareholders, 1977–1986,* page 66.

[9] Lowenstein, *Buffett,* page 51.

[10] Kaufman, *Soros,* page 158.

[11] *Ibid.,* page 126.

[12] Slater, *Soros,* page 139.

[13]Kaufman, *Soros*, page 158.

[14]Jay Palmer, "Market Mover," *Barron's*, November 6, 1995, page 33.

[15]*Ibid.*

[16]Train, *Money Masters*, page 194.

[17]*Ibid.*, page 194.

[18]Soros, *Soros on Soros*, page 86.

[19]www.anecdotage.com/index.php?aid=4595

[20]Kaufman, *Soros*, page 128.

[21]Hagstrom, *Warren Buffett Way*, page 128.

Chapter 20

[1]Hagstrom, *Warren Buffett Way*, pages 172–173.

[2]Soros, *Soros on Soros*, page 17.

[3]Lowe, *Warren Buffett Speaks*, pages 102–103.

[4]Lowenstein, *Buffett*, page 256.

[5]Michael Goldberg, quoted in "The Warren Buffett You Don't Know," *Business Week*, July 5, 1999, page 58.

[6]Berkshire Hathaway Annual Meeting, 2000.

[7]Kilpatrick, *Of Permanent Value*, pages 415–416.

[8]Devon Spurgeon, "Envelope Please: Warren Buffett Hints at Successor," *Asian Wall Street Journal*, October 19, 2000, page 11.

[9]Anthony Bianco, "The Warren Buffett You Don't Know," *Business Week*, July 5, 1999, page 58.

[10]Soros, *Soros on Soros*, page 18.

[11]*Ibid.*, page 52.

[12]*Ibid.*, page 21.

[13]*Ibid.*, page 58.

[14]*Ibid.*, pages 55.

[15]*Ibid.*, page 53.

[16]Kaufman, *Soros*, page 141.

[17]Soros, *Soros on Soros*, page 18.

[18]Kaufman, *Soros*, page 230.

[19]Soros, *Soros on Soros*, page 62.

[20]Brent Schlender, "The Bill and Warren Show," *Fortune*, July 20, 1998, page 46.

[21]Berkshire Hathaway Annual Report, 2003.

[22]Kent, *Money Talks*, page 212.

Chapter 21

[1]Soros, *Soros on Soros*, page 246.

[2]Reynolds, *Thoughts*.

[3]Kaufman, *Soros*, page 205.

[4]*Ibid.*, page 206.

[5]Soros, *Soros on Soros*, pages 53–54.

[6]Kilpatrick, *Of Permanent Value*, page 647.

[7]Warren Buffett, "1990 Letter to Shareholders," *Letters to Shareholders, 1987–1995*, page 78.

[8]Warren Buffett, "1984 Letter to Shareholders," *Letters to Shareholders, 1977–1986*, page 87.

[9]Kilpatrick, *Of Permanent Value*, page 537.

[10]Lowenstein, *Buffett*, page 75.

Chapter 22

[1]www.time.com/time/asia/asia/magazine/1998/981123/spotlight.html

[2]Kilpatrick, *Of Permanent Value*, page 632.

[3]Soros, *Alchemy*, page 12.

[4] Warren Buffett, "1992 Letter to Shareholders," *Letters to Shareholders, 1987–1995*, page 108.

[5] Lowenstein, *Buffett*, page 20.

[6] Kilpatrick, *op. cit.*, page 669.

[7] Warren Buffett, Berkshire Hathaway Annual Meeting, 2000.

[8] Berkshire Hathaway Annual Report, 2003.

[9] Kaufman, *Soros*, page 148.

[10] "The Man Who Moves Markets," *Business Week*, August 23, 1993.

[11] www.ixpres.com/twolff/moneyquotes.htm

[12] Kaufman, *Soros*, page 122.

[13] Soros, *Alchemy*, page 13.

[14] Soros, *Soros on Soros*, page 246.

[15] Soros, *Alchemy*, page 302.

[16] Soros, *Soros on Soros*, page 196.

[17] *Ibid.*, pages 244–245.

[18] Kaufman, *Soros*, page 323.

[19] Soros, *Alchemy*, page 23.

Chapter 23

[1] Warren Buffett, "1989 Letter to Shareholders," *Letters to Shareholders, 1987–1995*, page 63.

[2] Kilpatrick, *Of Permanent Value*, page 67.

[3] Mihaly Csikszentmihalyi, *Flow: The Psychology of Optimal Experience* (Harper Perennial, New York, 1990).

[4] Train, *Midas Touch*, page 95.

[5] *Sunday Times*, London, March 14, 1993.

[6] Schwager, *Market Wizards*, page 254.

[7] Scott Sterling Johnston in Tanous, *Investment Gurus*, page 150.

[8] Robert P. Miles, *The Warren Buffett CEO* (Wiley, New York, 2002), page 108.

[9] Reynolds, *Thoughts of Chairman Buffett*.

Chapter 24

[1] Kilpatrick, *Of Permanent Value*, page 113.

[2] John Train, *Money Masters*, page 156.

[3] Lowenstein, *Buffett*, page 92.

[4] *Ibid.*, page 149.

[5] Lowe, *Warren Buffett Speaks*, page 98.

[6] Schwager, *Market Wizards*, page 30.

[7] Kaufman, *Soros*, page 86.

[8] Schwager, *Market Wizards*, page 165.

[9] Schwager, *New Market Wizards*, page 63.

[10] Miles, *The Warren Buffett CEO*, page 61.

[11] www.rivkininstitute.com.au.

[12] Tanous, *Investment Gurus*, page 65.

[13] Schwager, *Market Wizards*, pages 44–45.

[14] *Ibid.*, pages 138–139.

[15] Tanous, *Investment Guns*, page 148.

[16] Peter Lynch, *One Up on Wall Street*, page 11.

[17] Kaufman, *Soros*, page 86.

[18] www.johnbudden.com/quotes.htm.

Chapter 25

[1]Soros, *Alchemy,* page 144.

Chapter 26

[1]Lowenstein, *Buffett,* page 311.

[2]Slater, *Soros,* page 66.

[3]Miles, *Warren Buffett CEO,* page 131.

[4]Kilpatrick, *Of Permanent Value,* page 671.

[5]*Ibid.,* page 30.

[6]Kaufman, *Soros,* page 94.

Chapter 27

[1]Mark Stevens, *King Icahn* (Dutton, New York, 1993), page 6.

[2]Quoted in *ibid.,* page 93.

[3]*Ibid.,* page 55.

[4]*Ibid.,* page 22.

[5]"Icahn, Company Scourge, Joins Hedge Fund Rush," *International Herald Tribune,* 4 August 2004.

[6]Nikki Ross, *Lessons from Legends of Wall Street,* page 178.

[7]*Ibid.,* page 209.

[8]*Ibid.,* page 183.

[9]John Train, *Money Masters of Our Time,* page 61.

[10]Victoria Murphy, "Old Dog, New Tricks," *Forbes,* May 28, 2001.

[11]This, all subsequent quotes, and the information in this section come from my interview with Bernhard in his Hong Kong office on June 28, 2004.

Chapter 29

[1]Kilpatrick, *Of Permanent Value,* page 673.

[2]Buffett, 2000 Letter to Shareholders, page 19.

[3]Lowenstein, *Buffett,* page 202.

[4]Schwager, *New Market Wizards,* page 202.

[5]Lowe, *Warren Buffett Speak,* page 69.

[6]Kaufman, *Soros,* page 80.

Chapter 30

[1]"Meg and the Machine," *Fortune,* August 11, 2003.

[2]Schwager, *Market Wizards,* page 167.

[3]Buffett, 1993 Letter to Shareholders, page 136.

[4]Harry Browne, *Why the Best-Laid Investment Plans Usually Go Wrong* (Morrow, New York, 1987), page 242.

[5]*Ibid.,* page 248.

Chapter 31

[1]John Train, *Money Masters of Our Time,* page 220.

[2]Kent, *Money Talks,* page 152.

[3]Schwager, *New Market Wizards,* page 133.

[4]Buffett, 2001 Letter to Shareholders, page 9.

Chapter 32

[1]Hagstrom, *The Warren Buffett Way,* page 225.

Index